SUFFRAGE DAYS

An exciting undertaking based entirely on new source materials. . . .
Of immediate importance to all those interested in the history of
women's suffrage movements in Britain, this book will make a major
contribution to its field.

Jane Rendall, *University of York*

Suffrage Days is an account of the British suffrage movement from
its inception until its victory in 1918. It is based on the activities of
seven individuals whose participation in the British suffrage movement is little known: Elizabeth Wolstenholme Elmy, Jessie Craigen,
Elizabeth Cady Stanton, Hannah Mitchell, Mary Gawthorpe, Laurence Housman and Alice Clark.

Through their stories and perspectives, Sandra Stanley Holton
uncovers a previously unacknowledged Radical–Liberal current in
the nineteenth-century movement; the transatlantic links between
Radical suffragists; the national and international significance of the
Women's Franchise League; some nineteenth-century origins of suffrage militancy; the relationship between emergent new masculine
identities and suffrage politics; and the complex relationship between
militant and constitutional suffragists. In a final chapter Holton
reflects upon the historiography of the suffrage movement.

Sandra Stanley Holton is Australian Research Fellow at the University of Adelaide and author of *Feminism and Democracy* (1986).

SUFFRAGE DAYS

Stories from the women's suffrage
movement

Sandra Stanley Holton

London and New York

First published 1996
by Routledge
11 New Fetter Lane, London EC4P 4EE

Simultaneously published in the USA and Canada
by Routledge
29 West 35th Street, New York, NY 10001
Routledge is an International Thomson Publishing company

© 1996 Sandra Stanley Holton

Phototypeset by Intype London Ltd
Printed and bound in Great Britain by
TJ Press (Padstow) Ltd, Padstow, Cornwall

British Library Cataloguing in Publication Data
A catalogue record for this book is available from the British Library

Library of Congress Cataloging in Publication Data
A catalogue record for this book has been requested

ISBN 0–415–10941–8
0–415–10942–6 (pbk)

For Bob, George and Flora

CONTENTS

CONTENTS

PLATES

ACKNOWLEDGEMENTS

I thank the University of Adelaide and the Australian Research Council for the fellowships which made this research possible. These two bodies, together with the Australian Academy of the Humanities and the Ian Potter Foundation also helped with travel and other research costs, and I thank them, too, for that support.

I am also grateful for the assistance given me by numerous libraries and archives over the past six years, including the staff of the Barr Smith Library at the University of Adelaide, the Mitchell Library Sydney, Murdoch University Library Special Collections, the National Library of Australia in Canberra, the Fawcett Library at the London Guildhall University, Friends House Library in Friends House, London, the British Library, London, the Archives of the British Library of Political and Economic Science at the London School of Economics, the archives of King's College, Cambridge, the Bodleian Library, Oxford, the National Library of Scotland in Edinburgh, the Edinburgh Public Library, the archives of the University of Edinburgh, the Sheffield Public Library and the Leeds Public Library in Yorkshire, Manchester Public Library, the Street Public Library in Somerset, the E. Sylvia Pankhurst Archive in the Institute of Social History, Amsterdam, the New York Public Library, the City of New York, Department of Records and Information Services, the Arthur and Elizabeth Schlesinger Library at Radcliffe College, the Special Collections of the libraries of Vassar College, the Special Collections of the library of the Northwestern University, Illinois, the Library of Congress, the Huntington Library in San Marino, the History Department of the Church of Christ, Scientist, Boston, the Mabel and Frederick Douglass Library, Rutgers, the University of New Jersey, and the Susan B. Anthony and Elizabeth Cady Stanton Project, now at Rutgers, the University of New Jersey.

Most especially, I must thank the trustees and staff of the Clark Archive for permission to draw on this private family archive.

Other researchers and historians have shown great generosity in sharing their knowledge with me, and I would like here to thank Margaret Barrow, Krista Cowman, David Doughan, Yvonne Fettweis, Muriel Fielding, Lesley Hall, June Hannam, Patricia Holland, Angela John, Pam Lunn, Mary Lyndon Shanley, the late Stephen Morland, Stephen Parker, Michael Roberts, Jill Roe, Anne Scott, Judith Smart, Tom Steele, Pat Thane, Greg Tobin and Rosemary van Arsdel. I am grateful to Philippa Levine and Jane Rendall, the originally anonymous readers of my preliminary draft, for providing such thoughtful and helpful suggestions for its improvement. Claire L'Enfant I thank for her patience and encouragement. I am grateful, too, for the interest and support of friends and colleagues in Adelaide, especially Margaret Allen, Jane Elliot, Robin Haines and Alison Mackinnon. They listened and responded to some of the ideas and material presented here, while Margaret Allen read through the final manuscript for me under considerable pressure of time. During the past few years the following conferences and seminars provided me with the opportunity to present earlier versions of my research, and the comments of other participants helped me revise that material for publication: the Women's Studies seminar, University of York, the Women's History seminar, the Institute for Historical Research, London, the London History Workshop, the 'Men's Share' project at the University of Greenwich, the Women's Studies seminar and the History Department seminar at the University of Adelaide, the Australian and New Zealand American Studies Association, the Australian and New Zealand British Historians Association, the Berkshire Conference of Women's Historians in the United States, the Suffrage and Beyond conference, Wellington, New Zealand, and the Mary Wollstonecraft 200 Conference at the University of Sussex in Britain.

Pam Burroughs communicated her enthusiasm for the Housman collection in the Street Public Library, while Janet Graham helped me with her knowledge of the local history of Street and its environs. I would also like to thank those who provided such kind hospitality during my numerous research visits to Britain in recent years: Mike and Jan Dougall, Janet Graham, June Hannam, Bronwen and Arun Holden, Polly and John Holton, Angela John, Mary Maynard, June and Michael Purvis, Pat Thane and Eileen Yeo. Irene Cassidy, Nesta

Holden and George Holton have each assisted from time to time with some of the research presented here.

My house is fortunate in having a resident cook of great skill, and I thank Bob Holton for his nourishing support – culinary, emotional and intellectual. Flora Holton I thank for keeping me laughing, especially in the last weeks of preparing this book for publication. George Holton provided such coffee that even the tiredest historian could not fall asleep over her word-processor.

ABBREVIATIONS

BSSSP	British Society for the Study of Sex Psychology
CCNSWS	Central Committee of the National Society for Women's Suffrage
CDA	Contagious Diseases Acts
CNSWS	Central National Society for Women's Suffrage
ILP	Independent Labour Party
LNA	Ladies National Association for the Repeal of the Contagious Diseases Acts
NSWS	National Society for Women's Suffrage
NUWSS	National Union of Women's Suffrage Societies
NUWW	National Union of Women Workers
NVA	National Vigilance Association
SDF	Social Democratic Federation
UDC	Union for Democratic Control
WCG	Women's Cooperative Guild
WEU	Women's Emancipation Union
WFL	Women's Freedom League
WILPF	Women's International League for Peace and Freedom
WLA	Women's Liberal Association
WLF	Women's Liberal Federation
WLL	Women's Labour League
WPPL	Women's Protective and Provident League
WSPU	Women's Social and Political Union

Plate 1   Hyde Park demonstration with Mrs Pankhurst and Mrs Wolstenholme Elmy, 1908. By courtesy of the Mary Evans/Fawcett Library.

INTRODUCTION

In old photographs of suffrage demonstrations from the early years of this century there occasionally appears a tiny, white-haired figure, still wearing the ringlets of a yet earlier period. Her presence seems anomalous among the 'militant suffragettes' of the early twentieth century, and immediately raises questions about the stereotypical images that attach to that designation. Both suffragists and anti-suffragists produced 'a series of representational "types" ' reflecting notions about 'womanliness' and 'unwomanliness', but this figure seems to fit with none of these.[1] Whatever the quaintness of her outward appearance, Elizabeth Wolstenholme Elmy had lived out radical new ways of being a woman. Her presence among the suffragettes of the Women's Social and Political Union (WSPU) illustrates the tenacity of many of those who initiated the campaign for votes for women in the mid-1860s. It testifies also to the equally hard-fought struggle by women to create new identities for themselves. Yet, though her name will be found in the index of almost every major study of the nineteenth-century women's movement, Elizabeth Wolstenholme Elmy has remained in the background, a ubiquitous but insubstantial figure.

In recent years, historians have become increasingly interested in the kaleidoscopic nature of the materials of history, 'a multitude of fragments, forming patterns that shift with the movement of the viewer'.[2] A shake of the kaleidoscope and different aspects of the historical pattern may move to the fore, altering our view of the relationship between the parts. Though the separate components of that pattern remain unchanged, the pattern itself may now look very different. This study explores what happens when the object of the historical gaze, in this case the suffrage movement, undergoes such a re-configuration. Millicent Garrett Fawcett, Josephine Butler, and

Emmeline Pankhurst will appear from time to time in what follows, but it is lesser-known participants in the British suffrage movement, like Elizabeth Wolstenholme Elmy, who provide the focus of my narrative.

So this book is in part a project of recovery – of reconstructing stories that have become largely hidden in the patterns formed by previous history-making. And the new prominence accorded such recovered stories produces, in its turn, a fresh pattern to the history of the campaigns for votes for women, sometimes imbuing long-known events with a meaning different from earlier accounts. An alternative dynamic to the suffrage movement is also thereby revealed – in the political significance which attached to personal life, to the webs of friendship, kinship and shared values which made up the suffrage movement, as well as the various party-political and factional loyalties to be found among suffragists. Such dynamics will be explored here in the lives of seven suffragists, active for some part of the campaign from 1865 to 1918, when women in Britain at last won the right to vote in parliamentary elections.

The first two chapters tell the story of how Elizabeth Wolstenholme, as she then was, came to join the women's movement, and the role she played in its early campaigns and organisations. The Bright circle, comprising a kinship and friendship circle of radical Quaker women, emerges as a source of strong support for the issues and strategies which Elizabeth Wolstenholme helped bring to the fore in these years. A new figure, Jessie Craigen, a working suffragist, is introduced in Chapter 3. She was among those who helped create a constituency for the suffrage movement which extended beyond the middle-class women's circles that initiated the first organised demand. She found some of her most long-standing friends among the circle of Radical suffragists within which Elizabeth Wolstenholme Elmy also moved. This chapter and also Chapter 4 bring an outside perspective on the British movement, that of Elizabeth Cady Stanton, a prominent figure in the women's movement in the United States. Her first-hand observations of the events in Britain have been surprisingly neglected by historians, but are an important source for revealing the extent and nature of Radical suffragism. In telling these stories, and showing how at times they came together, the distinctive nature of the Radical suffragist conception of the citizenship of women is explored, especially as it related to the legal and economic status of married women. And certain continuities between earlier radical movements and the nineteenth-century suffrage movement emerge, while a more complex origin for the militancy of the twentieth-century movement is suggested.

Chapter 5 turns to the emergence of a new presence within the suffrage movement from the 1890s, in working-class recruits from the socialist and labour movements. Hannah Mitchell, formerly a dress-maker, was among the earliest members of the Women's Social and Political Union after it was formed in Manchester in 1903, having already become a well-known figure in local socialist and labour circles. Mary Gawthorpe, a schoolteacher who became one of the best-loved speakers and organisers of the twentieth-century movement is introduced in the next chapter. Appointed as an organiser of the Women's Social and Political Union in 1906, she encountered both Elizabeth Wolstenholme Elmy and Hannah Mitchell at one of the militants' best-remembered demonstrations within the House of Commons. Subsequently, Hannah Mitchell's path diverged from that of Mary Gawthorpe and Elizabeth Wolstenholme Elmy, requiring an analysis of the nature of 'militancy', and of the Women's Social and Political Union.

Chapter 7 introduces Laurence Housman, a journalist, playwright and novelist, who lent his skills to the movement through a range of suffrage organisations established by artists and writers. The place of men in the suffrage movement has been a neglected aspect of its history, and Laurence Housman left evidence of some of the tensions and issues to which their presence gave rise. His story suggests, also, how women's suffrage raised questions about the nature of masculinity, and the links between masculine identities and masculine sexualities. Chapter 8 brings into the narrative Alice Clark, a Liberal Quaker industrialist, and a member of the third generation of the Bright circle to take an active part in the suffrage movement. She eventually joined the leadership of the constitutional wing of the movement, the National Union of Women's Suffrage Societies, in the same period that she also began her pioneering research on the history of women's work.

In Chapters 9 and 10 the stories of Mary Gawthorpe, Laurence Housman and Alice Clark are woven together so as to convey something of the complexities and cross-currents evident in the suffrage movement from 1912 onwards. The last chapter looks at the separate paths taken by those of the seven characters examined who lived on after the parliamentary suffrage was won for women in 1918. Each of these seven was linked to the others, in the chains of friendship, kinship, love and comradeship which helped make the suffrage movement – each knew at least one of the others personally, and shared friends with them. They did not, however, form, in life, a distinct grouping of their own making. They come together here as figures in a story that I, as historian, have put together. There was a congruence to the seven individual stories, however, which suggested the pattern I make with them, a pattern which also reveals significant, if previously neglected, filaments in suffrage history. The common filaments which link their stories together are most especially evident in the entwining of formal politics and the politics of personal life; of gendered identities, conceptions of citizenship, and the passions of love and friendship in these several stories.

Where possible, I have drawn on their own accounts of the suffrage movement, for five of the seven attempted their own history-making – in recollections, in biography or in brief studies of the suffrage campaigns. All left some evidence concerning their own day-to-day understanding of and experience in the movement, in the form of letters, speeches or pamphlets. And for each, the suffrage movement was only one of many interests and activities. So the picture of the seven individuals presented here is partial in every sense, focusing on only one part of a life, and drawing on representations which reflect the assessment of the subjects themselves. My title, *Suffrage Days*, was chosen to convey, also, the golden aura of nostalgia which often surrounded this period in the memory of suffragists. Looking back, they generally recalled their participation in the votes-for-women campaigns as either a transformative experience, or the high point in their lives, or both. At the time, however, there was also sometimes a darker side to suffrage campaigning, a side revealed more clearly in contemporaneous documents than in works of memory. This account attempts to convey, then, something of that duality – of the gold and the black of suffragism, of both the traces of the actuality and the subsequent reflections left by my subjects concerning their suffrage experience.

The choice of these seven suffragists also reflects the availability of sources of various kinds: there is published biographical material on each of the seven subjects, some of it autobiographical; there are also significant collections of letters from all of the subjects, except Jessie Craigen and Hannah Mitchell; there are the documents left by the numerous suffrage organisations in which each was involved – annual reports, pamphlets, journals, minute books. This history would not have taken the form or presented the arguments it does, however, but for the location of a quite new source of manuscript material among the papers of the Clark family. Both my methods of selection, and the use to which I have put such sources, raise issues central to current debates about the way histories are made, and I reflect on these questions at greater length in the concluding section of the final chapter. Some readers may prefer to turn first of all to that discussion. For now, I tell a story.

1

FROM 'SURPLUS WOMAN' TO INDEPENDENT PERSON

Elizabeth Wolstenholme and the early women's movement

We have only a limited knowledge of the early life of Elizabeth Wolstenholme Elmy (1833–1918). Much of this comes from a short article written in 1895 by 'Ellis Ethelmer', a pseudonym often used by Ben Elmy, whom she married in 1874. The picture it paints is thus based on intimate knowledge and is one to which, presumably, she had lent her approval.[1] It is a representation which provides, then, a valuable insight into the identity she built for herself. Here the young Elizabeth Wolstenholme is depicted as typical of those 'surplus women' around whom early discussion of 'the woman question' often centred in the mid-nineteenth century. Women, that is to say, who had shown themselves superfluous to the needs of society, in failing to find a husband, and in being otherwise without the means to maintain their middle-class status. By her late twenties, however, this account shows that Elizabeth Wolstenholme had, through her own example, done much to challenge the assumptions which lay behind such an understanding of the place of women in society. She had recreated herself as an 'independent person'.[2] From this position she began a long career as a 'woman emancipator'. In old age she celebrated, in her own writings, the emergence of those she dubbed 'insurgent women', the 'militant suffragettes' of the Women's Social and Political Union, formed by her friend, Emmeline Pankhurst, alongside whom she spent her last years of active campaigning.[3]

Her presence illustrates some of the continuities between certain currents within mid-nineteenth-century radicalism, out of which the women's movement grew, and the militant suffragism of the twentieth century. An appreciation of such continuities has been lost, at least in part, because of the way figures like Elizabeth Wolstenholme Elmy were 'written out' of the history of the suffrage movement. One who worked closely with her at the turn of the century has argued: 'The work of Mrs Elmy has never been sufficiently recognised, because she was frowned upon by the official suffragists, though she had quite the most able mind and memory of any nineteenth century woman.'[4] To understand why she was frowned upon by some among the leadership of the women's movement requires exploring the story of her personal life, and mapping her friendship circles, as well as a survey of her career as an activist. And this in turn brings a fresh perspective on the history of the women's movement.

Sylvia Pankhurst, daughter of Emmeline and herself a militant, came to know Elizabeth Wolstenholme Elmy well, and recalled a 'tiny Jenny-wren of a woman, with bright bird-like eyes, and a little face, child-like in its merriment and its pathos, which even in extreme old age retained the winning graces of youth'.[5] This fond characterisation reflects the affection which its subject inspired in many. But it belies a personal history of continual, and occasionally painful and dangerous, confrontation with notions of conventional femininity in order to create new opportunities and ways of being for women. The challenging appearance of the militant suffragette has sometimes been read as reflecting a brash new form of popular politics, or as symptomatic of a serious social malaise. But it served also to represent the final release of women from that dependent, passive identity which had informed notions like that of the 'surplus woman'.

The material reality that had supported this notion was the demographic imbalance between the sexes revealed by the 1851 Census. This had established that unmarried women far outnumbered potential husbands, a situation neither new in itself, nor one which necessarily had to mean hardship for women. But new aspirations to gentility grew in the early decades of the century, requiring that middle-class women no longer join in family enterprises or work for a living. In consequence, few received the education and training necessary to enter middle-class occupations. Many of these occupations were anyway closed to them, as were the universities. And middle-class men in turn became less ready to marry as the financial means required to support new notions of gentility grew. By the mid-nineteenth century, then, the failure of a middle-class woman to secure a husband–provider for her adult life, or the death of her provider, be he father, husband or brother, brought social marginality and economic vulnerability, if not extreme hardship. Many women fortunate enough to enjoy the security of wealth found themselves condemned to a limited life of entertaining, visiting and letter-writing, pursuits which by convention took precedence over the only acceptable 'work' they might find for themselves, as voluntary labourers in the field of philanthropy and social service. Those without either a provider or wealth of their own had to support themselves as best they might, within the constraints that prevailing notions of respectability and femininity had placed upon them.

Not all middle-class women, then, were leisured or wealthy or purely domestic in their pursuits. Many had to work for a living, and many established alternatives to married life, sometimes in the distinctive female communities which became a feature of later nineteenth-century society. Teaching offered one of the very few respectable occupations in which a middle-class woman might earn a living and establish herself as an independent person. It was by this means that Elizabeth Wolstenholme dealt with her lot as a 'surplus woman'. With only limited capital, some education, and greater natural abilities she pursued an occupation which also allowed her to prepare other young women for alternatives to a dependent or 'superfluous' future. By the early 1860s, when she was in her late twenties, she had already won for herself considerable standing in the Manchester region where she spent most of her life, and had helped establish supportive organisations of like-minded women. Her professional concerns brought her into contact with the earliest sustained efforts to establish a women's rights movement.[6]

She was among the first to join the Kensington Society formed in 1865, as a corresponding member.[7] This debating society brought together women with a special interest in improving education and work opportunities for their sex, but it also provided the forum in which the question of women's suffrage was revived. In the previous two decades, it had been an issue taken up only by the most radical, notably by Chartists like the Quaker, Anne Knight. Even within such circles it had proved controversial, and impossible in that period to sustain as an organised demand. From this point in her life Elizabeth Wolstenholme becomes more visible to us, not simply because she now began to acquire a greater public presence, but also because of what her choice of friends and associates may tell us about her own outlook and interests.

The women's rights movement in the latter part of the nineteenth century was built upon kinship and friendship circles among middle-class women. The Kensington Society itself arose out of the activities and interests of the Langham Place circle, an informal grouping of women which had gathered around two friends, Barbara Leigh Smith

(1827–91) and Bessie Rayner Parkes (1829–1925). Philippa Levine has recently suggested that 'the feminism of these women was more a lifestyle than merely a form of organised political activism',[8] and certainly it encompassed a wide range of activities, concerns, and needs among the women who made up its membership. The circle gained its name from a club for women established by Barbara Leigh Smith and Bessie Rayner Parkes in Langham Place, where a register for women's employment was maintained. A wider audience was reached through a periodical, the *English Woman's Journal*, in which a wide range of issues affecting women was discussed. Individual women had been making the case for improvement in women's status and opportunities for over two centuries. In the late eighteenth century the ideas of the French Revolution had prompted the English Jacobin, Mary Wollstonecraft, to write her classic work, *A Vindication of the Rights of Woman*. In the early nineteenth century advanced radicals, notably the Owenite socialists and some of the utopian communities of the 1830s–40s, had attempted to address these questions in short-lived social experiments, and William Thompson, prompted by the experience of his companion, Anna Wheeler, had produced another classic text, in his *Appeal on Behalf of One Half the Human Race*. . . .

But it was mid-nineteenth-century, middle-class radicalism which initially provided the organisational basis for a sustained movement for women's rights. Barbara Leigh Smith and Bessie Rayner Parkes shared family backgrounds of religious dissent and political radicalism. Both were from Unitarian families with a long involvement in reform movements. Their fathers and grandfathers had been part of the same intellectual and political currents which had formed the ideas of Mary Wollstonecraft on the rights and wrongs of women. They, too, had been notable radicals, sympathising with the American and French revolutions, opposing the slave trade, and advocating greater democracy in Britain. Barbara Leigh Smith had also been introduced, through the friendship circle of her aunt, Julia Smith, to a group of radical women, again Unitarians, though together with some Quakers, who had begun to advocate women's rights in the 1840s. This was a circle that one otherwise sympathetic observer felt carried 'radicalism to a romantic excess'.[9]

One of the principal humanitarian concerns shared by this circle was the abolition of slavery, and this question brought them into contact with reformers in the United States. When the World Anti-Slavery Convention met in London in 1840, it was confronted by a divided American movement, and a delegation from the section led by William Lloyd Garrison which included women. Abolitionism did not prompt the same degree of public fervour for women's rights among British women radicals as it did among their American counterparts. But the refusal of the convention to acknowledge the standing of American women delegates brought a sympathetic response from British women radicals. Anne Knight wrote to women abolitionists back in America that their example had 'lighted a flame' among British women who previously had 'thought not of *our* bondage'.[10] Out of this experience, friendship networks between British and American women abolitionists were established, which, as we shall see later, were to prove a valuable link between the suffrage movements in both countries.

The world of male middle-class radical politics provided further important training for many who came to the fore of the early women's movement. Mary Howitt, another Quaker radical and writer associated with this circle, warned a friend: 'Thou shalt find us desperate Radicals, Anti-Corn Law League, universal suffrage people.'[11] Barbara Leigh Smith, like many other pioneers in the suffrage movement, gained her first experience of active campaigning in the Anti-Corn Law League of the 1840s, the first organisation to encourage middle-class women's participation in the political process. Such interests were encouraged by her father, who would allow his children to join the company when radical political colleagues, like John Bright, one of the leaders of the League, visited their London house. Elizabeth Wolstenholme was just too young to have taken an active part in the campaigns of the League, but even so, forty years on, she too could still remember 'watching with deep emotion the great Manchester procession in celebration of the repeal of the Corn Laws'.[12]

Such kinship and friendship circles among middle-class women provided, then, valuable links back to earlier generations of radicals, as well as a forum for challenging ideas concerning the position of women. But more than this, they promoted the creation of purposeful networks, as one circle rippled out to bring contact with others, thereby extending links with male reforming elites and providing the foundations for an organised women's movement. Such informal circles provided, too, an experience of sexual solidarity, and the emotional and moral support which was needed to sustain the unconventional and often controversial undertakings involved in any campaign for women's rights at this time. The intense 'romantic friendships', like that between Barbara Leigh Smith and Bessie

Rayner Parkes, were often the most valued experiences of women's lives in this period and provided yet further bonds.

Anna Jameson, one of the most popular writers of her day and a particular influence on Barbara Leigh Smith, put forward through her lectures and writings in the 1850s a fresh perspective on the emancipation of women. She argued for a 'communion of labour' between men and women, in public as well as in private life, for the duty and rights of women to carry the roles they undertook in the domestic sphere out of the home, into a wider sphere beyond. Such arguments not only undermined the prevailing notion of quite separate spheres for men and women, they also established a bridge between women's rights demands and more generalised movements for social reform. And they claimed for women particular qualities, knowledge and aptitudes as essential to any proper reordering of society, something additional to and differing from the masculine contribution which determined public life at that time. To be sure, such arguments rested on a notion of sexual difference that continues to provoke controversy among feminists to this day. But it was an argument which insisted on the common humanity of men and women in the possession of a moral sense and the capacity to reason, while also claiming the public value and significance of womanly roles and duties.[13] In this idea, such advocates of women's rights were drawing on a different experience and understanding of domestic life from our own. Domestic life was not then so fully characterised by the privacy and separation from community life it now represents, and many of the day-to-day tasks of middle-class women, especially their philanthropic activities, were of considerable social, not merely personal, significance. Whereas present-day historians have often emphasised the constraints and restrictions imposed on women in this period, Victorian women's rights activists themselves frequently saw opportunities to improve the position of women by expanding these accepted roles.

But nor were women's manifest wrongs ignored or neglected. Anna Jameson also guided Barbara Leigh Smith into her first organised campaign, to reform the marriage laws as they affected women. Anna Jameson had herself been a victim of these laws, when she was left penniless by the death of her estranged husband in 1854, although it had been her earnings as a writer which had largely supported their family. Under English common law a married woman was defined as a 'feme covert'. By this doctrine of coverture, a woman who married lost the civil standing of the 'feme sole'. Her legal personhood was subsumed under that of her husband, and was only regained if she became widowed. One consequence of this was that her husband became the owner of any property which she brought with her into the marriage, and of any wealth which she subsequently acquired, including earned income, unless this property had been protected through the establishment of a trust prior to marriage. Though a new companionate ideal of marriage had been developing over the previous two centuries, the legal basis of marriage retained these remnants of an older patriarchal ideal, producing what has most aptly been described as 'a curdled mixture of domestic contradictions'.[14] As we shall see, the position of the married woman became a central concern also for Elizabeth Wolstenholme, and shaped her approach both to the citizenship of women, and to women's suffrage (for the first was a larger issue altogether than the second). The Married Women's Property Committee, established by Barbara Leigh Smith in 1855, has been seen as signalling the 'real beginning for the women's movement'.[15] It also attracted the interest of male reformers in the recently instituted Social Science Association, an organisation which became a valuable forum for raising a variety of women's rights issues in the years to come.

Not surprisingly, perhaps, this campaign also took on a significance for the personal lives of those involved. Barbara Leigh Smith wrote to Bessie Rayner Parkes of her own strong desire for a husband and children, but asked 'Where are the men who are good? I do not see them.' In her turn Bessie Rayner Parkes confided in her journal her own feelings on refusing a proposal of marriage: 'A single woman is so free, so powerful.' To her mind only 'an intense love' might make marriage an option, 'but *that alone* in the present state of society'.[16] Many in these circles were at this time attracted by the ideas of socialist thinkers such as Fourier, who rejected conventional marriage in favour of free sexual union. Barbara Leigh Smith was herself the child of such a union. Her close friend, George Eliot (the pseudonym of Marian Evans), also lived as the common-law wife of another writer, Henry Lewes. In the midst of her campaign to reform the marriage laws, Barbara Leigh Smith proposed a similar union between herself and the already-married publisher, John Chapman. But her father, to whom she was very close, rejected any such scheme, and Barbara Leigh Smith appears not to have questioned either the double standards or the patriarchal authority represented by such an intervention. Elizabeth Wolstenholme was to meet equally stern opposition when she, in her turn, sought a free union some years later.

Meanwhile, the campaign for married women's property rights ran aground in 1857, when some of the worst abuses in the law were removed by a new Matrimonial Causes Act. But even before this Barbara Leigh Smith and Bessie Rayner Parkes had begun to expand their examination of women's situation. Above all, they insisted on the importance of work 'for every human being regardless of sex', defining work not simply as paid employment but as 'the productive application of talent'.[17] Together they founded the *English Woman's Journal*, in 1858, which Bessie initially edited, through which their ideas and interests found a broader audience, out of which grew the Langham Place circle of women seeking to improve the social position of their sex.

Concern to expand women's opportunities for employment also led to a related campaign for improved educational provision. When Bessie Rayner Parkes published her 'Remarks on the Education of Girls' it prompted a diatribe in the *Saturday Review* against 'strong-minded' women which was to be repeated by opponents throughout the nineteenth century, opponents for whom dependence and ignorance were synonymous with femininity. It was this question which first brought Elizabeth Wolstenholme into contact with the circle around Barbara Leigh Smith Bodichon (she married in 1857) and Bessie Rayner Parkes. Emily Davies (1839–1921), the single daughter of a Newcastle churchman, was another whose interest in promoting better employment opportunities and education for women led to her friendship with Barbara Bodichon and her subsequent move to London. There she waged a campaign for better schools and entry to university for women, a campaign in which she was aided by Elizabeth Wolstenholme. Both women shared a sense of grievance at the limited educational opportunities which had been provided for them as compared to their brothers, both had confronted a future as a 'surplus woman'.

'Ellis Ethelmer' tells us how Elizabeth Wolstenholme's mother, daughter of a Lancashire cotton-spinner, had died shortly after her birth. Her father, a Methodist minister in Eccles, also died while she was still a child, though not before re-marrying and enlarging his family further. The needs of a large family of small means meant that as a girl she was subjected 'to a domesticity so rigorous' that any kind of reading was frowned upon. She enjoyed just two years of formal education, at the Moravian School, Fulneck, near Leeds, between the ages of fourteen and sixteen, an education which reflected the strictness of that sect, but which would also have been more intellectually stimulating than that provided for most girls in this period. After this she undertook some teaching from her home, while continuing to educate herself. The trustees of her father's small estate refused her request to be allowed to pursue further study at the Bedford College, where Barbara Leigh Smith was beginning her education as a painter. In contrast, and with an 'unjust disparity', Joseph Wolstenholme, Elizabeth's older brother, was sent to Cambridge. There he studied mathematics, eventually completing a doctorate and pursuing a successful career as an academic. While he enjoyed the privileges of life as a Cambridge fellow, Elizabeth was advised by her trustees to invest the small capital remaining to her in a 'high-class boarding school' – an indication not only of their perception of her lesser right to an education and the restricted professional openings for women, but also of the low qualifications then thought adequate to teach young women, even in the better girls' schools.[18]

It was in this way that Elizabeth Wolstenholme became, at the age of nineteen and largely self-taught, the headmistress of a school at Boothstown, near Worsley. This 'desperately precarious undertaking' was one which offered 'perhaps the only livelihood honourable to herself and useful to humanity' as an unmarried, middle-class woman of small means.[19] We know very little about this period of her life, but she was evidently a dedicated teacher. Her philosophy of education appears to have been a broad one which recognised the need to prepare children for the adult world of work, but saw this as best achieved by fostering the intellectual development and aptitudes of each individual. She had little time for the debate, even then current, over the relative merits of vocational training as opposed to academic learning, for she believed there to be 'a meeting point in which all are reconciled'.[20]

In arguing for improved education for girls she took issue with those parents who regarded it as a matter of little importance, especially those who could see no economic advantage in it, or who ignored its other benefits for their daughters. She characterised the consequences of such an outlook in these terms: 'A woman must remain ignorant because, to her, knowledge has no practical, that is commercial value. She is idle because she is ignorant. She becomes frivolous or vicious because she is idle.' Elizabeth Wolstenholme insisted that, as a fact of life, education was as much an economic necessity for girls as for boys: 'The practical exclusion of girls from the highest educational advantages . . . is in very many cases equivalent to a sentence of lifelong pauperism and dependence.' She rejected the assumption that women would marry and be maintained by their husbands:

> Nothing is more plainly to be seen by those who will open their eyes than these three things: − 1. That a very large minority of women do not marry. 2. That of those who do marry, a very considerable proportion are not supported by their husbands. 3. That upon a very large number of widows . . . the burden of self-maintenance and of the maintenance of their children is thrown.[21]

By the mid-1860s, the Schools Enquiry Commission was beginning to investigate educational provision for the middle classes. Elizabeth Wolstenholme was one of the signatories to a successful submission to the inquiry, prepared by Emily Davies, which argued that it should also investigate the state of girls' education. Early in 1866, she became, along with Emily Davies, among the first women ever called to give evidence to a Royal Commission. In this period, too, she began to contribute papers to the Social Science Conference on the education of girls. In this forum for reformers, she put forward a programme for advancing women's education which included establishing a high school in every major town, and similar institutions in rural areas, with small boarding houses nearby so that the benefits of home life might be maintained for those girls who had to leave their families to go to school. Like most women activists of this period, she had a high appreciation of the value of domestic life, especially as the most effective site for the moral training of the young. In order to advance the position of women, she sought more than access to male institutions as they already existed. Indeed, she evidenced considerable disdain for the general run of boys' boarding schools and grammar schools, as at best inadequate, and at worst, corrupting of the young.

Elizabeth Wolstenholme believed that women might manage these things better, especially if their domestic experience and knowledge were also brought to bear on the profession of teaching. She also believed teaching to be a highly skilled occupation, one which itself needed to be taught. She hoped to see it become a profession in its own right, rather than merely a temporary resort for the indigent middle class, as it was so often regarded at this time. Her method was to encourage mutual aid and cooperation among women teachers, to which end, in 1865, she established the Manchester Board of Schoolmistresses. Her example was soon emulated in other towns in the north-west, and these organisations together, and under the leadership of a Liverpool headmistress, Anne Jemima Clough (1820–92), established courses of advanced lectures for women in this region during 1867. Such efforts were furthered also by the formation of the North of England Council for Promoting the Education of Women. Its president was Josephine Butler (1828–1906), wife of the principal of Liverpool College, an institution itself involved in a new initiative to provide a co-educational series of lectures for advanced students.

The North of England Council eventually became something of a rival to the committee formed by Emily Davies and Barbara Bodichon for the founding of a university college for women in Cambridge. The aim of Emily Davies's scheme was to establish a separate college which would provide a university education equivalent in terms both of curriculum and assessment to that available in the men's colleges. The approach of the North of England Council was somewhat different. Its immediate aim was to establish some kind of examination to follow the series of advanced lectures for women which had proved such a success. Though this would not be the equivalent of a university degree it would provide women teachers with a formal qualification. This was a need which many, including Elizabeth Wolstenholme, saw as a pressing one for women teachers themselves, but which also promised longer-term benefits in the improvements which might then follow in the education that such teachers were able to provide in girls' schools.

Emily Davies remained sceptical of this scheme because she feared that such a lesser qualification would establish permanently second-rate standards of education for women. She also disliked in principle Anne Jemima Clough's claim for women's 'special needs' in education, or any belief that a proper provision must be 'womanly' in approach and content. The North of England Council, on the other hand, was influenced by the views of some of the Cambridge lecturers providing its programme of advanced lectures, and also at this time seeking significant reform and modernisation of the university curriculum. Such views fostered an equal scepticism among members of the North of England Council with regard to Emily Davies's scheme, which sought to imitate this questioned curriculum in university education for women. The North of England Council succeeded with its goal of securing a special Cambridge Higher Examination for women, based on a more modern curriculum, and Elizabeth Wolstenholme herself sat for the examination in 1869, winning honours. The advanced lectures for women led subsequently to the founding of

Newnham College in Cambridge with a distinct curriculum of its own. Meanwhile, Emily Davies pushed ahead with her particular vision of equality in higher education in the women's college she established at Hitchin, which subsequently became Girton College.

The question raised by these different approaches, then, was how best to recognise the differing needs and ambitions among women in any single reform? Those who supported the approach of Emily Davies tended to emphasise the right to equality of provision for women from the wealthier families whose sons made up the student bodies of the ancient universities. The approach of the North of England Council reflected, in contrast, the pressing concerns of those who earned their living from the education of girls. Elizabeth Wolstenholme's aim, for example, was to address quickly both the present under-qualification of most women teachers for their profession, and the need of these same women to protect their employability in a labour market which was about to see significant change. Another member of the North of England Council, Millicent Garrett Fawcett (1847–1929), similarly pointed out that few of the women with the most pressing need for advanced education had the resources to support themselves in Cambridge for several years. So while the approach of the North of England Council may appear less committed to the full equality sought by Emily Davies, it was also less exclusive in its applicability, more extensive in its reach. It addressed itself to the problems of a larger body of women, and sought also to make opportunities for advanced education as widely available as possible. Moreover, members of the North of England Council intended the lectures for women merely as a stop-gap. Their ultimate aim was the equal entry of women into existing institutions. Hence, Elizabeth Wolstenholme also became an advocate of opening up technical education to women, and of co-education in secondary schools.

As the movement for women's rights began to expand in yet more numerous directions, and as an increasingly various body of women was recruited into that movement, differences among women inevitably gave rise to further such tensions and divisions, and there emerged an ever widening spectrum of opinion on women's rights. At one extreme were those, like Elizabeth Wolstenholme, generally advocating policies which were more, rather than less, inclusive; which would address the needs of as wide a body of women as possible. At the other were those, like Emily Davies, who generally took existing male elites as their model, and sought women's recognition within those elites. In between was a large body of moderate opinion which tended to look at such questions pragmatically. It sought approaches which promised the best immediate outcome, and which took note of particular external circumstances of relevance, for example, the party-political balance within the House of Commons. Such varieties in outlook and approach were to become particularly divisive in the campaign for women's suffrage, another campaign in which Elizabeth Wolstenholme was to play a notable part. Here, once again, she helped articulate and advocate a more inclusive conception of the citizenship of women.

Though women's suffrage was not an entirely new demand, it was among the most controversial to be mooted in the nineteenth-century women's movement. In questioning an ideology of 'separate spheres', which identified public life as the domain solely of men and which would confine women to the realm of the domestic, it challenged the existing relation between the sexes in a most fundamental way. More particularly, it sought to end the male monopoly of political representation in the House of Commons. In the 1860s the issue was revived, initially in the columns of the *English Woman's Journal* and in a debate at the Kensington Society in 1865. The question had taken on a fresh urgency with the election of John Stuart Mill to parliament that year. He was the intellectual guide for a new generation of Radical Liberals, among whom Elizabeth Wolstenholme and many of her colleagues counted themselves. He declared his support for women's suffrage during his campaign for the seat of Westminster, and a number of the Kensington Society worked in this election on his behalf. One of Elizabeth Wolstenholme Elmy's fondest memories in old age was her attendance at Mill's election meeting, where he put the issue of women's suffrage before voters.

Nearly all fifty members present at the Kensington Society debate on the question in November 1865 voted in support of women's suffrage. But Emily Davies cautioned against forming a committee to pursue the demand, especially in the terms used by Barbara Bodichon: 'I find nothing irritates men so much as to attribute tyranny to them. . . . Men cannot stand indignation, and though of course I think it is just, it seems to me better to suppress the manifestation of it.'[22] She also feared that such a radical demand would attract 'wild people', who would proceed by 'jumping like kangaroos', and so damage pre-existing undertakings. When the Liberal government announced a forthcoming Reform Bill in March 1866, Barbara Bodichon secured an undertaking from John Stuart Mill that he would present a petition requesting the inclusion of women in the proposed extension of the franchise, if she were able to obtain at least a hundred signatures. Even then Emily Davies maintained the unwisdom of moving on this issue. It took a speech supporting the inclusion of women in the franchise by Disraeli, the Conservative leader, to convince her that the time was indeed right to pursue the enfranchisement of women.

Now there was divided council on how to formulate this fresh demand on behalf of women. It was the view of Emily Davies that the franchise should be sought only for single women and widows, those women, that is to say, who could demonstrate the 'independence' which had long formed the basis to claims for citizenship. John Stuart Mill's step-daughter and amanuensis, Helen Taylor (1831–1907), acknowledged that there might be a certain wisdom in focusing on the disfranchisement of women property-owners, for property remained the qualification for the vote even in the new Reform Bill. As Helen Taylor put it, seeking the vote for women who could satisfy the same property qualifications required of male voters was certainly less challenging than 'the much more startling proposition that sex is not a proper ground for distinction in political rights'.[23] But Helen Taylor also accepted the view of her step-father, Mill, that the petition should incorporate no principle of exclusion which differentiated between men and women, as any limitation of the demand to unmarried women and widows would have done. She successfully advocated a form of words within the petition which argued that 'the possession of property in this country carries with it the right to vote in the election' and that 'the exclusion from this right of women holding property is therefore anomalous'.[24] This represented a compromise which, though it effectively excluded married women under coverture, did not *expressly* do so. A refusal to take any deliberately exclusive stand on this issue marked the approach of Radical suffragists like Elizabeth Wolstenholme for the remainder of the century, while the subsequent readiness of more moderate suffragists expressly to write married women out of the demand gave rise to some of the bitterest disputes among suffragists. For the time being, however, the compromise form of the petition satisfied both sides.

Elizabeth Wolstenholme was among the initial subscribers to the committee formed in London, and she also immediately set about establishing a similar group to forward the project in Manchester. Among those who gathered to her support were Ursula Bright and her husband, Jacob. Surprisingly little is known about this couple. He was a local industrialist and a younger brother of John Bright, by this time one of the elder statesmen of middle-class radicalism. Jacob Bright's advanced liberal outlook had led him away from the Society of Friends, although his closest associates within the women's movement remained his own Quaker sisters and sisters-in-law. Ursula Bright was a wealthy woman in her own right, the daughter of a successful Liverpool merchant, William Mellor. Her love of fine dress and outspoken directness became a by-word among her more restrained Quaker kin, who none the less showed a fond tolerance for this warm, if somewhat strident, personality. Others in the women's movement were to find her overbearing, and high-handed, but her husband remained almost universally liked and respected by allies and enemies alike, and proved perhaps the most consistently active member of parliament on behalf of women's emancipation in the following decades.

Among the earliest members of the Manchester committee was Richard Pankhurst, a radical lawyer at this time much involved in the workers' education movement and other advanced causes in Manchester. He lacked the means of wealthy reformers like the Brights, and his radicalism proved an insuperable hindrance to his ambitions for a parliamentary career. But he, too, remained among the most stalwart in his commitment to women's rights, contributing his professional knowledge to advance the women's cause through the courts and Parliament, and drafting the first solely women's suffrage bill. In subsequent decades he was joined in the suffrage campaigns by his wife, Emmeline, and she in her turn was followed by their children, most notably their three daughters, Christabel, Sylvia and Adela. This group of Manchester Radicals provided Elizabeth Wolstenholme with her closest associates for the next twenty years or so.

Almost single-handedly she collected, as the first secretary of the Manchester committee, over 300 of the 1,499 signatures which appeared on the petition that John Stuart Mill presented to the House of Commons on 7 June 1866. Her efforts went unacknowledged, however, in subsequent histories which chose to ignore the role of such Radical suffragists in the formation of the demand for votes for women. This is only the first of many instances where the contribution of Elizabeth Wolstenholme and her closest associates became 'written out' of the history of the suffrage movement.[25] For it is clear that they and the London committee, under the leadership of Emily Davies, became increasingly at odds. The Liberal government fell in the summer of 1866 without having secured passage of its Reform Bill, so this opportunity to test support for women's suffrage was lost.

The following months saw large demonstrations on behalf of a wider suffrage, culminating in the Hyde Park riots.

In February 1867, after Elizabeth Wolstenholme moved and established another school at Moody Hall, Congleton in Cheshire, the Manchester Society elected a new secretary in Lydia Becker (1827–90). This signalled no change in its Radical complexion, however, and Lydia Becker remained among the closest allies of Elizabeth Wolstenholme Elmy and Ursula Bright in the leadership of the women's movement for a number of years to come. She, too, was a Lancashire woman born and bred, though partly of German descent. Until then her life had been altogether more retiring, as an unmarried daughter in the home of well-to-do parents. She had enjoyed the benefits of a private education and travel in Europe, and was widely read. In consequence she had become something of an expert in horticulture, winning a gold medal for one of her scholarly papers in 1862. Her own intellectual leanings led her to establish the Ladies' Literary Society in Manchester in 1867, though such interests were soon supplanted by her involvement in the suffrage campaign.

Lydia Becker's introduction to the question of women's suffrage came through a paper which Barbara Bodichon read before the Social Science Conference in Manchester in October 1866. It inspired her to write her own article on the issue, one which she sent to Emily Davies for advice as to possible publication, who forwarded it to Elizabeth Wolstenholme as secretary of the Manchester Society. She in turn persuaded her colleagues there that they should publish 10,000 copies of the paper as a pamphlet, and invite this capable new convert on to their committee. Shortly, as we have seen, Lydia Becker herself became its secretary, and in this position, and subsequently also as editor of the *Women's Suffrage Journal*, which first appeared in 1870, she became a commanding presence in the national leadership of the suffrage movement.

Lydia Becker's letter book for 1868 suggests close and fond friendships between her and both Elizabeth Wolstenholme and Ursula Bright. It also suggests that she felt at one with the Manchester Radical–Liberal circles to which this work had introduced her, in the tensions among suffragists that became ever more evident. John Stuart Mill and Helen Taylor have been credited with fomenting many of these tensions. Certainly, Mill had disliked the informal basis of the initial petition committee in London, which had resulted in policy-making and management of the campaign by a small clique. He had also argued for excluding men from any suffrage organisation to increase women's confidence and autonomy – though not averse himself to manipulating the policies of such an organisation behind the scenes. Emily Davies, for her part, believed it advantageous to have the advice and active support of men in public life. Her preferred method was to work through small, informally constituted groups of like-minded people, who might effectively organise for change through contact with and pressure upon those influential men sympathetic to their cause. The demonstration of large-scale support was not important to the task, as she conceived of it.

Emily Davies was also increasingly wary of the 'radical proclivities' of some of those brought on to the London committee, and dismayed by the influence of Radical–Liberals. She became especially concerned at any possible identification with the Reform League, which was promoting the Reform Bill, especially after the Hyde Park riots in the summer of 1866. She wrote to Barbara Bodichon at this time: 'It clearly will not do to identify ourselves too closely with Mill.'[26] As a consequence, for the first few years of the campaign John Stuart Mill and Helen Taylor worked far more closely with the Manchester committee. It was the Manchester petition, for example, which Mill chose to put before the new session of Parliament in 1867, so that the London petition, in consequence, attracted far less notice.

The 'quiet section' of the suffrage leadership around Emily Davies found itself increasingly the subject of bitter criticism. By the summer of 1867 it agreed to withdraw, and leave the London suffrage society 'under the direction of the Radical section of the party'.[27] Emily Davies was in any case now very much immersed in her efforts to establish a women's college at Cambridge, and though Barbara Bodichon continued to keep in close touch with the new suffrage society, and to express her support and enthusiasm for the suffrage cause, she too decided to focus her energies on this goal. A fresh London committee was then formed at the home of Clementia Taylor (1810–1908). A farmer's daughter and former governess, she had been involved in a wide range of reform causes, going back to the Anti-Corn Law League of the 1840s. P. A. Taylor, her husband and the MP for Leicester, was also known to be 'an advanced radical', once described as 'anti-everything'. Their radicalism extended beyond Britain, including, for example, Italian independence and reunification, and they became the lifelong friends of Mazzini. Clementia Taylor had also been especially active in the anti-slavery cause. By this time, her home, Aubrey House, had become a centre for middle-class, non-conformist radicalism in London, and she had been among the signatories to the original women's suffrage petition which was gummed together in her library.[28] But she reported to Helen Taylor how the other members of the London committee had viewed her as 'a dangerous, go-ahead, revolutionary person', so that she had felt herself to be 'a Pariah' among them.[29] She found herself the only remaining member of that original committee, but joined now by others more congenial to her point of view. Among those invited to the inaugural meeting of the new society was Millicent Garrett Fawcett, whose sister Elizabeth Garrett had been aided by her close friend, Emily Davies, in her pursuit of a medical education. Their recently deceased sister, Louisa Smith, had been the nominal secretary of the original London committee. At this time Millicent Garrett Fawcett was only newly married to the blind MP and Cambridge economist, Henry Fawcett, another of John Stuart Mill's admiring followers in Parliament. This new committee was dominated by women from such circles of middle-class radicalism. None the less, to begin with the new London Society sought to establish as broad a political base as possible for its work and included among its number Conservatives like Frances Power Cobbe. But the tensions proved too great, and Frances Power Cobbe soon resigned, along with others of like mind.

The Radical kinship and friendship circles evident in the formation of the Manchester and London Societies also provided much of the leadership for further suffrage societies being formed at this time in Scotland and the west country. Members and relatives through marriage of the Bright family had been among the original subscribers to both the London and Manchester committees. Margaret Bright Lucas, sister of John and Jacob Bright and a leading temperance campaigner, now joined the committee of the new London Society. Meanwhile her sister, Priscilla Bright McLaren, was helping to found the Edinburgh Society, and often represented it at joint meetings in London. The Brights' sisters-in-law, Mary and Anna Maria Priestman and Margaret Tanner, and their nieces, Lilias and Anne Ashworth, as well as John Bright's daughter, Helen Priestman Bright Clark, were all to the forefront in the suffrage societies which were formed in Bristol and Bath the following year.[30] At the suggestion of the Manchester Society, these local bodies came together in 1867 in a loose federation, the National Society for Women's Suffrage (NSWS).

The women's suffrage amendment to the Reform Bill sought by John Stuart Mill was rejected in the House of Commons, and so women had no share in the extensions to the franchise introduced in 1867. None the less, shortly afterwards a Manchester shop-keeper, Lily Maxwell, found herself included in error on the voters' roll. With Lydia Becker's encouragement she cast a vote – one on behalf of Jacob Bright. Lydia Becker then set about organising the registration of other women with the necessary property qualifications on the electoral rolls being prepared for the general election of 1868. She used the argument that under Brougham's Act of 1850 the term 'man' was to be interpreted in all statutes as including women, unless otherwise specified. Accordingly women were enfranchised by existing legislation. This interpretation was challenged in the courts, however, and ruled incorrect in the judgment given in Chorlton v. Lings in November 1868. Only fresh legislation now would secure the vote for women. In 1870 Jacob Bright introduced to Parliament the first bill aimed at giving women the parliamentary franchise. It had been drafted by his colleague on the Manchester committee, Richard Pankhurst, and provided for all words importing the masculine gender in franchise legislation to include females. It embodied, therefore, the compromise formulation of the demand around the principle of sexual equality, a formulation which, as Elizabeth Wolstenholme later recorded, had the advantage of avoiding 'the vexed question of unmarried women' (though it remained the case that only single women would have qualified for the vote under such an act).[31] The bill did not gain a majority in the House of Commons, but its supporters declared themselves encouraged by the number of votes which it had attracted.

These early efforts to secure votes for women brought one significant advance. In 1869, Jacob Bright successfully moved an amendment to the Municipal Corporations Bill so as to include women in the terms there established for certain local government franchises. As a result women were enabled to participate formally in public life, albeit at a local level, almost fifty years before they gained the parliamentary franchise. Moreover, a precedent had been set which was speedily acted upon once more. The school boards established by the Education Act of 1870 not only allowed women with the necessary property qualifications to vote, but also to stand for election. Emily Davies, Lydia Becker and Elizabeth Garrett Anderson shortly after became among the first women to be elected to public office as members, respectively, of the Manchester and London school boards. Over the next two decades women steadily advanced their right to participate in local government, as new franchises and new offices were opened up to them.

Plate 2 Elizabeth Wolstenholme Elmy. By courtesy of Manchester Central Library Local Studies Unit (M50/2/21/28).

2

'THE REVOLT OF THE WOMEN'
Sexual subjection and sexual solidarity

Elizabeth Wolstenholme had already formed herself as an 'independent person' by the time she encountered a like-minded community in the Langham Place circle and the Kensington Society. Such independence rested both on a professional career and the civil status of a single woman, that of 'feme sole'. It was an independence she had sought to reinforce in herself, and foster more generally among her sex, through the formation of associations with other professional women, continuing self-cultivation, and involvement in the campaigns to extend women's rights and opportunities which were well underway by the end of the 1860s. Such independence was hard-won and vulnerable. And this vulnerability increased, as we shall see, when Elizabeth Wolstenholme became an employee of the movement she had helped create, for it was a movement which became increasingly bitterly divided over differing conceptions of the citizenship for women.

Elizabeth Wolstenholme's closest colleagues remained the Radical suffragists of the Manchester–Liverpool region, and she helped articulate and strengthen the Radical suffragist perspective on women's claims to citizenship.[1] This was a perspective, first, which denied property-holding as the only signifier of that 'independence' on which radical claims to citizenship had so long been based. Instead, drawing especially on the work of John Stuart Mill, it grounded civil rights in the human capacity for reason and moral judgement. Yet again, this was an inclusive approach, and often led Radical suffragists to support universal suffrage – the vote for all adults, women and men – though their primary concern remained the removal of the sex disqualification.

The Radical suffragist perspective also brought with it a more

27

extensive agenda than franchise reform, for it recognised the embodied nature of citizenship. From this viewpoint, women's claim to the vote was undermined by other aspects of their civil status, most notably in marriage laws which robbed the feme covert of her former rights over her own body. So, for Radical suffragists, ending coverture was as important a matter as the vote for securing the full standing of women as citizens. The divisive potential of the differing civil status of married and single women had been evident from the very beginning of the suffrage movement. Moderates were prepared to leave aside the issue of coverture, and seek the vote only for single women, whom they viewed as a vanguard for their sex. Radical suffragists, however, took the married woman as the fullest measure of women's subordination, and believed there could be no emancipation for women while this particular group remained so oppressed. The 'equal rights' formula advocated by John Stuart Mill was a compromise which could not fully satisfy the ambitions of Radical suffragists, for such a measure would have left the large majority of married women disfranchised, as legally incapable of holding the necessary property qualifications for the vote. Very soon after collecting the first women's suffrage petitions, then, Radical suffragists moved also to revive the campaign for reform of the laws relating to married women's property. In this way the suffrage campaign lent a fresh imperative to reform of the marriage laws, revealing more clearly the fact that married women suffered a double disqualification from the franchise – that of sex, and that of coverture.

Here again Elizabeth Wolstenholme was to the fore. In December 1867, together with other members of the Kensington Society, she approached the Social Science Association with a memorial signed by 300 women of note, asking this body to take up the question of reform of the married women's property laws. The Social Science Association agreed to do so, and within a matter of months had drafted a bill to give married women full rights over their property and person. Elizabeth Wolstenholme also became the 'moving spirit' in the formation of a new body, the Married Women's Property Committee.[2] Here again Radical suffragists, and especially those in the north-west, were a notable presence.

Writing to invite Helen Taylor to join its general committee, Elizabeth Wolstenholme explained that the headquarters of the new body would be in Manchester as most of its provisional executive committee, which included Josephine Butler and Richard Pankhurst, lived in or near that city. She also offered an indirect criticism of

London suffragists by suggesting the unfeasibility of being able to bring together such a group in the metropolis.[3] In accepting this invitation, Helen Taylor expressed the view common among Radical suffragists that: 'women cannot in the present state of opinion work at reforming too many points'. She also praised the 'short and emphatic terms' in which the demand was formulated.[4] The Married Women's Property Bill was introduced by Jacob Bright in 1869, but by the time of its passage in 1870 it had been savagely amended during its process through parliament. Married women gained some significant new rights over their property, perhaps most notably in terms of their earnings, but these rights none the less remained circumscribed and the doctrine of coverture still prevailed. As a consequence this measure failed to end the double disqualification of married women from the franchise. Elizabeth Wolstenholme described it as 'retaining the old unjust principle, and applying partial remedies for some of its worst abuses'.[5] As we shall see in subsequent chapters, bringing an end to the doctrine of coverture remained among her most pressing commitments for the remainder of the century.[6]

Family life and sexual relations, not simply parliament and the franchise, became the ground over which Radical suffragists waged the battle for the citizenship of women – so much so that a number of historians have recently begun to argue that such questions became 'a concern fundamental to nineteenth century English feminism'.[7] But as new rights were being won from the 1860s, fresh injustices were simultaneously being created, and these fresh wrongs served only to compound the inter-relatedness of formal politics and personal life in the eyes of Radical suffragists like Elizabeth Wolstenholme. At the Social Science Conference in Bristol in 1869 she heard two medical men, Charles Bell Taylor and Charles Worth, launch a public campaign against the Contagious Diseases Acts. There she learnt that this legislation, which had been introduced in 1864 and extended by two further acts in 1866 and 1869, required women to undergo medical examination, if suspected of prostitution in certain designated military and naval districts. Those diagnosed as suffering from a venereal disease were then placed under compulsory medical surveillance in a lock hospital until considered cured. A prison sentence with hard labour was among the penalties for non-compliance with the Acts. The legislation contained no similar sanctions against any man who might similarly be a source of infection, while the designation of a woman as a prostitute rested simply on the word of a policeman. Moreover, diagnosis of such disease remained uncertain and in contention among medical men in Britain at this time, and there was as yet no certain cure for syphilis. This legislation, then, was both ill-conceived and inequitable, but more than this, it represented a significant assault on the civil liberties of all women, for simply by walking in certain areas a woman might become subject to the provisions of the Acts.

As a result of the airing of these issues at the Social Science Conference, a National Association for the Repeal of the Contagious Diseases Acts was formed. Women were not invited to its initial meeting, and so Elizabeth Wolstenholme's response was to organise a similar opposition among women. She contacted her old friend, Josephine Butler, already known for her rescue work among prostitutes in Liverpool, and similarly convinced that reform of sexual relations was central to the goal of women's emancipation. Josephine Butler might stand at the head of any women's campaign against this legislation as someone with an established philanthropic reputation in this field, and as 'a matron with the experience and standing of a wife and mother'.[8] In this particular matter, paradoxically, married women had a greater freedom to speak out publicly than single women. Josephine Butler was also known to be religiously devout, an evangelical who was still looking for some great work to assuage her grief at the accidental death of her small daughter some years before. After reflecting on the summons from Elizabeth Wolstenholme, she came to the conclusion that here was the call for which she had been waiting. Fighting for repeal of the Contagious Diseases Acts became for her, and for many other women, 'a great crusade' in the years that followed.[9]

Such a campaign was one certain to provoke controversy, given the social taboos of the day. It also aroused strong resistance from the establishment, in the form of the church, the military, and the medical profession. Josephine Butler needed the support of women recognised both for an intrepid commitment to justice, and for maintaining the highest standards of modesty and piety. So, she sought the counsel of those Quaker women, notably among the Bright circle, who had already come forward in support of the vote and married women's property rights. They possessed a long experience of campaigning for moral and political reform, as abolitionists, temperance workers and supporters of the Anti-Corn Law League.

When Josephine Butler first put this issue before them, she recalled, their response had been unequivocal: 'Well, we must rouse the country . . . so gentle, so Quakerly, yet convinced that we three poor women must rouse the country.'[10] Together they called a gathering of concerned women in the meeting house in Leeds. Elizabeth Wolstenholme and Ursula Bright were among those who attended alongside Quaker women. Out of this initiative came the Ladies National Association for the Repeal of the Contagious Diseases Acts (LNA), which, as Josephine Butler recorded, included as some of its most tenacious supporters 'all the sisters and other relatives' of John Bright, 'all the leading ladies of the Society of Friends'.[11] She herself provided the charismatic leadership which stirred so many eminently respectable women to join a campaign that was shocking both in terms of its public response, and in what it revealed of the underside of society. It was women from 'the peace-loving, but combative Society of Friends', however, and most notably Margaret Tanner and her sister, Mary Priestman, who saw to the central management of the campaign on a day-to-day basis 'in their own calm, practical manner', with the support and aid also of Anna Maria Priestman.[12]

All three Priestman sisters by this time lived in or near Bristol, where they shared with Elizabeth Wolstenholme a mutual friend in Mary Estlin, widely known in these circles as one of the earliest and firmest supporters among British abolitionists of William Lloyd Garrison and the 'immediatist' approach to ending slavery. Other members of the Bright circle, including their niece, Helen Priestman Bright Clark, also lived in the west country, as did her cousins, Lilias and Anne Frances Ashworth. Just as these kinship and friendship circles had provided networks important to the formation of a women's suffrage movement, so too they now became the foundation for Josephine Butler's campaign against the Contagious Diseases Acts. Ursula Bright, Priscilla Bright McLaren, Margaret Bright Lucas, Anna Maria Priestman and Helen Priestman Bright Clark lent their names to its governing body, and helped with the work of local committees.[13]

Involvement in this agitation required considerable care initially. Anna Maria Priestman reported of her work alongside Mary Estlin and Elizabeth Wolstenholme during the 1870 Social Science Conference that 'our cause is such a secret one'.[14] It also required courage and self-assurance of a new order, and Elizabeth Wolstenholme in turn subsequently recalled of Mary Estlin's efforts at this time: 'how brave and true she was to CDA when so many were timid'. Very shortly, however, the LNA began more directly to confront the male monopoly of parliamentary politics. In selected constituencies it began to put up its own candidates in opposition to supporters of the legislation, and in this way, for example, defeated Colonel Storks in two attempts during 1870 to become a Member of Parliament. Such activities exposed women repealers to the violence and thuggery which was a common aspect of elections at this time. During their first campaign in Colchester against Colonel Storks, for example, Josephine Butler and her colleagues were chased from the town by a set of brothel-keepers and their bullies. On another occasion they were fortunate to escape unharmed when the hay-loft where they were holding their meeting was set ablaze by opponents. Threats of sexual violence were another trial, and Josephine Butler recalled: 'the indecencies of the men, their gestures, and threats, were what I would prefer not to describe'.[15]

One Member of Parliament testified to the problems which the campaigns created for politicians: 'We know how to manage any opposition in the House or in the country, but this is very awkward for us – this revolt of the women. It is quite a new thing; what are we to do with such an opposition as this?'[16] The LNA intervention in elections highlighted the brutality and corruption which remained a characteristic of political processes in Britain. It promoted quite new political alliances, most notably between middle-class women and those organisations of working-class men which sought to resist legislation that threatened especially their own womenfolk in those poorer working-class communities that were most subject to the Acts. The activities of the LNA also revealed conflicts of interest between men and women of the governing classes. Such tensions were evident even within circles of middle-class Radicals and reformers. Such women, accustomed to working for radical causes alongside fathers, brothers and husbands for a generation and more, now often encountered an unexpected antagonism to their claims from those they assumed would be their natural allies. The prevarication, obstruction, and ridicule which they met with from men in their own circles provoked great bitterness.

In this the experience of Priscilla Bright McLaren was not exceptional. She was devoted to both her brothers, but perhaps especially to John, whose companion and housekeeper she had been in the years after his first wife died. She had forwarded his political career, like many other women in their family circle, through sewing, fundraising, and canvassing, not to mention the care she provided for his small daughter. Similarly, in her subsequent marriage she had supported her husband in a political career which took him from the Anti-Corn Law League, through public office as Lord Provost of

Edinburgh and a wide range of reform activities including abolition and temperance, to a seat in the House of Commons. For Priscilla Bright McLaren, commitment to repeal of the Contagious Diseases Acts was all of a piece with her longstanding radical politics and with her continuing liberal principles, but she was increasingly disillusioned by the response to this question from among the men of her circle. She reported to the niece she had helped raise, John Bright's eldest daughter, Helen Priestman Bright Clark, how their support in Parliament was proving uncertain. She recorded, too, how her close friend, Clementia Taylor, suffered at P. A. Taylor's initial 'want of clearness of vision' on the question. At one of the Taylors' regular evening soirées for Radical MPs and their wives, Priscilla Bright McLaren had finally found herself unable any longer to suppress her own outrage. Overhearing a conversation between two men which reflected commonly dismissive or complacent attitudes on the question, she intervened to declare: 'What is unjust can never be right – what is wrong can never be good.'[17]

Priscilla Bright McLaren became a fervent advocate of ladies-only meetings on this legislation: 'Women meeting women – I mean ladies – at which we can speak freely of the false idea of morality in which our *gentlemen!* are educated and in which they live.' In this she did not mean to deny the value of meetings for working-class women, which she believed to be especially important to prevent further extension of the legislation. But she drew from her own experiences an intensified sense of middle-class women's particular responsibilities in this matter: 'we require [that] the ladies of the country [be] plainly told how their male friends live and what they believe'.[18] Anna Maria Priestman was similarly incensed by the opposition which had met the suffrage and anti-Contagious Diseases Acts campaigns in the early 1870s from many of the 'screaming gentlemen' who were to be found even among Radical–Liberal circles.[19]

Such tensions promoted among middle-class Radical suffragists a growing sense of solidarity with women of the working class, and a developing analysis of women's wrongs in terms of all women's shared membership of a subordinated sex-class. Some such sense led Elizabeth Wolstenholme, Lydia Becker and Josephine Butler to combine in 1871 to form yet a further body, closely associated with the LNA but broader in scope, the Committee for Amending the Law in Points Injurious to Women (CALPIW). The initial prompt had been a measure of infant life protection the sanctions of which fell harshly on women, especially the mothers of illegitimate children.[20] Out of this committee grew, the following year, an associated body, the Vigilance Association for the Defence of Personal Rights, the aim of which was 'to uphold the principle of perfect equality of all persons before the law, irrespective of sex or class'.[21]

The campaigns for repeal of the Contagious Diseases Acts had already shown the potential for solidarity between women from differing backgrounds. The common oppression of women under the laws which regulated family life and sexual relations formed the ground of such solidarity. But Radical suffragists also saw links between women's economic subordination and their sexual exploitation – prostitution was, from this perspective, the direct outcome of women's limited opportunities in the labour market. Moreover, the work of organisations like CALPIW and the Vigilance Association brought a growing awareness among suffragists of conflicts of interest between working-class men and women. Elizabeth Wolstenholme noted this problem, for example, in relation to the growing body of legislation which aimed to 'protect' women by restricting their employment in processes or occupations deemed detrimental to their well-being. When she asked the Trades Union Congress to receive a deputation of women on the matter of its sponsorship of such measures, she was refused. Reflecting on this rebuff, she commented: 'the legislation proposed is to apply to women only and in no case to men. . . . Yet men decline to hear what women have to say on a matter exclusively affecting themselves.'[22] Anna Maria Priestman expressed similar doubts about the mutuality of interests among men and women in the workplace: 'It is clear that the interests of working women are not represented by the class of men to whom they belong – and therefore so long as the men have votes and the women have none the industrial position of women must be at a disadvantage.'[23]

It is not surprising, then, to find that a number of Radical suffragists, including Anna Maria Priestman and other members of the Bright circle, responded to a call by Emma Paterson to promote trade union organisation among working women.[24] The intention was to emulate recent developments in this area in the United States, and in July of 1874 Emma Paterson founded the Women's Protective and Provident League (WPPL). Shortly after she reported on this initiative to the Social Science conference meeting in Bristol, and it was in this city that the first of the organisations to be sponsored by the WPPL, the National Union of Women Workers, was established. Anna Maria Priestman, Mary Priestman, and their friend, Mary Estlin were all active in its formation, and members of their family and friendship circles made up a significant group on its committee.[25]

Very soon, the National Union of Women Workers (NUWW) established branches also in Yorkshire through a corresponding member, Alice Cliff Scatcherd (1842–1906). The wife of a textile factory owner in the Leeds area, Alice Scatcherd was another Radical suffragist-repealer critical of the existing nature of marriage. This she signalled by refusing to wear a wedding ring, or to attend marriage services in the established church, in which a vow of obedience was required from women.[26] Ben Elmy, Elizabeth Wolstenholme's Congleton neighbour, was another of the corresponding members of the NUWW, and came to know some of her old friends among the Bright circle through its activities. The NUWW also had links with the Bright circle through Lilias and Anne Frances Ashworth who were members of its committee, while among its subscribers were Margaret Bright Lucas, Josephine Butler and Clementia Taylor. Millicent Garrett Fawcett was one of its trustees.

The aims of the WPPL have been described as 'essentially those of a Friendly Society with trade union overtones'.[27] The NUWW followed its parent organisation in this respect. Middle-class benevolence informed the spirit of class cooperation which it promoted, and a middle-class ethos is evident also in its provision of club facilities, aimed at 'rational recreation' and working-class self-improvement. Membership was also open to housewives, indicating some wish to recognise women's unpaid labour in the home. Equally, maternity benefits were limited to married women, suggesting an orientation towards the 'respectable' working class. The promoters of the NUWW sought to strengthen the case against protective legislation for women by advancing the unionisation of women workers. They believed that the organisation of solidarity and mutual aid among women workers might provide a voluntaristic alternative to what they preferred to term 'restrictive' (rather than 'protective') legislation. This was made clear in the submissions which various members of the NUWW, including Anna Maria Priestman, Alice Scatcherd and Ben Elmy, made to the Royal Commission on the Factory and Workshop Acts in 1875. Evidence was offered that existing shop and factory legislation served to take jobs away from women, and to reduce the wages they could command. Another witness for the NUWW, Dr Elizabeth Dunbar, argued further that much of the unpaid domestic service required of women in their homes was far more damaging to their health than most factory work available to them.[28] In sum, then, the NUWW, like its parent organisation was 'marked by a strange mixture of feminism, trade unionism and middle-class attitudes'.[29]

The WPPL has been described as adopting 'a very moderate policy', for example, in making no provision for strike or lockout benefits.[30] This was also the case with the NUWW. Yet though many of the unions established by the WPPL proved short-lived, the NUWW survived for at least twenty years, suggesting that it was meeting at least some of the needs of its members. And like the WPPL, it also successfully supported women in a number of strikes and lockouts in these years. Alice Scatcherd, of the Leeds NUWW, helped organise women during a six-week lockout in Dewsbury, for example, establishing a union which was able to negotiate a victorious return to work. She reported to Lilias Ashworth, of the Bristol NUWW committee, the 'business-like habits' she found among the working-class women she had encountered there, noting how practical and capable she had found them. Her letter also suggests that while the NUWW had no provision for the payment of benefits during such industrial disputes, wealthy women like Lilias Ashworth used acts of personal benevolence to relieve the distress occasioned by the loss of wages. It is clear, too, that through such shared activities middle-class women were able to put the issue of the suffrage before working-class women's groups on a more regular basis.[31]

But in the same period that grounds for cross-class solidarity among women were being articulated, the middle-class leadership of the movement became more and more bitterly divided. The personal life and broader political values of Elizabeth Wolstenholme now became the focus for some of these tensions. She had become a convert to free thought while she was still a headmistress in Manchester.[32] Subsequently, she no doubt welcomed the arrival in the neighbourhood in 1869, of Ben Elmy, at one point a Vice-President of the National Secular Society. She had felt it necessary to refuse several senior appointments in her profession given her 'growing thought concerning matters of orthodoxy', for religious instruction remained an important part of girls' education.[33] No doubt, in these circumstances, she especially welcomed an opportunity to change career, and to take up the paid secretary's position recently established by the Vigilance Association at an annual salary of £300. Her friend, Mary Priestman, reported: 'She will live in

London and devote herself to Parliamentary work for which she is wonderfully fitted',[34] and certainly Elizabeth Wolstenholme's knowledge and understanding of parliamentary procedure was to become a by-word in the movement thereafter.

This appointment also allowed her to give fuller expression to the broader approach to securing the citizenship of women which she shared with other Radical suffragists. As she saw it:

> It is of no avail to expend enormous effort in the attempt to get rid of one legislative embodiment of the evil principles we are fighting [in this case, the Contagious Diseases Acts] whilst leaving untouched other equal abominations and allowing fresh developments of evil to spring up on every side.[35]

In the meantime, divisions had begun to appear among middle-class Radical suffragists. The formation of the LNA, and the link this represented between the demand for women's suffrage and for repeal of the Contagious Diseases Acts, first of all brought a breach with John Stuart Mill and Helen Taylor. Mill himself opposed this legislation but argued against any such close association between the two questions, emphasising the distasteful nature of the issues raised by the movement for repeal. He also sought to undermine the credibility of repealer-suffragists by suggesting their lack of womanliness and gentility in warnings that their 'noisy activity' could only appear 'indelicate and unfeminine' and threatened 'an enormous loss with the public in general'.[36] From 1870 the Manchester Society and John Stuart Mill were also at odds over the best strategy for pursuing women's suffrage itself. He believed that the vote against the 1870 bill showed that public opinion was not yet ready for a purely women's suffrage measure, and counselled against any reintroduction until substantial support at the constituency level had been organised. A meeting of delegates of all the member societies of the NSWS met in the middle of 1870 to debate some of these issues, and agreed to accept his plan for building up constituency organisations. But it also decided in favour of reintroducing the women's suffrage bill the following year, contrary to his advice.

John Stuart Mill and Helen Taylor resigned from the Manchester Society, and now focused their attention on the London Society. Mill began actively to conspire against the northern Radical suffragists, 'the obnoxious set' whom he accused of importing 'common vulgar motives and tactics' into the suffrage movement by linking it to the movement for repeal.[37] The resignation of the secretary,

Caroline Biggs, together with other repealers including Clementia Taylor, was achieved. Mill was anxious to bring Clementia Taylor back into the society as its secretary, however, for he confessed that without her any London committee 'must be a usurper'. He believed her to be more tractable than the other repealer-suffragists: 'Her bitterest enemy could not accuse her of being a strong-minded woman.' But she proved otherwise, and from then on worked alongside the Radical repealer-suffragists of the Manchester Society. Millicent Garrett Fawcett was also sympathetic to the cause of repeal, though her husband, like Mill, felt the campaign ill-advised. For a while Mill thought she might also become an enemy on the London committee. He found 'she has a prosaic literal way of looking at things' and was 'apt to be a little doctrinaire'.[38] But as her friend and biographer, Ray Strachey, recorded: 'Deliberately, and after careful consideration, she stood aside from it [the repeal campaign], and though this decision cost her a great effort, she believed to the end of her life that it had been right.'[39]

The Radical repealer-suffragists in their turn sought to gain control of the movement nationally. Late in 1871, on the initiative of the Manchester Society, a new Central Committee of the NSWS was created, with Jacob Bright in the chair. The NSWS remained a loose-knit organisation which left individual societies largely autonomous and independent, while providing a London headquarters where policies and campaigns could be planned in unison. But by creating this central body the provincial societies strengthened their position with relationship to the London Society, and all the major provincial societies within the NSWS affiliated to it. The London Society, for its part, refused to join the Central Committee, but it had been further divided by this development, and most of the women Radicals now withdrew from its leadership. Mill himself became president of the London Society, and Helen Taylor a vice-president, but it was now only a hollow shell, and one ironically, given Mill's earlier advice, dominated by men. As he himself admitted, there were few prominent women any longer who would join its committee. Millicent Garrett Fawcett was one who did remain loyal to Mill, however, and attempted to broker a new unity among suffragists by promoting the replacement of Jacob Bright as the leader of suffrage MPs, but without success. Mill himself continued to attack the 'Bright and Becker set' for a 'total want equally of good taste and good sense', and to blame them for the defeats met by the suffrage bill when it was reintroduced on a number of occasions in the early 1870s.[40]

It was in the context of such increasingly bitter tensions among suffragists that changes in the personal life of Elizabeth Wolstenholme took on particular significance. The 'Bright and Becker set', of which Elizabeth Wolstenholme was a part, itself began to divide in the mid-1870s, putting Elizabeth Wolstenholme's career and livelihood under threat as it did so. It was the new parliamentary situation of 1874 which set Lydia Becker increasingly at odds with her colleagues among northern Radical suffragists. The general election that year had brought the defeat both of the Liberal government, and of Jacob Bright who for the time being lost his seat in parliament. The views of the Conservative government now in power, and of Conservative suffragists in the House, led to proposed changes in political strategy. Initially, debate focused on how to formulate the demand for votes for women. William Forsyth, the Conservative MP who replaced Jacob Bright as leader of suffragist opinion in the House of Commons, insisted on altering the wording of the suffrage bill so as explicitly to exclude married women.

Though she regretted such a limitation, Lydia Becker advocated a pragmatic acceptance of the new situation in parliament. Elizabeth Wolstenholme and Jacob and Ursula Bright, in contrast, vehemently opposed any such retreat from principle. Jacob Bright declared that he would rather wait a further ten years than support such a measure, while Lydia Becker dryly confessed herself unimpressed by his 'unselfishness at the expense of the 800,000 widows and spinsters' who would have been enfranchised under the proposed bill.[41] In the brief history of the suffrage campaigns, which she published in the 1890s, Elizabeth Wolstenholme saw this as Lydia Becker's greatest failure in leadership, and blamed the weakness of the suffrage movement for the remainder of the century on the divisiveness of the Forsyth proviso.[42]

These personal and party political tensions turned into open division over more extensive changes in Lydia Becker's attitude to the claims of married women. She is supposed once to have protested to Emmeline Pankhurst: 'Married women have all the plums of life!',[43] a perception not shared by many of her married colleagues. On the other hand, she had worked consistently and hard on the Married Women's Property Committee up until 1873, and had once said: 'I think that the notion that the husband ought to have headship or authority over his wife is the root of all social evils. It is a doctrine demoralising alike to men and women.'[44] She had also argued forcibly against the double burden carried by married working women, insisting that men should take 'their fair share of domestic duties'.[45]

From this time onward, however, Lydia Becker reversed her position, seeking not only to re-formulate the demand for the vote only in terms of single women, but seeking also to bring an end to the work of the Married Women's Property Committee. Whereas previously she had been at one with Elizabeth Wolstenholme on the need to maintain this campaign after the passage of the unsatisfactory act of 1870, she now set out a case for suspending the work of the Married Women's Property Committee: 'The best plan would be to pay off our liabilities and rest on our oars.' She pointed out the sympathy within the newly elected Conservative government for a limited measure of women's suffrage, but also its opposition to any further extension of married women's property rights. She advocated, in consequence, a concentration on the women's suffrage issue, and declared of married women's property law reform: 'I should be strongly averse to any attempt to re-open the question in the House of Commons *until women have votes*' [her emphasis].[46] This approach proved unacceptable to most of her closest colleagues, however.

After a short period of reduced activity, the Married Women's Property Committee began again to press for further reform. Lydia Becker remained on the committee but no longer took an active role in its work. She also began to encounter opposition, led by Ursula and Jacob Bright, to her new approach to the suffrage demand. Priscilla Bright McLaren regretted such division, and the personal antagonisms which it increasingly reflected, writing to Helen Priestman Bright Clark: 'I wish Miss Becker and Aunt Urlie [Ursula Bright] were a little different – especially the latter.'[47] The disaffection of some within the Bright family circle went even further, and led Lilias Ashworth and her sister, Anne, to align themselves increasingly against their aunt and uncle. They joined their old friend, Millicent Garrett Fawcett, in supporting the change of direction taken by Lydia Becker.

This division was not simply one between married and unmarried women, then – Millicent Garrett Fawcett, a married suffragist, lent her support to Lydia Becker, while Elizabeth Wolstenholme, as yet unmarried, opposed such a shift in focus to the needs of the single woman. It was not conflicting self-interest among suffragists which was at the heart of these tensions, but differing conceptions of women's citizenship, and of strategies to achieve it. To those who would exclude married women from the suffrage demand, acceptance of the Forsyth proviso separated the 'realists' from the 'extremists', the truly non-partisan from Liberal Party loyalists. To the Radical suffragist point of view, however, the exclusionist approach appeared narrow, directed by Conservative Party interests, and a hindrance to any genuine achievement of citizenship for women. This was to be the first of many such disputes among suffragists in which Elizabeth Wolstenholme and her closest colleagues continued to challenge the more cautious approach of those like Lydia Becker and Millicent Garrett Fawcett.

In late 1875, many of these tensions became centred on Elizabeth Wolstenholme herself, and her future role in the women's movement. At this time it became evident to circles beyond her closest friends and colleagues that Elizabeth Wolstenholme's radical outlook extended also to her personal life. In 1874 she had married her Congleton neighbour, Ben Elmy, sometime schoolmaster, minor poet and man of letters, but at this point a silk-crepe manufacturer in that town. As 'Ellis Ethelmer' he recorded it as a marriage 'by registration . . . in which no degrading proviso of "obedience" is extracted from the wife'.[48] But this was only one of the significant aspects of the Elmys' matrimonials. In fact, their marriage had begun some time earlier as a free union, a choice consistent with their shared commitment to secularism.[49] Certainly, Annie Besant's account of the secularist view of marriage 'as something far higher than a union "blessed" by a minister' is consistent with the Elmys' originally free union, with their defenders' accounts of their informal marriage, and with the kind of views about sexual passion later to be put forward in the works of 'Ellis Ethelmer'.[50] Another factor in their decision may also have been Elizabeth Wolstenholme's combination of libertarianism and opposition to existing family law. By choosing a free union she both refused any official sanction for her personal life, and avoided demotion to the status of 'feme covert'.

The strain of her position appears, however, to have been taking a toll on her health in the spring of 1874. Mary Priestman undertook the care of her old friend at this time, and Mary Estlin commiserated with her in her efforts: 'It grieves me to know she is so weak. . . . Poor dear, she draws out one's sympathy and one's vitality in no ordinary measure – nothing ever seems to "stay put" (as the Americans say) with her.'[51] Initially the Elmys' informal marriage appears to have been known to only a few of their closest friends, though Elizabeth Wolstenholme was openly acknowledging her *plans* to marry in the summer of 1874. She evidently also felt cause for concern in some of the expectations aroused by this news: 'Mr Elmy and I are constantly pained by the assumption of our friends that our marriage must needs involve cessation of interest and activity in our works. That can never be.' She indicated, also, that she wished to combine marriage with a continuation of her professional life, even if this meant living apart from Ben Elmy for much of the time: 'If V.A. [Vigilance Association] work in London is given up – of course I should be free to go down to Congleton – but that could never mean idleness or apathy – only a varied form of action.'[52] She made it clear, then, that she had no wish to retire into domestic life, even should she leave London for Congleton.

Her evident anxiety over reception of the news of her plans to marry may have reflected also the increasing hostility she was then experiencing from some among the suffrage leadership. At least part of this antagonism arose from her links with the northern Radical suffragists, who continued to contest the leadership of the movement, and to resist the exclusion of married women from the demand. Such considerations clearly informed the antagonism towards her evident in a letter written by Lilias Ashworth, whose sympathies, as we have already seen, were with Lydia Becker's change of view, and not with that of her aunt, Ursula Bright. Reporting on movement business to Anna Maria Priestman in mid-1874, she said she had been unable to find time to see Elizabeth Wolstenholme when she was in London, suggesting a deliberate snub:

> We have been much annoyed with her. She has been far too busy stirring up ill feeling against the Suffrage Bill owing to the proviso. . . . [the new Forsyth proviso which for the first time expressly excluded married women from a suffrage bill] In trying to spread around the rumour that there are divisions in the suffrage camp she injures *all* our women's questions. Poor thing! I believe she thinks we have all deserted her (I mean the suffrage women).[53]

Further anxieties began to grow among her colleagues when Elizabeth Wolstenholme did not attend the annual meeting of the Vigilance Association in Bristol in mid-October 1874 as expected. She was, in fact, by this time over five months pregnant, and she and Ben Elmy had been persuaded to go through a formal marriage only days before at the Kensington Register Office. Ursula Bright, it is said, eventually persuaded the couple to this step with the argument that to refuse would be to harm the cause they had so long served. The marriage was witnessed by Emilie Venturi, who had worked alongside Elizabeth Wolstenholme in both the repeal campaigns and the Vigilance Association, and who was herself something of a sexual renegade as a divorced woman. The Elmys' son, Frank, was born in January 1875.

Elizabeth Wolstenholme's closest colleagues presumably hoped that the matter might now be forgotten. Those in Bristol suffrage circles were generous in their response. Anna Maria Priestman received this report of Ben Elmy, after he had stayed at the house of Mary Estlin in 1875:

> I cannot tell you how pleased I am with him. The very first evening I had the pleasure of making his acquaintance I went home feeling that life was richer and more worth having, for meeting such a man. He is a real true, noble-minded man, and full of righteous zeal and indignation at the bad things of this world.[54]

But the couple's affairs also continued to be the subject of gossip. Sophie Courtauld, the aunt of P. A. Taylor and a close friend of the Priestman sisters and of Mary Estlin, commented: 'I don't think, were I Miss Wolstenholme, I should thank my lover for a consideration for me that would prevent our marriage.'[55] The formal marriage of Elizabeth Wolstenholme Elmy evidently did not put an end to such comment, and by the end of the year which followed, she found herself the subject of an orchestrated campaign against her continuing public association with a movement she had helped found.

The prompt for this attack remains unclear. Possibly much of the hostility against her stemmed from her close association at this time with secularism and republicanism. In June 1875, Ben Elmy arranged for Annie Besant to come and give two lectures in the Congleton Town Hall, the first called 'Republicanism' and the second on 'The Value of Christianity'. The town clerk sought to cancel these arrangements, without success. Other opponents attempted to raise a rousing chorus of 'God Save the Queen' at the end of the first lecture, but as 'Ajax' reported in the *National Reformer*: 'Loyalty to the Brunswicks is apparently not very flourishing in Congleton.' This was not the case, however, among sections of the suffrage leadership, for whom such anti-monarchical views would have confirmed their fears concerning the Elmys' extremism. These fears, in turn, must have appeared fully justified the following year when both Annie Besant and Elizabeth Wolstenholme Elmy were stoned in Congleton, when they attempted a further series of secularist lectures, while Charles Bradlaugh engaged in a tussle with a local tradesman and well-known wrestler, whom he succeeded in worsting. The *National Reformer* reported laconically that the hymn 'Safe in the Arms of Jesus' was now 'quite a war song' among their opponents, who attempted to drown out the speakers with their singing.[56]

It may simply have been that in the late summer of 1875, now recovered from what had been a difficult birth and having adopted her married name, Elizabeth Wolstenholme Elmy returned to an active role in the movement.[57] Possibly this alerted unfriendly colleagues who had not been privy to the earlier scandal, or further antagonised those hostile to her who assumed she had retired permanently into domestic life. Certainly, the controversy was to centre on her possible reappointment as secretary and member of the executive committees of the Vigilance Association and the Married Women's Property Committee. Whatever was the case, it was the circumstances of her marriage which provided the grounds for the concerted attacks on Elizabeth Wolstenholme Elmy's position in the women's movement which occurred in late 1875. Josephine Butler undertook her defence and was eventually constrained to admit that she had known of the original free union between the couple. A card circulated among those who led the attack and put Josephine Butler's view of the matter in these terms:

> They have sinned against no law of Purity. They went thru' a most solemn ceremony and vow before witnesses. I knew of this *true marriage before God – early in 1874*. It would have been a legal marriage in *Scotland*. They *blundered*; but their whole action was grave and pure. The English marriage laws are impure. Marriage under English law is an *unholy* thing as far as the law is concerned. It sins against the law of purity *indeed*. It is a species of legal prostitution the woman being the man's property. Many of us live *above* that hateful law[58]

Such a defence gave expression to the kind of militant stance towards existing institutions and practices which many in the movement thought exaggerated and harmful. It reflected an essentially revolutionary approach to the emancipation of women through repeal of the Contagious Diseases Acts, reform of the married women's property laws and the enfranchisement of women, which together entailed a dismantling of the existing order of sexual relations. Hostility to the subordinated position of women in the marriage laws was shared by many of the most radical within the movement. Emmeline Goulden is said to have offered Richard Pankhurst a similar free union only a few years later. Yet others rejected the wearing of wedding rings and veils, and the adoption of husbands' last names as symbols of the subordination of the married woman. So Elizabeth Wolstenholme was not alone in her outlook, though it was one which it proved impossible always to live by, even among sympathetic colleagues.

Mutual incomprehension marked the two sides of the controversy. Josephine Butler's account bore this annotation in another hand: 'All this about the marriage law is quite beside the mark I think',[59] suggesting once more a narrower conception of the citizenship of women among the opponents of the Radical suffragists. Isabella Tod, one of the leaders of the suffrage movement in Ireland who was active in this attempt to expel Elizabeth Wolstenholme Elmy from her prominence within the movement, searched around to find her own explanations for these events. She evidently did her utmost to make a charitable reading of them, but it was a bizarre one which indicated the breadth of the division between the two outlooks:

> I do not for a moment forget the great services Mrs Elmy has in times past rendered to the cause of women. On the contrary, I look upon her to some extent as a victim, for I feel convinced that when she took this fatal step her mind had given way, and that alienation was produced by too constant and exclusive attention to the painful subject of the Contagious Diseases Acts and the cognate matters that fall into the department of the Vigilance Society.

Isabella Tod was worried, too, at the way Josephine Butler had maintained her own counsel on the matter, only sharing her knowledge under considerable pressure, and holding back even longer about her knowledge of the original informal marriage: 'It was only after a second letter from me, I am afraid a sharp one, that Mrs Butler gave me the information – but *that* is the only thing that saves the scandal from being utterly unbearable.'[60]

Such pressure persuaded Josephine Butler not to pursue plans to recommend that Elizabeth Wolstenholme Elmy be appointed secretary to the Vigilance Association, at the forthcoming annual meeting in Liverpool. But she insisted her colleague's name be retained on its executive committee. Even so, at the meeting Isabella Tod and others of like mind moved Elizabeth Wolstenholme Elmy's exclusion also from that role. Their votes for her exclusion were matched by those against from Ursula Bright, Jacob Bright, Emilie Venturi and Lucy Wilson. Only Josephine Butler's casting vote from the chair ensured the failure of this attempt to censure and exclude Elizabeth Wolstenholme Elmy.

Isabella Tod reported an even worse reversal at the meeting of the Married Women's Property Committee in Manchester the next day: 'The most awful scene that I have almost ever witnessed, the bitterest part of which to me was the language and action of people whom I have hitherto so truly admired and esteemed as Mr and Mrs Jacob Bright.' She reported that most of the anger had been directed against Lydia Becker who had argued for a check of the marriage registers, to establish whether or not the couple were now legally married:

> At least that was the pretext, but I cannot help feeling that so much wrath could not be expended on that matter, except from a consciousness that no more defensible ground could be taken and that the facts could not be denied.

Only she and Lydia Becker this time voted for Elizabeth Wolstenholme Elmy's removal as secretary. Isabella Tod then gave in her resignation, threatening that the Irish committee might in future act independently on the issue.[61] Lydia Becker also finally withdrew from the committee during this year, as she saw the end to her hopes for the suspension of the campaign for reform of the married women's property laws.

Afterwards, Josephine Butler attempted to protect the Elmys from further harassment by reporting that they had since 'expressed a desire to live very quietly in Congleton and not be made prominent'.[62] None the less, Millicent Fawcett continued to pursue the matter, and wrote directly to Elizabeth Wolstenholme Elmy on this 'very painful subject'. Here she suggested that 'the circumstances connected with your marriage and what took place previous to it . . . has been and is a great injury to the cause of women'.[63] Though she did not agree with those who had sought to exclude Elizabeth Wolstenholme Elmy from the committee of the Vigilance Association, she did urge that by resigning as secretary of the Married Women's Property Committee 'you could in some measure repair the injury' which she believed the scandal had done to the movement. Not altogether consistently, she also joined Isabella Tod in a threat to reveal the details of the controversy to their parliamentary supporters.

Elizabeth Wolstenholme Elmy refused to be intimidated and continued to work closely with other Radical suffragists, especially Ursula Bright. But her name disappears from the reports of both the Vigilance Association and the Married Women's Property Committee until the end of the decade. Sylvia Pankhurst recorded that the Elmys continued to be the focus of 'unpleasant stories' within the women's movement, because of these events and their subsequent involvement in the sexual reform movement. Ben Elmy, for his part, 'intensely resented and never forgave' the interference of his wife's colleagues in their private life, whilst among some suffragists his reputation remained 'as black as though he had been the devil himself'.[64]

In effect, Elizabeth Wolstenholme Elmy's desire to retain her standing as a 'feme sole' along with a sexual union had been thwarted by some among her colleagues within the movement, and at some cost, both personal and financial. She continued to resist what she saw as false considerations of respectability and political expediency, considerations which guided the activities of her detractors in the years to come. She continued to raise questions and issues which many thought too provocative, too advanced, too revolutionary in their implications. The bitter feelings aroused by her marriage took many years to dissipate, while the Radical perspective of her own close circle continued to separate its members from those like Lydia Becker and Millicent Garrett Fawcett, whose vision of women's emancipation was altogether less challenging.

3

A 'STRANGE, ERRATIC GENIUS'

Jessie Craigen, working suffragist

The market squares and village greens of the north saw a new figure enter the suffrage scene in 1879, lumbering and somewhat odd in appearance, but one who cast a spell over the audiences of working people who came to hear her. Accompanied only by her dog, Tiny, Jessie Craigen traversed the countryside, hiring a bell-ringer to spread news of her arrival in town, and holding impromptu open-air meetings outside factory-gates, or wherever she might gather listeners. Her presence challenges a common perception of the nineteenth-century women's movement as one of narrow middle-class perspectives. The attitudes of it leadership might on occasion evidence an ignorance of, or lack of sympathy with, the problems of the less fortunate among their sex. Yet, as we have seen, there were issues on which women might identify with each other across divisions of class, and there was also a growing recognition of sources of strength to be found among working women. Lydia Becker, for example, once declared:

> What I most desire is to see men and women in the middle classes stand on the same terms of equality as prevail in the working classes – and the highest aristocracy. A great lady or a factory woman are independent persons – personages – the women of the middle classes are nobodies, and if they act for themselves they lose caste.[1]

Working-class support took on a particular urgency in these years. The return of a reforming Liberal government was anticipated at the next general election, and a further Reform Bill was expected to be part of its programme. Among men, agricultural workers and pitmen in the colliery villages of the north generally remained disfranchised, and Radicals and labour leaders were beginning to press for a householder franchise. To reach working-class audiences effectively, the suffrage movement needed organisers with an under-standing of the lives of working-class women. It also needed speakers who could take its message out of the drawing room and city hall, and who could build bridges between the middle-class leadership of the movement, and potential working-class supporters. Jessie Craigen had already been doing this on her own initiative when Alice Scatch-erd first sought her help in 1879 in preparations for a forthcoming major suffrage demonstration at the Free Trade Hall, Manchester. She was only one of a number of working women who found employment in the suffrage movement in the years that followed.

Jessie Craigen was the daughter of a Scottish seaman and an Italian actress. Her father had died while she was still an infant, and her mother returned to the stage. There, Jessie Craigen had begun her working life at the age of four, as a fairy in a pantomime. It was through her training for the stage, a training she is said to have received from Madame Lucia Vestris, that Jessie Craigen developed the powerful and magnificent speaking voice which subequently she put at the service of a number of reform issues, including women's suffrage. As a young woman, it appears, she turned her back on the stage when 'religious scruples took hold of her'. Instead, she turned her talents to public lecturing, initially for the temperance move-ment, and thereafter also for women's enfranchisement. Her career began with a series of public meetings which she addressed in the north of England in 1870.

During the following years, she also played a role in the work of the Women's Protective and Provident League, forming a trade union in Aberdeen which gradually attracted women employed in jute and cotton factories there, and which remained in existence well into the 1890s. But it was as a suffrage speaker that this 'strange, erratic genius' came to national prominence, when she directed her efforts especially towards building up working-class support for the women's movement: 'Amongst the miners in Cornwall, the agricultural labourers in Dorsetshire, the colliers of South Wales, the factory hands of Lancashire and Yorkshire, the miners of Durham and the north, she seemed equally at home.' Every so often Lilias Ashworth or Lydia Becker would receive bundles of petitions, 'very genuine and very dirty'.[2] Initially, she undertook such work without pay, seeking only the occasional five-pound note to cover her living expenses.

Jessie Craigen came to greater prominence only in 1879, as we have already seen, and her campaigning in these months reflected the Radical suffragist approach of uniting repeal and suffrage agitation, expecially in seeking working-class support. Alice Scatcherd reported to the annual meeting of the Manchester Suffrage Society in 1879 that Jessie Craigen was undertaking a series of meetings which combined both issues. Some were women-only events, directed particularly at working-class women, among whom she collected a petition of over 1700 signatures. Lydia Becker was so impressed with the impact which Jessie Craigen made on audiences, that she in turn employed her as a speaker for a series of meetings for women electors. These were held in the poorest wards of Manchester, shortly before the November local elections. She wrote to Priscilla Bright McLaren after one of these occasions when, she reported, Jessie Craigen had 'held the meeting enchained by her grand voice and her strong and witty words'. Her description of this contact with an audience of working-class supporters imbued it with the significance of a religious conversion. The audience, she explained, had been:

> all poor women, and, as it seemed on both sides of politics . . .
> I can't tell you how my heart went out to those women; and
> to see them look at me – oh, it was really sacred – awful; it
> was as if I received a baptism. It has been a new life to me to
> know and feel the strength there is in those women – when
> so many fall away from us and leaders desert us; but in those
> women there is a force which, gathered together, led, organ-
> ized, and made manifest, is enough to lead us to victory. It
> has given me such a sense of strength and happiness.[3]

Priscilla Bright McLaren, in her turn, employed Jessie Craigen to help organise the series of major demonstrations being planned in principal cities over the course of the next two years.

Jessie Craigen's first appearance among the national suffrage leader-ship occurred at the first of these, a 'Demonstration of Women', at the Free Trade Hall, Manchester in February 1880. It was a meeting advertised for women only, and, like the others in the series, aimed to bring together women of all classes and conditions. Men were allowed in on this occasion only as spectators in the galleries, and required to pay half-a-crown for the privilege. One eye-witness recalled it as 'a night never to be forgotten'. The dense crowd wishing to take part was made up almost entirely of women, some of whom were said to have walked ten, even twenty, miles to attend.

An overflow meeting had to be organised nearby, with Margaret Bright Lucas presiding, and even then thousands, it was claimed, were turned away. Priscilla Bright McLaren chaired the main meeting and welcomed the assembly by declaring that it all seemed to her like a dream, 'but only a grave reality could have brought so many women together', suggesting once again the combination of suffrage and repeal agitation which had mobilised such support. She reminded her audience that they were in a hall built 'in the cause of freedom'. Harking back to her participation in the Anti-Corn Law campaigns of the 1840s, she recalled that she herself had learned her first 'politic lessons' within its walls.[4]

Jessie Craigen's contribution came at the end of the meeting 'when her heavy, uncouth figure rose, and, sending forth a voice that pealed like a sonorous bell over the vast multitude, roused up their enthusiasm, till every one had risen from their seats in one united burst of cheering'. Jessie Craigen's speech on this occasion reveals something of her rhetorical skills, and of the appeal which she made to women's consciousness of themselves both as members of a sex-class, and of a sex which differed in socially valuable ways from men. To begin with she declared that women 'in the nature of things' were unable to resort to riot, turbulence and violence to demonstrate their wish to become citizens – in fact, she declared such a claim in itself showed 'that the reign of mere brute force is wearing to a close'. The Free Trade Hall had been built on the site of the Peterloo massacre in 1819, when a peaceable demonstration was violently crushed by armed force. Referring to this link with past radicals, Jessie Craigen declaimed: 'On this ground sixty years ago, the blood of women was spilt for freedom' while presently women met to 'lift up their voices in peace and security to claim their share of the liberty', so marking 'the progress of the people from midnight to morning'. But she placed the greatest emphasis on 'the unity of womanhood in which our claim is made'. Though she acknowledged that suffragists were 'separated by many barriers of caste, creed, and education', she insisted also that this could not 'separate the hearts of womanhood that beat in unity. . . . In the name of this common womanhood we are gathered here tonight, rich and poor, educated and untaught, to raise our voices together to ask for justice.' It was in the sufferings of women that such unity was to be found: 'Gentlemen can be bad husbands as well as poor men. The money that should sustain a household can be melted in champagne as well as in beer or whiskey.' Equally, she declared, 'The mother love is also one. The richest woman here tonight that is the mother of children loves them dearly; the poorest does no less.' In particular, she argued, 'the laws which wrong the mother's love are an outrage to the common womanhood by the bond of which we have all been drawn together here'. Reflecting on the demonstration afterwards in the *Women's Suffrage Journal*, 'JHC' celebrated the sense of solidarity which it had created: whereas previously women 'struggled and suffered in solitude' and 'drank their own tears in silence', now 'we see each other's faces, the sun is shining, and the road is plain before us'.[5]

Jessie Craigen's ability to play an audience was evident also in the appeal she often made to local pride, and regional and ethnic rivalries. At the Free Trade Hall, for example, she mentioned how her girlhood had been lived in the environs of the Houses of Parliament, and remarked that Big Ben had to take its time from Greenwich, elaborating her point thus: 'Here in the North is the political Greenwich; we in the North set the political time of day.' If the north agreed that women's claim to the vote reflected 'the true sun of justice', then it was hoped they should soon hear ' "Big Ben" strike the hour that makes women free citizens in their native land'.[6] When Jessie Craigen spoke at a similar major suffrage rally at the Colston Hall, Bristol in 1880, Anna Maria Priestman declared her performance 'splendid'. Once again, Jessie Craigen demonstrated her capacity to appeal to particular concerns and values in her audience. She must have known that Quaker and Unitarian women dominated the movement in the west of England, and she focused her speech there on the 'physical force' argument against women's suffrage, which based claims to citizenship on the capacity to bear arms. There she insisted that women did engage in warfare, but only ever in defence of themselves and their children. Aggressive war-making she declared to be barbaric, and looked forward to the establishment of international courts of arbitration. She stressed, also, that women were victims of war equally with men, and that this provided one of the reasons why they sought the vote. She saw the proper role of government as the defeat of brute force in human affairs, and insisted that rights of citizenship should rest on the 'moral and intellectual capacity' of individuals, in which women were the equals of men. Indeed, to cheers from her audience, she added that 'morally, I think we are a great deal better than men'.[7] From this time the Priestman sisters became some of Jessie Craigen's most steadfast friends among the leadership of the women's movement. They found in her

speaking powers 'all that could be desired', even though they acknowledged among themselves, and with a certain glee, both the
outlandishness of her appearance, and the uncaring attitude she
showed towards middle-class proprieties, as in her choice of
lodgings.[8]

The Priestmans, and other Radical suffragists, were less happy,
however, with attempts yet again to adopt a restricted formulation
of the demand for women's enfranchisement. Once more this issue
threatened the unity of the movement. Jacob Bright, on his re-
election to parliament in 1876, had briefly succeeded in re-instating
the equal rights compromise formulation. Illness forced his retire-
ment as suffrage leader in the House of Commons shortly afterwards,
however. His replacement, another Liberal MP, Leonard Courtney,
brought forward a somewhat different compromise. This was one
which formulated the demand in terms of seeking the parliamentary
franchise for all women who had gained a local government vote in
the preceding decade. It proved acceptable to the London Society,
which at last agreed to join the Central Committee. The NSWS
might now claim, formally at least, to represent a fully unified
movement on behalf of women's suffrage. Helen Blackburn, who
had been the secretary of the Central Committee since 1874, now
became secretary of the NSWS, while Lydia Becker became its
parliamentary secretary, a position which allowed her great influence
over the development of political strategy in the campaigning which
preceded the 1884 Reform Act. Such a reformulation of the demand
continued effectively to exclude married women, even if it did not
do so expressly or by reference to the doctrine of coverture. In this
context the ending of coverture took on a fresh urgency in the eyes
of Radical suffragists.

Perhaps this, together with the reunion and the fresh optimism of
these years, explains the re-emergence of Elizabeth Wolstenholme
Elmy among the leadership of the women's movement, for in 1880
she was once again openly acknowledged as secretary of the Married
Women's Property Committee (during the previous few years she
had continued in this role, but anonymously). Securing further
reform in this area remained an uphill struggle for, as Priscilla Bright
McLaren told the Social Science Conference that year, their
opponents recognised all too well that 'it was a question of power.
They could not bear that the wife should have power.'[9] Elizabeth
Wolstenholme Elmy's name had disappeared from the committee of
the Vigilance Association after the controversy at the end of 1875,

although it had remained under the control of her old allies among the Radical suffragists, including Ursula and Jacob Bright, Emilie Venturi, and Clementia and P. A. Taylor, together with a younger generation of the Bright circle, including Priscilla Bright McLaren's sons, Charles and Walter McLaren, and J. P. Thomasson, son-in-law of Margaret Bright Lucas. Now, the acceptance of Elizabeth Wolstenholme Elmy back into an open role in public life became evident also in the work of the Vigilance Association. Lucy Wilson had been another of her defenders in 1875. When she became founding editor of the monthly journal which the Vigilance Association began to publish in 1881, its columns included regular contributions from Elizabeth Wolstenholme Elmy. These ranged over a wide number of issues, but she took this opportunity to raise repeatedly the question of the position of married women.

First and foremost, she returned to her attack on the 1870 Married Women's Property Act as 'a mere palliative and protective measure'. In response to those opponents who said that an end of coverture would reduce marriage to 'a mere chumming together' she insisted that 'human love, and the affection of husband and wife, of parent and child, are deeper and more permanent facts than any system of legislation whatsoever'. Any such 'truly natural relation', she argued, was 'accidental and not essential' under the present conditions of marriage. She noted that 'hitherto, the heavens have not fallen when law has endeavoured to ally itself with justice', and urged that indeed reform could only strengthen marriage.[10] Perhaps she was offering a personal testimony when she wrote that such a revolution in the marriage relationship was happening despite the state of the law: 'In every happy home the change is complete. There no husband claims supremacy, and no wife surrenders her conscience and her will.' Only in such marriages, she claimed:

> the true unity, that of deep and lasting affection, which law can do nothing to create, but which bad law has done much to weaken and destroy, reigns alone, making of the rich and diverse elements of human nature a whole so sweet that those who have ever tasted such happiness can but trust and strive that it shall one day become universal.[11]

Elizabeth Wolstenholme Elmy did not limit her discussion of the position of married women to property issues, however. Her articles drew attention also to the limited power of the law in securing adequate maintenance for wives and children from husbands and fathers. She presented evidence also of the failure of magistrates to implement those protections which now existed for married women, especially with regard to the granting separation orders on the grounds of physical abuse, or the recognition of their recently won rights over their own wages.[12] Inequalities in the divorce law, and in the law relating to the custody and guardianship of children, also remained a major concern for her.

The high optimism and unity which marked suffrage campaigning in 1880 was soon under threat, however. Many Radical suffragists like Anna Maria Priestman found Leonard Courtney's approach to the question of votes for women altogether 'too patient'.[13] But they had supported Lydia Becker's decision to promote no separate women's suffrage bill, and to concentrate instead on securing a women's suffrage amendment to the anticipated Reform Bill. It was rather the implementation of this strategy which provoked frustration and dissent among Radical suffragists. To begin with, it soon became clear that Lydia Becker's plans were influenced more by her assessment of Conservative Party concerns and aims, than any commitment to the broad programme of reform promised by Gladstone's government. As she explained to Lilias Ashworth Hallett, once a Liberal Reform Bill was brought forward, they could surely count on Conservative support for a women's suffrage amendment, so as to 'give women landowners votes as a counterpoise to the men labourers'. Rather than looking to participate in the government's reform project, then, she aimed at 'making ourselves disagreeable' at every point, seeking to 'mix up our question' with as many parts of its parliamentary programme as possible, so as to convince Gladstone that he could not ignore the question.[14]

Not only was such an approach uncongenial to Radical suffragists, it also neglected to realise their own potential for influencing the government, through their extensive family and friendship links with the leadership of the Liberal Party. On the one hand, the personal and party loyalties of Radical suffragists led them to place their hopes in the Liberal government, and the principles for which it claimed to stand. They also had a much more intimate knowledge of the workings of the Liberal Party, and channels of influence unavailable to Lydia Becker, who sometimes evidenced some resentment at her own standing as an 'outsider' in these circles. Such knowledge, on the other hand, meant Radical suffragists became increasingly anxious about the Liberal government's failure to take up their question, after its return to power in 1880. From such a perspective, it seemed both ill-advised and wasteful not to direct the main efforts of the suffrage movement toward swinging the Liberal Party behind their demand. Increasingly, they acted on their own initiative to stir up support within the rank-and-file of their party, and to put pressure on its leadership through the public representations of women close to its leadership. Lydia Becker, for her part, became increasingly antagonistic to efforts which she saw as undermining her authority as the parliamentary secretary of the NSWS, and thwarting her preference for, and role in, manoeuvrings among sympathetic politicians behind-the-scenes.

She proved especially hostile to any attempt to link the suffrage cause organisationally with the Liberal Party. Anna Maria Priestman was among those who saw matters quite differently. She believed that as a consequence of the strategies pursued by Lydia Becker, the suffrage societies, including her own local society in Bristol, had become inert to a degree which she found 'disgraceful'.[15] She chose, then, to take a quite fresh approach to the question, and in 1881 established a Women's Liberal Association in Bristol, among the first such organisations in the country to make women's suffrage a 'test question' for candidates in parliamentary and local government elections.[16] Similar associations sprang up elsewhere in the months that followed, in which Radical suffragists were always to the fore. These bodies provided an alternative basis from which this section of suffrage opinion was able to pursue its own preferred strategy of working up popular support for their cause, especially among the rank-and-file of the Liberal Party.

Like other Radical suffragists Anna Maria Priestman believed that the claim for women's suffrage was inextricably entwined with the question of democratising the franchise for men. Indeed she clearly felt this offered the most realistic approach to women's suffrage, and she advocated, unsuccessfully, that the suffrage leaders attempt to join forces with Joesph Arch, the leader of the Agricultural Workers' Union. She wrote: 'we shall win with our poor brothers, the agricultural labourers – and I hope we shall use our new power to help to do them good – poor things', a statement which incorporated at one and the same time both a middle-class paternalism and a sense of solidarity with another oppressed group.[17] The origins of the Women's Liberal Associations lay not in Anna Maria Priestman's sense of loyalty to the Liberal Party or to her class, but rather in the growing disillusion experienced by herself and other Radical suffragists. This disillusion extended not only to their party and the men who dominated it, but also to their more cautious colleagues in the suffrage movement and the more restricted perspective on women's emancipation which they held. The formation of the Bristol Women's Liberal Association reflected, then, a commitment to upholding the principle of sexual equality in the face of opposition and hostility among male Liberals. It was motivated also by a desire to realise more effectively the potential for union between the women's cause and plebeian radicalism in a truly popular campaign for women's suffrage. The women's suffrage movement enjoyed a renewed vigour in these years by drawing on such sources of support. In the west of England, for example, Anna Maria Priestman was able to raise £1000 to fund a 'systematic', three-year plan of suffrage work there and in Wales, in preparation for the anticipated Reform Bill.

Like Elizabeth Wolstenholme Elmy before her, however, Jessie Craigen became a victim of the growing tensions within the suffrage leadership over these new directions. She, too, found that paid work for the movement might also bring attempts to limit her freedom of action and of speech, and that the favours of her suffragist employers could prove erratic, uncertain and personally hurtful. Wealthy women, accustomed to dominance and control in relationships with servants, found it difficult always to respect the independence of those less fortunate women who, of necessity, could offer only paid service to the movement. In Jessie Craigen they encountered someone of such deeply held convictions and so passionate a nature that misunderstandings and conflict were inevitable. We have already seen how her 'uncouth' dress, manners and bearing might occasion remark. As she came to prominence as a suffrage speaker there were attempts to make more of a 'lady' of her, albeit with scant success. Alice Scatcherd, for one, came to regret the way their more conventional colleagues had put Jessie Craigen into 'silk dress and lavender kid gloves'.[18] She believed it had raised false expectations in Jessie Craigen, and undermined her capacity to appeal to a wider audience. For her part, Jessie Craigen was to endure much heartache, constant chivying, and an increasingly precarious livelihood, as she became embroiled in antagonism and rivalries among her middle-class patrons.

In her obituary it was recalled how the 'wayward soul' of Jessie Craigen was one which:

could brook no constraint or control: the calm, dispassionate ways of the Women's Suffrage Committees were irritating to her, and she swept along her way to Home Rule, to anti-vaccination, and other questions in which she could let her passionate emotions have full play.[19]

Such an assessment masks a much more complex reality, however. By the spring of 1881 Jessie Craigen's star was evidently in the descendant as far as the more moderate national leadership of the movement was concerned. By this time, she was in the employ of the Ladies National Association (LNA), and no longer appeared prominently in reports of women's suffrage campaign activities published in the *Women's Suffrage Journal*, suggesting some cooling towards her on the part of Lydia Becker, its editor. Possibly the short period of imprisonment which Jessie Craigen underwent at the time was a cause of concern. But it seems likely that Jessie Craigen's growing friendship with Helen Taylor was another cause of her alienation from Lydia Becker, for the two women had earlier regarded each other as rivals for the leadership of the suffrage movement, and by this time apparently refused to appear on the same platforms. By the early 1880s Helen Taylor maintained close relationships with only a few of the Radical suffragists among the Bright circle, most notably with the generally liked and conciliatory Priscilla Bright McLaren, and was otherwise alienated from the work of the suffrage societies. In these years, she immersed herself instead in alternative aspects of Radical politics, most especially the question of home rule for Ireland. Her connection with the Irish Land League only served to reinforce the 'dark surmises' about how her presence on its platforms might 'retard our suffrage movement'.[20]

Initially, Helen Taylor resisted friendship with Jessie Craigen. Anna Maria Priestman remarked on her attitude at this time as 'rather cat's pawish', and it seems that others in the Irish Land League were also attempting to woo Jessie Craigen away from the LNA.[21] If so, such efforts were successful, for during 1881 Jessie Craigen turned away from the women's movement for a time, and put her talents to the service of the Irish cause instead. Such work was fully in accord with her own views, for she was evidently as committed to Irish freedom as she was to the emancipation of her sex. However, she soon found herself at cross-purposes with Helen Taylor. This time the pain of parting was intensified by the passionate love she felt for her patron.

The ending of their friendship followed a characteristically unequivocal voicing by Jessie Craigen of her own assessment of Irish politics, after she had gone to Ireland as an open-air speaker on behalf of the Land League in 1882. She declared that the Irish leader, Charles Stuart Parnell, had 'sold himself to the ministry', that is to Gladstone's government, and was now intent on breaking up the Land League to further his own political ambitions. This was an assessment which Helen Taylor rejected, and from then on she refused any further friendship with Jessie Craigen. In a last plea for reconciliation, Jessie Craigen wrote this to Helen Taylor: 'I made a great sacrifice for the Irish cause. I gave up my situation and threw myself on the world without a penny and without a friend: but it was to fight for the liberty of the people and not to put political tricksters into power.' Helen Taylor had since refused to read any letter from her, and so Jessie Craigen arranged for someone else to write this one in the hope that it might restore their friendship: 'I wish you to have this explanation in order that you may know that I am as true to my principles as I am to you; that my actions are not dictated by caprice, but that I follow as well as I can the light of truth.' She concluded with this declaration: 'I love you more than life. I want nothing of you except that you will let me be a comfort to you as you used to tell me once that I was.'[22]

Such romantic friendships were commonplace among women in the ninteenth century and had not yet acquired their later character- isation as sexual deviancy. What was less common was the formation of such passionate commitment between women from two such differing backgrounds. It would appear that Helen Taylor expected such devotion to include subordination also to her own political assessments and goals, an expectation her protogée had been unable to satisfy. Helen Taylor remained resolute in abandoning Jessie Crai- gen, and it was once more to her friends among the Bright circle that Jessie Craigen turned, both for consolation and practical help. Together, they arranged that she be re-employed in the campaign for repeal of the Contagious Diseases Acts. Priscilla Bright McLaren wrote to Helen Taylor with this news, telling how Jessie Craigen remained 'dreadfully upset' over the ending of their friendship. Pris- cilla Bright Mclaren also told how at first Jessie Craigen had refused the new work found for her out of a sense of solidarity with Helen Taylor, believing that 'the Women's Suffrage ladies' had put them both 'out of court' so that 'she could not think of being taken into favour unless you were'. In a gentle but pointed reprimand Priscilla Bright McLaren commented: 'We women have much to learn yet to defend each other's independence of opinion and action.'[23] In the meantime, while Anna Maria Priestman fussed about finding Jessie Craigen a more suitable wardrobe in which to return to her work for the women's movement, Priscilla Bright McLaren saw to it that Jessie Craigen once again found a place as a speaker at major suffrage demonstrations.[24]

By the end of 1882, then, Jessie Craigen was again on the platform of a large suffrage demonstration, this time in Glasgow. An eye-witness account has been left of the occasion by Elizabeth Cady Stanton, a leading figure in the suffrage movement in the United States who was also among the platform party. She had come to know the Priestman family over forty years earlier, when she had visited Britain to attend the World Anti-Slavery Convention of 1840. Her return to Britain was also the occasion of the marriage of her daughter, Harriot Stanton Blatch, to an Englishman. During her time in Britain, she renewed her friendship with the Priestmans, and found a welcome, too, among other Radical suffragists of the Bright circle. On this occasion she was the guest of Priscilla Bright Mc-Laren. Her report of the event tells how Jessie Craigen chose to emphasise her Scottish background as part of an appeal to the national pride of her audience. She and an Irish speaker used the occasion for 'firing bombshells into English policy, to which the audience responded with wild enthusiasm'. Elizabeth Cady Stanton recorded: 'I was astonished, for even in America you never hear such whole-sale criticism of England.' The meeting erupted when Jessie Craigen declaimed 'England never conquered Scotland but we gave them a King' for then 'the audience just shouted, rose to their feet and waved their handkerchiefs all over the house, all those on the platform rising and waving until arms ached' – and Elizabeth Cady Stanton waved happily along with the rest.[25] Afterwards Pris-cilla Bright McLaren sent her a copy of a 'laughable cartoon' record-ing the event, adding 'I think they have done you the best of anyone, they have given you some force of character.'[26] This force of character was to leave its mark on the British movement, and Jessie Craigen and Elizabeth Cady Stanton were to meet again, this time in circum-stances which provided further evidence of the deepening divisions between British suffragists. Once again, both Jessie Craigen and Elizabeth Cady Stanton ranged themselves alongside other Radical suffragists and against the moderate leadership, and once again the question at issue was the exclusion of married women.

Like the Radical suffragists who became her close colleagues,

Elizabeth Cady Stanton saw marriage as the keystone of women's subjection, and she was able to celebrate with British suffragists the passage of a further Married Women's Property Act in November 1882, shortly after her arrival in Britain. With this measure Ursula Bright and Elizabeth Wolstenholme Elmy had sought to bring about the end of coverture, but once again they had been defeated in this object by amendments made to the bill as it passed through the House of Commons. None the less, the measure did mark a significant expansion of married women's capacity to hold property, and hence of their potential to qualify for the franchise. Alice Scatcherd organised a testimonial from the National Society for Women's Suffrage, thanking the two women for this advance, and Ursula Bright responded with a leaflet which argued for the inclusion of married women in the suffrage demand:

> Now that she can make contracts, and be sued for the breach of them; now that she can be rated like any other woman or man; now that she can possess every qualification which gives a vote to any man. . . . I ask, Is she to be excluded from your claim?[27]

But the forces of moderation remained in the ascendant, and Ursula Bright began to organise a protest at a forthcoming London demonstration. Jessie Craigen, who was to be on the platform, undertook to seek an amendment to the women's suffrage resolution which was about to be put by suffrage MPs before Parliament, 'as a preliminary skirmish' in the campaign to have women included in the anticipated Reform Bill. Ursula Bright could not herself attend the meeting and so she asked Elizabeth Cady Stanton to support Jessie Craigen on the inclusion of married women.[28] To accomplish her challenge, Jessie Craigen ignored the authority of the chair and took over the platform in order to argue for the expansion of the parliamentary resolution so as to include married women.[29] Though her amendment was ruled out of order, the furore which followed appears to have prevented a proposal to reformulate the demand in a way which would have explicitly *excluded* married women. Susan B. Anthony recorded: 'I heard strong protests against the way Mr Mason [the MP who was about to put a women's suffrage resolution to Parliament] disclaimed all intention of enfranchising married women. He carried the matter too far even for the most timid.'[30] Resignations and 'storms', 'protests and passions' followed, as the 'extremists' continued to press their demand.

Elizabeth Cady Stanton agreed to confer with Ursula Bright and her supporters. The meeting resulted in 'a great ferment' when she lent her support to the demand for the enfranchisement of all qualified women, married and single. Elizabeth Cady Stanton not only advised the dissidents, but attempted also to strengthen the resolve of those among her friends in the Bright circle who were equivocal about such a challenge. Her diary recorded that she had written to Priscilla Bright McLaren, Margaret Bright Lucas, and her daughter, Kate Thomasson, urging on them:

> the wisdom of broadening their platform. I impress on them the fact that to get the suffrage for spinsters is all very well, but their work is to elevate the position of women at all points, and that in calling to every form of injustice and laying bare every inequality they take the shortest way to educate women into rebellion and self-assertion. That the married women of this movement in England consent to the assumption that they are through marriage, practically represented and protected, supported and sheltered from all the adverse winds of life, is the strongest evidence of their own need for emancipation.[31]

Priscilla Bright McLaren hesitated, however, to follow such advice, realising the divisive effect it might have at this critical time. She replied to her American friend: 'I abhor the idea of degrading marriage as much as my sister Ursula Bright by any positive prohibition of right because of marriage.' But she also expressed firmly the view that 'the real reformer must be willing to climb step by step'. She was impatient of 'the cat and dog work' which continued between Lydia Becker and Ursula Bright, yet only six months later this most generous-hearted and conciliatory of Radical suffragists also lost patience with the moderate leadership and declared: 'I shall go in strong for married women now.'[32]

More and more even the most conciliatory among the Radical suffragists felt it necessary now to defy the views of Lydia Becker on how best to secure a women's suffrage amendment to the forthcoming Reform Bill. Instead of secret machinations among parliamentary cliques in the capital, they sought to demonstrate popular support for their cause. Alice Scatcherd and Priscilla Bright McLaren continued the organisation of large suffrage demonstrations in each of the major cities, and continued to argue: 'We must have working women in to show it is the people's cause.'[33] Similarly, Helen Priestman Bright Clark used her standing as John Bright's daughter in an attempt to appeal over his head, and over those of other members of the Gladstone government, to the rank-and-file of their party. The occasion for this challenge was provided by a major Reform demonstration in Leeds, to be presided over by John Bright. In this instance, Radical suffragists found themselves opposed both by leading members of their party and the leadership of the suffrage movement. Priscilla Bright McLaren reported to Helen Priestman Bright Clark: 'all our friends are bowing the knee to thy Father's wilfulness and dare do nothing'. Her niece, in her turn, reported on 'wire-pulling' by the Manchester NSWS to try to prevent the appointment of herself and other Radical suffragists as delegates to the conference: 'I concluded it might be because as Miss Becker could not go as a liberal, she wished no other woman to go.' Subsequently, she reported: 'Somebody has succeeded in frightening away all the women except us four who resolutely refused to be frightened.'[34]

In the event, Alice Scatcherd helped orchestrate the appointment of women delegates so that finally they numbered nine, including herself. She also reported that 'in the end I had my complete way with a Cobden and a Bright speaking', for Jane Cobden joined Helen Priestman Bright Clark in calling on the conference to endorse the inclusion of women in the Reform Bill.[35] Susan B. Anthony was among those who travelled north to enjoy the spectacle and recalled how the audience 'hushed into a profound silence' when John Bright's daughter rose to speak, with 'an effect on the audience which was thrilling'. Helen Priestman Bright Clark told the convention that while the women there put their hope in the Liberal Party 'all of its members were not yet converted to true liberalism'. What Liberal women sought was 'a real and honest household suffrage'.[36] When the vote was taken on the women's suffrage resolution, only 30 of the 2000 delegates voted against the daughters of Bright and Cobden. Priscilla Bright McLaren was among those who fully endorsed the role in this demonstration of the niece who was also as a daughter to her:

> I cannot doubt for a moment that the impulse came from above and that thou was quite right and thy father wrong. It is he who ought to keep silence when he sees all his women relations for women's suffrage.[37]

Radical suffragists and the moderate leadership also failed to see eye-to-eye on a proposal which Elizabeth Cady Stanton and Susan B. Anthony put before British colleagues, shortly before they returned to the United States in November 1883. They urged that the time was right for the formation of an international suffrage organisation to facilitate the sharing of ideas and experience. Lydia Becker and those around her remained sceptical of the idea, warning that it had been taken up by 'some injudicious people'. Almost certainly, it was Ursula Bright they had in mind, and even promoters of this new initiative like Priscilla Bright McLaren had to confess: 'I am not quite sure that Aunt Urlie [Ursula Bright] may not be using this as an annoyance – but there is not real proof of this yet.'[38]

The Bright circle, unsurprisingly, proved the most receptive to the plan, and Priscilla Bright McLaren, Margaret Bright Lucas and Ursula Bright took up the challenge during their farewell meetings with the American suffragists in November 1883. It was agreed to establish an international organisation based in the United States, with corresponding committees in other countries. Out of this was to come the first international conference of women's suffragists, in Washington in 1888. The conference was arranged so as to coincide with the fortieth anniversary of the Seneca Falls convention which had marked the formal beginnings of a women's rights movement in America. It is noteworthy that the more moderate leadership of the suffrage movement in Britain consistently failed to accord this formalisation of international networks among women's movements the same significance as their Radical suffragist colleagues. Possibly the international context was more important to the latter precisely because of their more marginal standing in their own country, serving as a valued endorsement of their distinct identity as the radical section of their particular national movement. But there was also a note of cultural, if not racial, superiority in this effort to join American and British suffragists in providing leadership for suffragists internationally.[39]

In the months that preceded the reading of the Reform Bill in 1884, the tensions and conflicts among British suffragists intensified still further. A number of Jacob Bright's relatives among the Radical suffragists attempted to restore him to the leadership of parliamentary suffragists, while one of his nieces, Lilias Ashworth Hallett, worked successsfully alongside Lydia Becker to defeat his reinstatement. Margaret Bright Lucas wrote to Anna Maria Priestman bewailing such ingratitude and disloyalty, suggesting that it reflected not hostility to Jacob Bright himself, but fear of the influence of Ursula Bright. Priscilla Bright McLaren was also distressed over 'such ungrateful conduct' towards her brother.[40] She professed still to feel 'a sort of tender sympathy and affection' for Lydia Becker, but she also increasingly saw her old colleague, and her niece, Lilias Ashworth Hallett, (whom together she described as the 'Dual Combine') as destructive influences on the suffrage movement.[41] And once again, Helen Priestman Bright Clark met opposition from Lydia Becker when she attempted to organise an interview between the prime minster and a group of leading Liberal women suffragists.

Other Radical suffragists like Anna Maria Priestman were equally unimpressed with the suffrage leadership's failure to work up grassroots support for their demand. Like Alice Scatcherd, she also stressed the importance of demonstrating working-class support and advocated a closer alliance with working-class leaders like Joseph Arch. She was further alienated by the open hostility which former Liberal allies like Lilias Ashworth Hallett were now expressing with regard to the movement for Irish home rule, and by Lydia Becker's anger at the continuing intervention of the Women's Liberal Association in the suffrage campaign.[42] In these ways the suffrage movement became virtually paralysed by inner turmoil and divided loyalties, as the Reform Bill was put before Parliament in the early summer of 1884.

By this time, the Liberal leadership, and most notably the Prime Minister, Gladstone, had made clear their determined opposition to any women's suffrage amendment. Under such pressure, those politicians in whom the moderate leadership of the suffrage movement had placed its trust began to waver in their commitment to the cause. Yet again, Priscilla Bright McLaren could only bemoan: 'Oh how badly the men are behaving.' When Gladstone made what she considered 'a most insulting speech' on the question of women's suffrage, Priscilla Bright McLaren reported that her own husband, the Liberal MP Duncan McLaren, 'looks very sorrowful for us. But every man's mouth is shut.' Once again she had to place her faith instead 'in a power above' for she was unable to believe 'that power *can* approve of what our men are doing'.[43] Even Ursula Bright felt constrained in such circumstances, so that Helen Priestman Bright Clark could report, 'Aunt Urlie is quite a new creature', keeping silent on the failure expressly to include married women in the suffragist amendment, though she remained convinced that such moderation could only result in disaster and defeat.[44]

Jacob Bright was able to prevent a complete rout, at least, for women's suffragists. He made it clear that he would himself introduce an amendment to the Reform Bill enfranchising women, should the 'official' one be withdrawn, as at one point appeared likely under government pressure. 'Brave Jake!', declared Priscilla Bright Mc-Laren, while adding 'Oh what foes are against us.'[45] Elizabeth Wolstenholme Elmy also sought to stiffen the resolve of suffragists in parliament with an open letter to all MPs. Here she recorded her own experience in campaigning for women's rights over the previous twenty years as one which led her to the conviction that men could never adequately represent women's interests: 'the great grievance of women is that the voice of men alone is listened to, the male interest alone is considered'. In such a situation it was impossible that 'the predominant influence of sex bias should not cause great and grievous wrong'. She also reaffirmed her conviction that should married women be excluded from any measure of women's suffrage, the outcome would be 'absurd, illogical, unjust, and indefensible'.[46]

Defeat was ensured when 104 supposed suffragists voted against the women's suffrage amendment to the Reform Bill. When the Bill was then thrown out by the House of Lords, the suffrage societies found themselves paralysed. Fears for the complete failure of this Liberal reform now ensured that no women's suffrage amendment was put forward when the measure was reintroduced, this time successfully. So the Liberal Party's Reform Act of 1884 compounded the exclusion of women from full citizenship by adding some two million to the numbers of male voters. When William Woodall brought forward a separate women's suffrage measure shortly afterwards he reintroduced a clause expressly disqualifying women under coverture. Jacob Bright immediately withdrew as one of the Bill's backers, but it was an addition in which the moderate leadership of the suffrage movement again acquiesced. Suspicion and hostility between Radical suffragists and the moderate suffrage leadership only intensified still further in such circumstances. Alice Scatcherd expressed the view that this return to an exclusionist formulation of the demand breached the constitution of the NSWS, confiding to Anna Maria Priestman: 'I feel as though Miss Becker were at the bottom of this.' She also reported the hopes of Millicent Garrett Fawcett and others that the NSWS would hold together 'and not go into Liberal and Conservative camps'. This seemed increasingly impossible to avoid, however, for she also found that those who supported the revival of the restricted formulation (i.e. excluding married women) 'speak of the present arrangement as "ordained" . . . whilst eight out of ten Liberal women do want to move on'.[47]

Such disunity and disarray brought a new vulnerability to those who earned their living as speakers and organisers for the suffrage movement, especially those working women who had generally found their sponsors among the Radical suffragists. As the hectic activity which had marked the years preceding the Reform Act was halted, and as Radical suffragists either withdrew or were increasingly excluded from the leadership of the local NSWS societies, such women faced a bleak future, and became a cause for considerable concern among their more well-to-do patrons. Throughout 1886, then, the Priestman sisters sought funds to help provide work for Jessie Craigen. Alice Scatcherd was herself engaged in a similar effort to establish an annuity for Mrs McCormick, formerly an organiser for the Manchester Society. She pointed out that Elizabeth Wolstenholme Elmy, too, was sorely in need of assistance at this time, in the midst of collecting petitions in support of the Infants Bill by which she aimed to extend the rights of mothers with regard to custody and guardianship of their children. Alice Scatcherd reported: 'Mrs Elmy has done without a servant two years in order to have money for public work – only has a woman once a week . . . till the Bill is law, it is heavy toil for Mrs Elmy.'[48] But this work would have to be undertaken in London, and it was felt that Jessie Craigen was not to be trusted on her own in the metropolis. As it proved impossible to find a working-class woman to act as her minder, this opportunity was lost.[49]

Alice Scatcherd, for one, thought it regrettable that Jessie Craigen would not go back to her old style of open-air meetings which had cost so little and proved so effective. So the Priestmans found it difficult to gather the sponsorship to fund further employment for Jessie Craigen, and hostility to their protégée's modes, manners and opinions was the principal source of such difficulties. W. T. Stead was called on to use his influence with Jessie Craigen. Her huckster's approach to public speaking was one source of grievance. She had been known both to 'spout from the top of cabs', and to use her professional engagements for private enterprise, for she also sold her vegetable cordials – no doubt a legacy from her career in the temperance movement – during her meetings. It was further claimed that she mixed one issue with another in her speeches, and could not be relied on to speak on the subject requested. In her discussions with W. T. Stead she rejected only this last allegation as 'a frightful lie'. And it appears that he had not found the courage to question her on another matter, that of 'bedroom blinds, which is a rather delicate subject'.[50] It seems that Jessie Craigen's standards of propriety also differed in some respect from those of her middle-class employers.

In an unaccustomed show of eating humble pie, Jessie Craigen agreed to the suggestion put to her by W. T. Stead that in future she work under 'a manager', go where she was told, and speak only on subjects as directed. She agreed to this last condition, however, only on the understanding that she was unable to say anything which 'conflicts with her innermost conviction of the truth'. Even so, it proved impossible to restore confidence in Jessie Craigen in some quarters. Margaret Bright Lucas, for example, a longstanding friend, as well as a leading figure both in the World Women's Christian Temperance Union and the LNA, now made it clear that she no longer had any confidence in Jessie Craigen as a reliable employee.

Jessie Craigen's quixotic approach to life worried even those who were less concerned with her failings as a respectable and moderate representative of their shared causes. For one thing, her defenders found themselves repeatedly bailing her out of debt. Francis Newman, the free-thinking brother of the cardinal, had long taken an active part in women's movement activities in the Bristol area, and reported himself grateful for the 'comfort and hope' which Anna Maria Priestman and Josephine Butler had been able to give him regarding Jessie Craigen's future. In his view she used her 'philanthropic intentions' as an excuse for irresponsibility in the management of her own affairs, so that he had found it necessary on one occasion to deliver the following homily: 'Philanthropy is a luxury to which we have to earn a right by first feeding, clothing and housing oneself.' None the less, he and others in Radical suffrage circles conscientiously contributed to the 'Jessie Craigen Lecture Fund' which Anna Maria Priestman established in 1886, and which appears to have kept going until the end of the decade.[51] Thereafter, Jessie Craigen disappears from the women's movement. Anna Maria Priestman reported their last encounter in 1898, when Jessie Craigen came to speak in Bristol against vivisection 'with overwhelming force and truth'.[52] She died the following year, in lodgings in Ilford.

4

'THE GRANDEST VICTORY'
Married women and the franchise

When Elizabeth Cady Stanton returned to Britain in November 1886 she found hopeful signs in an increasing forcefulness within the women's movement, 'even here in slow old England'. She was impressed with a younger generation now coming to the fore, and warned 'of one thing men may be assured . . . the next generation will not argue the question of women's rights with the infinite patience we have displayed this half century'. Priscilla Bright McLaren also saw grounds for optimism: 'We see everywhere women rising to a much higher moral and intellectual stature than twenty years ago.'[1]

But Elizabeth Cady Stanton observed also the ever-deepening divisions within the British movement, a disunity occasioned not only by soured relationships among its own leadership, but also by events outside. In 1886 the Liberal Party itself split between the supporters of Gladstone's policy of home rule for Ireland, and those who rejected such a solution to the Irish question. The latter group broke away to form the Liberal Unionist Party. For the next twenty years the Liberal Party enjoyed only brief periods back in power. Neither the Radical suffrage section of the movement, nor the Bright circle avoided the fresh divisions which this brought to their movement. The main body of Radical suffrage opinion, including Ursula and Jacob Bright, Richard and Emmeline Pankhurst, Alice Scatcherd, the Priestman sisters, Helen Priestman Bright Clark, Charles and Walter McLaren (the MP sons of Priscilla Bright McLaren), remained committed to home rule. If anything, their loyalty to the Liberal Party was intensified by the split, despite the unhelpfulness of the 'Grand Old Man', Gladstone, to the suffrage cause. Priscilla Bright McLaren, though she had the deepest sympathy for Ireland and its grievances, felt home rule would produce only further violence. Like her dying husband, Duncan McLaren, she advocated instead the establishment of an imperial parliament, whereby *all* nations presently subject to British dominion might find representation and autonomy. Together with Lilias Ashworth Hallett and Millicent Garrett Fawcett she now became a Liberal Unionist. Other Radical suffragists like Elizabeth Wolstenholme Elmy were simply confirmed in their hostility to all partisanship within the women's movement. Such partisanship, they believed, brought only divided loyalties, and greater susceptibility to the manipulation and duplicity of male politicians. For her, Gladstone remained the Grand Old Humbug, though, for the time being, she continued to find her most congenial associates among the Gladstonian Radical suffragists.

After the defeats and turmoil of 1884–6, many Radical suffragists, including Anna Maria Priestman, concentrated their efforts on the Women's Liberal Associations, withdrawing more and more from the suffrage societies themselves. The numbers, strength and influence of local Women's Liberal Associations had greatly increased since their beginnings in the early 1880s, as new electoral legislation and the greatly extended franchise made the voluntary election work of women ever more important to their party. In 1886 the local WLAs became unified within the Women's Liberal Federation, recognition of the greatly expanded scope and functions of women's political organisations. But these developments in themselves had meant a large influx of women into the organisation who were not prepared to give the same primacy to the suffrage cause as those who had founded the original societies. Radical suffragists like Anna Maria Priestman and her friends and kin among the Bright circle had now to battle to ensure that women's suffrage remained to the fore of the programme of the Women's Liberal Federation, and that its growing power and influence was put to support the suffrage cause.

Radical suffragists also now struggled to keep their perspective on women's emancipation to the fore in the Vigilance Association. In 1884–5 opinion among its members on whether to include or exclude married women from suffrage measures had gone back and forth. But when William Woodall once more introduced a suffrage bill expressly excluding married women in 1886, its journal published Elizabeth Wolstenholme Elmy's view that the measure served 'simply to create a fresh privileged class, at the cost of imposing a new disability on every married woman – doing this, moreover, in the most grossly insulting manner, since the law of "coverture" invoked for their exclusion is undoubtedly the grossest, the most oppressive, and the most degrading of the legal wrongs of which women have to complain'.[2]

The moral panic of the latter half of the 1880s also provided a fresh source of discord in the women's movement in general, and the Vigilance Association in particular, when a new direction emerged on issues of moral reform. This 'social purity' perspective reflected the alarm which followed the sensationalist exposé of child prostitution. In a series of articles in 1885, the editor of the *Pall Mall Gazette*, W. T. Stead, told how, with the support and aid of Josephine Butler, he had set about buying a child from a London procurer. His articles resulted in the formation of the National Vigilance Association (NVA) in which some of the national suffrage leadership figured prominently, including Millicent Garrett Fawcett. The NVA sought to deal with problems such as prostitution and the employment of children in music halls through repressive legislation. Its members also attempted to gain control of local watch committees through women's increased role in local government, so as to ensure greater enforcement of regulations by the police. For a time, Josephine Butler lent her name to the new NVA, though she was soon alienated by its pursuit of policies which she felt undermined the civil rights of women, and treated harshly those who for her were the victims, not the agents, of sexual disorder. Opponents of the 'social purity' approach, including a number of Radical suffragists, reconstituted the old Vigilance Association under the new title of the Personal Rights Association, and Elizabeth Wolstenholme Elmy advanced further in her public re-acceptance when she was elected on to its executive committee.[3]

The moral panic prompted by W. T. Stead's revelations was further fuelled by the Jack-the-Ripper murders in London's East End, and the trial of Oscar Wilde on charges of homosexuality. It was a moral panic which continued to have an impact on the women's movement, most especially in Radical suffrage circles, for some years to come. For 1886 also saw the downfall of a leading Radical, Sir Charles Dilke, after the salacious revelations which followed his naming in a divorce case. It was Charles Dilke who had supported Jacob Bright when he introduced the first women's suffrage measure to be put before the House of Commons in 1870, and some had expected that he might one day become a Liberal Prime Minister.

Loyalty to, or rejection of, Charles Dilke as he attempted re-build his political career provided further grounds for discord among Radical suffragists. This also proved to be the case when Charles Parnell, the Irish Nationalist leader, suffered a similar downfall over a divorce scandal in 1890. Many, like Ursula and Jacob Bright, Emmeline and Richard Pankhurst, and Elizabeth Cady Stanton had little time for the hypocrisy they perceived in the scandal-mongering which surrounded these events, and remained loyal to their old friends. Others were less tolerant of men they felt had selfishly harmed the causes they claimed to serve, and whom they suspected of a cynical manipulation of whatever continuing loyalty they were able to command.

During her return to Britain in 1886, Elizabeth Cady Stanton found herself once again most in sympathy with Radical suffragists like Ursula Bright, and at odds with the moderate leadership of the British movement. It continued to take little interest in the plans for the international conference of suffragists which was to meet in Washington in 1888. Elizabeth Cady Stanton recorded, in consequence, 'a very unpleasant interview' with Lydia Becker and some of her supporters over their continuing refusal to cooperate in the venture. Instead, she turned to Priscilla Bright McLaren and Anna Maria Priestman to help her organise a British delegation.[4] This proved an oddly assorted group which included the Radical suffragist, Alice Scatcherd, the social purity campaigner, Mrs Ormiston Chant, and May Dilke, the widowed sister-in-law of Charles Dilke. May Dilke's inclusion in the British contingent proved the cause of yet further controversy. The scandal around Charles Dilke had implicated her mother and her sister, who were each accused of having been his mistress. Suggestions of May Dilke's own irregular life since her husband's death had similarly become the subject of speculation and gossip. The presence of May Dilke as a representative of the British women's movement so outraged Helen Taylor that she made it the grounds for her own withdrawal from participation in the international conference. It had been intended that Helen Taylor, as John Stuart Mill's step-daughter, should be among those to address a Senate Committee on Women's Suffrage while in Washington, so her withdrawal appeared all the more regrettable to the organisers of the convention. Both Elizabeth Cady Stanton and Priscilla Bright McLaren pressed Helen Taylor to adopt a more open-minded view of the matter, with no success. Elizabeth Cady Stanton made her own position quite clear by travelling back to the United States for the conference in the company of May Dilke.[5]

By the end of 1888, the tensions within the British movement could no longer be held in check by the national leadership, and there was a successful move to alter the rules of the National Society for Women's Suffrage. The new rules allowed for the affiliation of any women's organisations which included women's suffrage among their objects. In the view of many, including Lydia Becker, such a change opened the way for the suffrage movement to be taken over by Women's Liberal Associations. Certainly, some of the main proponents of change were leading Liberal suffragists, including Priscilla Bright McLaren's son, Walter, and his wife Eva McLaren, while many of the leading opponents were Liberal Unionists like Millicent Garrett Fawcett and Lilias Ashworth Hallett. These last two joined with Lydia Becker in establishing an alternative society which held to the old rules of the NSWS. The 'new-rules' society called itself the Central National Society for Women's Suffrage (CNSWS), while, altogether confusingly, the new 'old-rules' organisation called itself the Central Committee of the National Society for Women's Suffrage (CCNSWS). Each was more conveniently referred to by the address of its central offices, as respectively the 'Parliament Street' Society and the 'Great College Street' Society.

Lydia Becker now designated her opponents in the Parliament Street Society as the 'left-wing' and 'extreme section' of the movement, and her own account of the split suggests that the exclusion of married women had once again been an issue dividing the two groups. Certainly, the Great College Street Society held by the explicit exclusion of married women from the demand. But it very soon became evident that the Parliament Street Society was not united on this issue. Its leadership attempted to resolve such differences by supporting both bills which explicitly excluded married women, as well as those formulated in terms of equal rights. But it refused to support the ultra-Radicals in promoting measures which expressly included married women. At the first annual meeting of the Parliament Street Society, the ultra-Radicals, led by Richard Pankhurst, attempted to achieve a compromise whereby it was at least to withdraw its support for measures which excluded married women. He met with no success.[6]

Elizabeth Wolstenholme Elmy had at last seen the extension of married women's rights over their children in the Infants Act, the passage of which she had secured almost single-handedly the previous year. At the time Alice Scatcherd had commented, with good reason: 'How that woman works!'[7] As so often in the past, Elizabeth

Wolstenholme Elmy now promoted a fresh initiative to ensure that married women were included in any future women's suffrage measure. With the support of Alice Scatcherd and Harriet McIlquham, she established a new suffrage society unequivocally committed to this end.[8] The Women's Franchise League became the first suffrage organisation in Britain to formulate its demand in terms which expressly included married women. Harriot Stanton Blatch, daughter of Elizabeth Cady Stanton, was among its earliest supporters. She linked the formation of the League to her mother's intervention in the British movement some six years before, when she had joined Ursula Bright and Jessie Craigen in urging just such a re-formulation of the demand. And certainly, the League drew on the transatlantic network formed by her mother's friends and colleagues for its early support, with both Elizabeth Cady Stanton and Isabella Beecher Hooker, another leading American suffragist, becoming corresponding members.[9] The links back to the abolition movement, and more especially with the Garrisonian conception of the reformer's role, was evident also in the contribution of William Lloyd Garrison the younger to the proceedings.

The League's leadership drew support from two generations of Radical suffragists and it was in this organisation that the Radical perspective on women's citizenship at last found full expression.[10] Political pragmatism was consistently eschewed in favour of holding to principle, most especially in the matter of including married women in the suffrage demand, and its programme was an expansive one by the standards of the existing suffrage societies. The exclusion of married women from the suffrage demand was, as we have seen, the main spur to its formation and Elizabeth Wolstenholme Elmy drafted a separate suffrage measure for the League to promote. The Women's Disabilities Removal Bill was brought before the House of Commons in 1889 and 1890. It included a clause which read 'that no woman shall be subject to legal incapacity in voting . . . by reason of coverture', making it the first women's suffrage bill which expressly included married women.[11] This marked a departure from the earlier support of Radical suffragists like Elizabeth Wolstenholme Elmy and Alice Scatcherd for the compromise formulation of the demand in terms of sexual equality, and their pursuit of the end of coverture as a quite separate campaign. It represented a shift to Ursula Bright's position, no doubt because of the continuing currency of measures which expressly excluded married women. There was also a growing conviction among Radical suffragists generally that women's suffrage was essential to any further advance in the rights of married women, most particularly the end of coverture itself. Alice Scatcherd expressed this view when she told the inaugural meeting: 'I, for one, am perfectly tired of joining societies which fight only for a little bit, a little shred, a little fragment of freedom.'[12] Increasingly, among such veterans and their younger colleagues, the vote became the key by which all further emancipation for women was to be achieved. They now sought to realise their Radical perspective on the citizenship of women through a single measure which would give all women, married and single, an equal civil standing with men, whether in the matter of marriage, the vote, or moral policing.

By the time of Elizabeth Cady Stanton's final visit to Britain in 1890, she had firmly aligned herself with the ultra-Radical suffragists around the Women's Franchise League. Lydia Becker had recently died, while Ursula Bright had moved into the League's leadership, so that, in Elizabeth Cady Stanton's estimation, she now stood 'at the helm of the woman suffrage movement on this side of the ocean'.[13] But the League itself now experienced internal tensions, at least in part as a consequence of Ursula Bright's presence. Shortly, Elizabeth Wolstenholme Elmy once again faced expulsion from an organisation she had helped found. Ursula and Jacob Bright had at first held aloof from the new society. Possibly, this reflected some hostility to Elizabeth Wolstenholme Elmy herself. In the years immediately preceding the formation of the Women's Franchise League, the Elmys had been at the forefront of the Fair Trade League. Their own modest income had been eroded with the sharp decline of the British silk industry, a decline they had come to believe could best be halted by the imposition of tariffs on foreign imports of silk. Jacob Bright, in contrast, remained among the firmest advocates of free trade, and had become the focus of a fierce and surprisingly personalised attack in leaflets written for the Fair Trade League by Elizabeth Wolstenholme Elmy in 1886.[14] Once again, forces external to the women's movement were undermining former unities within it, as longstanding liberal certainties and orthodoxies began to unravel.

But Elizabeth Wolstenholme Elmy feared the entrance into the League of Ursula and Jacob Bright for other reasons. She believed it had been engineered by Richard and Emmeline Pankhurst as part of a plan to re-establish the political career of Charles Dilke, a mutual friend of both the Brights and the Pankhursts. A new political role was being sought for him, one which might combine women's rights issues with the emerging desire for the independent representation of labour in Parliament. Elizabeth Wolstenholme Elmy, as always, believed it wisest to keep the suffrage issue clear of the divided loyalties which might result from such exterior goals, and was also contemptuous of the political ambitions of Charles Dilke. She now met opposition from among the League's leadership, opposition which claimed she was unbusiness-like in her management of League activities. She herself felt that such criticism had been worked up by Florence Fenwick Miller with the aim of replacing her in the paid post of secretary.[15] Florence Fenwick Miller (1854–1935) was another of those 'platform women' of working-class origins who had made a career for herself in the women's movement over the previous decade or so, and who, like Elizabeth Wolstenholme Elmy and Jessie Craigen, depended upon it for her living.[16]

Elizabeth Wolstenholme Elmy, for her part, argued that much of the blame for some of the less-than-successful undertakings of the League lay with its committee, which she claimed had given her 'minimal help' and support. Perhaps more significantly, she had increasingly found herself at cross-purposes with Alice Scatcherd. As a joint founder of the League, she appears especially to have resented the demands which the wealthier Alice Scatcherd, in an honorary role as treasurer, made upon her time as the League's paid secretary. Elizabeth Wolstenholme Elmy complained that both she and her assistant, Romola Tynte, had experienced 'brutal' treatment from their employers, though she excluded Ursula Bright from any responsibility for this. Romola Tynte had apparently been 'worked and worried' into a dangerous illness from which she was still recovering in the October of 1890, while Elizabeth Wolstenholme Elmy recorded that she also had been 'really ill' as a result of these strains. Though she did not know it at the time of her dispute with the League's committee, she subsequently found that an anonymous and slanderous leaflet, purporting to provide a history of her life, had been circulated during the controversy, one in which she reported: 'I am presented as greedy and self-seeking, whereas I was sacrificing everything, time, money, health and strength, life itself for the cause I believed in.'[17]

After resigning as secretary of the League, Elizabeth Wolstenholme Elmy stayed with Harriot Stanton Blatch and Elizabeth Cady Stanton in preparation for a special executive committee meeting which she hoped would resolve her differences with its leadership. But when the committee refused to re-instate her as secretary, she resigned from the League altogether.[18] Thereafter the office of secretary of the League appears to have remained an honorary one. Elizabeth Wolstenholme Elmy now focused her energies once more upon the Fair Trade League, clearly deeply hurt at what she saw as a lack of recognition of the part she had played in the reforms so far achieved by the women's movement, and refusing for the time being any further role in that movement: 'When any one of the women who so insulted and wronged me can show such a record, I may begin to believe in her zeal.'[19] Ben Elmy's business continued to fail, costing them £80 a year, and proving impossible to sell, so that the loss of her own income was no doubt all the more bitter to her. She hoped, instead, to earn a living by free-lance work as a journalist.

Meanwhile, Harriot Stanton Blatch became the League's joint honorary secretary with Ursula Bright in 1891. The records which remain of the League's activities under its new leadership suggest that it continued to conceive of itself principally as the voice of Radical suffragism, committed to a more advanced programme than the more moderate societies, deliberately linking itself to the international women's movement, most especially to the movement in the United States, and pursuing new sources of support for the demand in the emerging labour and socialist movements. This it did principally by providing speakers on women's suffrage for radical clubs, progressive clubs and branches of the Women's Cooperative Guild.[20] But from this time it saw itself equally as an organisation of women Liberals, and the Women's Liberal Federation now became a main focus for many of its activities.[21]

The League has left few records. The few details provided of its finances in the only surviving minute book suggest that Alice Scatcherd, and to a lesser extent Ursula Bright, were its financial mainstays.[22] A generous reading would suggest that it only ever attracted at most a membership of a few hundred. Nor does the central executive appear to have kept in very close touch with those local branches which were established, largely in London and in the region of Leeds. Indeed, the work of the League in the Leeds area seems to have run virtually autonomously under the direction of Alice Scatcherd, while individual members of the executive on several occasions undertook activities in the name of the League for which they only subsequently sought endorsement.[23] But such indices cannot provide a proper measure of the success or significance of the League.

Radical agitation was what gave the League both its identity, and its rationale. It acted as the conscience of Radical suffragism, constantly keeping this perspective before audiences both within the women's movement and within popular politics, though without seeking to become a mass movement in itself. This was the character of the League as presented, for example, by Ursula Bright when describing its work to an international audience at the World Congress of Representative Women organised during the Chicago World Fair of 1893. Here the Women's Franchise League's special commitment 'in plain language to ask for votes for married women' was emphasised, with the declaration that 'the legal position of the wife in England is a scandal to civilisation'. Ursula Bright also laid claim to 'a much broader and bolder' approach than 'the ordinary suffrage societies'. The programme which she outlined was indeed an extensive one: equal political rights and duties; equal educational opportunities; equal wages for equal work; equal access to paid, honorary or elected public office; equality under family law; equality in the rights and liabilities of contract.[24]

Undoubtedly though, the League's work also evidenced an unwavering loyalty to Gladstone, and to a Liberal Party which repeatedly thwarted the suffrage demand. In this same paper, Ursula Bright offered a somewhat lame explanation for this situation, pointing to the League's altruistic dedication to the cause of Irish home rule, and seeking instead to direct her audience's attention to the 'timid counsels' which would exclude married women from the claim, counsels which she blamed on the 'narrow prejudices of Tories or second-hand Liberals'. In so doing, Ursula Bright was attempting to address, if not directly, those critics of the League who would dismiss it simply as a women's auxiliary of the Gladstonian Liberals. While she demonstrated effectively that her suffrage organisation was one committed to a broader conception of women's citizenship, she failed convincingly to answer the charges of the League's subordination to Liberal Party faction-fighting. Perhaps the better to establish the radical credentials of the League she also noted in her conclusion: 'The leaders of the working men are almost to a man on our side.'[25]

This link with the labour movement was clearly central to the approach to suffrage campaigning for a number of the League's leadership. By this time the League might on occasion look for support from the campaign for the eight-hour day, for example, and much of its work was directed to organising working-class support for the suffrage demand. Alice Scatcherd's association with women's trade unionism has already been noted, and at the League's inaugural meeting she argued:

> There are only two great questions presently before the public. These are the labour question and the women's question. And when we come to consider these questions really they are united; for it is largely on the economic condition of woman that her freedom in the future will depend.[26]

Here she was giving expression to a new perspective on women's rights which proved especially influential in the work of the League, one linked to Radical conceptions of the claim to citizenship.

This new perspective emerged in Radical suffragist argument in the early 1880s, and based claims to citizenship on the labour of women. At the same time, it adopted a broad definition of labour, so as to include every kind of women's work – in reproduction and sexual labour, as well as the workplace; in unpaid as well as in paid labour. May Dilke put forward just such an understanding of women's claim to citizenship in these years, to counter the militaristic account which was so often used as an argument against votes for women. She argued, for example, that women in childbirth put their lives at risk equally with men called on to do battle, insisting that the maintenance of society rested not on warfare but on labour in all its forms. Though it was the case that much of women's labour went unpaid, it was 'quite as fundamental a part of civilised life as the paid labour of men'. Moreover, she argued, women were also increasingly entering the paid work-force, and therefore needed their own voice in the making of laws which controlled the labour market.[27]

Harriot Stanton Blatch characterised such understandings of the citizenship claims of women as an 'economic' approach, one which attended especially to the need of working women for the vote. It was an approach which appealed especially strongly to ultra-Radical suffragists, and which clearly informed much of the work of the Women's Franchise League.[28] This new 'economic' perspective within the women's movement sometimes also linked women's rights to a critique of social relations in general under capitalism, and emphasised the need to unite industrial women workers with middle-class women in the campaign for the vote. Here again Fabians like Harriot Stanton Blatch were an especially important influence. She later recalled how she had explained her involvement in campaigns for women's rights to fellow Fabians, Beatrice and Sidney

Webb, in these terms: 'Women are the source of the race. Its supreme moulders. To do that work efficiently, they must be politically and economically independent beyond all call. Free they cannot be under capitalism: the capitalistic system and feminism are at war.'[29]

The new directions taken by the League under the leadership of Ursula Bright, Alice Scatcherd, Emmeline Pankhurst and Harriot Stanton Blatch were not congenial to others among its originators, however. Shortly, Harriet McIlquham was sharing some of the concerns voiced by Elizabeth Wolstenholme Elmy the previous year. As a Liberal Unionist, Harriet McIlquham must have felt some dismay at the growing influence of Gladstonian–Liberal interests on the policies and practices of the League. Elizabeth Wolstenholme Elmy had expressed to her a growing conviction that 'the Bright–Pankhurst alliance' would prefer that women failed to gain the vote that century than that the governing Conservatives and Unionists 'should have any credit for it'.[30]

Elizabeth Wolstenholme Elmy's letters also reveal how difficult the period after her resignation had been for her. In March 1891 she recorded 'winter has been so "cruel and hard" and I have found it hard to exist at all'. She declared she would be grateful once her son, Frank, were established in life, 'to lie down and rest for ever – Life has been a weary burden'. But the spring days of 1891 also saw her spirits lifted considerably by a court decision which very shortly led her, with Harriet McIlquham, to form yet another organisation committed to improving the position of women, especially married women. The case in question, R. v. Jackson, also known as the Clitheroe case, had resulted in a judicial ruling that a husband did not have the right to imprison his wife in order to secure his conjugal rights over her. In Elizabeth Wolstenholme Elmy's view, this judgment sounded the death knell of the doctrine of coverture: 'It is the grandest victory the women's cause has yet gained, greater even than the passing of the Married Women's Property Act.'[31] By eroding to some degree the submersion of a married woman's legal personality, it also served to further undermine the case for excluding women under coverture from the suffrage demand.

It was this unanticipated victory in the courts which prompted Elizabeth Wolstenholme Elmy to resume an active role in the women's movement, initially through a series of letters to the press on the question, letters which she shortly issued as a pamphlet. The response they prompted led her to feel that the time was right to start a new organisation. The objects of the Women's Emancipation

Union (WEU) were virtually the same as those of the Women's Franchise League. It was more a matter of emphasis that distinguished them. The WEU was altogether more explicit in the link it made between the rights of married women over their own persons, and the pursuit of full citizenship for all qualified women. Elizabeth Wolstenholme Elmy had been among the first publicly to raise the issue of rape-in-marriage, albeit somewhat tentatively, during the 1880s, an issue which had been only implicitly addressed in the programme of the Women's Franchise League. The WEU was alone in making more explicit this aspect of the question, and in linking it to the achievement of citizenship.[32]

Another distinctive element in early WEU pronouncements lies in its conception of itself as an organisation only for 'real workers'. This emphasis reflects not so much a wish to appeal to working-class support (something undoubtedly more evident in the activities of the Women's Franchise League), as the determination of Elizabeth Wolstenholme Elmy to campaign only alongside those who promised a dedication to the cause which might match her own. To maintain her own authority among WEU members, she took up her role as secretary in an honorary capacity. Although initially she had agreed that a small salary might be attached to the office should funds prove sufficient, she later retreated from this. She never accepted a salary for her work as secretary of the WEU, although eventually her own poverty led her to accept occasional small honoraria in recognition of such service. 'Worker' was for her, then, essentially a moral, not an economic category. Her adoption of this term also sometimes revealed a bitterness in the distinction she made between those 'workers' who dedicated their lives to the cause, and wealthy women who only 'played' with it, and used their wealth to make mischief by exerting arbitrary, fickle or unscrupulous control over the movement. She expected WEU members to expend without stint their time and energies in the cause, and she expected those with wealth to give as the campaign required, and without attaching any conditions to such contributions.[33]

Elizabeth Wolstenholme Elmy's unhappy experience in other organisations also led her to emphasise the role of a small, closely-bound circle of like-minded colleagues in the campaigns of the WEU. At one point, for example, she sought to pre-empt the role of the WEU's governing council, through the creation of an 'inner Cabinet' of those in whose support she felt she might place complete trust. Similarly, the WEU never seems to have sought a large

membership or an extensive network of branches. Elizabeth Wolstenholme Elmy frequently evidenced an unease about such possibilities,
fearing the multiplication of committees which must follow as a
hindrance to rapid and effective action, as well as a potential source
of division and discord. She measured the effectiveness of the WEU
in terms of the numbers of constituencies in which it had contact
with someone she considered a 'worker', rather than those where
there was a fully fledged branch. Similarly she measured the influence
of the WEU in terms of its 5000 'occasional correspondents', rather
than its subscriptions.[34]

Most significantly for practical purposes, the WEU differed from
the Women's Franchise League in its greater flexibility concerning
the formulation of the women's demand. At its formation, the WEU
upheld the inclusion of married women in the demand, preferring
the broad formulation embodied in the Women's Disabilities
Removal Bill which Elizabeth Wolstenholme Elmy herself had
helped to draft. It never lent its support to any bill which expressly
excluded married women. When there was no immediate alternative,
however, the WEU was prepared to campaign on behalf of measures
which would bring less than full equality in the franchise laws. In
the view of Elizabeth Wolstenholme Elmy, any measure was to
be supported which breached women's total exclusion from the
parliamentary franchise, providing it did so in a way which offered no
endorsement for the doctrine of coverture. In contrast, the Women's
Franchise League refused to countenance any measure which did
not expressly include married women, or which fell short of full
equality. It was this issue which provoked a direct confrontation
between supporters of the two organisations, and perhaps the most
notorious episode in the League's history, in 1892.

Early in that year a Conservative MP, Sir Albert Rollit, introduced
a new women's suffrage bill. This was not an equal suffrage measure,
but it would have enabled women who already had local government
franchises to vote in parliamentary elections also. It was, however,
yet again a compromise with conservative opinion. But some married
women were by this time voting in local elections, and were therefore implicitly included in its provision. In consequence, Elizabeth
Wolstenholme Elmy was prepared to offer support for the bill. She
began to lobby on its behalf all the more energetically when it
became clear that the League intended to 'do their utmost to stop
it'. When she explained her own willingness to support any measure
'which did not explicitly exclude and insult any class of women',

Harriot Stanton Blatch responded by accusing English women in general of an 'utter want of principle'. For her part, Elizabeth Wolstenholme Elmy felt the position of the League was 'very silly, but it is not my place to advise them'.[35] The League's rejection of such a bill was further evidence of the ultra-Radical stance which Ursula Bright and her supporters maintained on this issue.

Elizabeth Wolstenholme Elmy continued to support Rollit's bill, whilst those she identified as 'fake suffragists, the Gladstonians' made a public stand against it. Ursula Bright, on behalf of the Women's Franchise League, issued a memorial to the Liberal leader, Gladstone, rejecting the bill and falsely claiming that it excluded married women. Matters came to a head at a major London demonstration held in support of the bill at the St James Hall in April. The Women's Franchise League issued the following call, signed by a number of its leadership including Ursula Bright, Alice Scatcherd, Emmeline Pankhurst, and Richard Pankhurst, alongside Helen Taylor, H. M. Hyndman and Herbert Burrows (the last two from the Marxist Social Democratic Federation), and George Lansbury: 'working men and women are urgently asked to attend in the interest of labour and justice to all'. They claimed that Rollit's bill was 'class legislation aimed to enfranchise only wealthy women, while excluding married women, and women lodgers'.[36]

Elizabeth Wolstenholme Elmy and her husband arrived early at the hall to prepare for the meeting, but found that their opponents had leafleted all the seats, and were about to take over the platform. Ben Elmy was in time to bar their way onto it from backstage. During the meeting itself, however, League supporters, led by Herbert Burrows, stormed the stage from the floor of the meeting, overturning the reporters' table in the process. Accusations and counter-accusations of violence flew between the two sides in the furore which followed. Elizabeth Wolstenholme Elmy had to plead with Harriet McIlquham not to resign from the WEU: 'We are all non-party women, married mothers, good speakers, earnest workers, and put women's suffrage above all.' She claimed that the press accounts had greatly exaggerated the uproar, that there had never been any danger of real violence, and that all the rowdyism had been on the part of their opponents, and especially 'Mrs Bright's socialists'. She also commented: 'It is satisfying to note that London working men and women are not readily gulled by mere clap-trap appeal to class prejudice', claiming that the League's supporters had numbered only about 200. The most significant aspect of the affair for her was the evidence the demonstrators had provided of 'a growing national danger' in their physical degeneration. She claimed that most of the demonstrators had been 'puny, undersized, ill-nourished youths', though they had 'made almost enough noise for 200 mad bulls'.[37]

The incident caused even greater unease among members of the League, even though Herbert Burrows and his supporters insisted that it was they, in fact, who had been the initial victims of violence at the hands of Ben Elmy. Some resignations followed, and Herbert Burrows was asked to provide the League's executive with his own account in writing, something which was apparently never forthcoming. Elizabeth Wolstenholme Elmy also reported that Harriot Stanton Blatch, who had been overseas during these events, entirely disassociated herself from Ursula Bright's memorial to Gladstone, and now lent her support to Rollit's bill, despite her earlier stand on the matter. She also resigned from the executive committee of the Women's Franchise League. Ursula Bright remarked to Emmeline Pankhurst on this defection: 'Of course she is not a strong soul like old Mrs Cady Stanton.'[38]

For Elizabeth Wolstenholme Elmy the event was evidence of the growth of 'the rowdy element in so-called Liberalism', and she warned her local colleagues against its spread from 'the metropolis of the south to that of the north' (Manchester). She declared:

> The Liberalism I believed in is dead and buried. Its murderers are Mr Gladstone, Mr Harcourt, Mr Labouchere and the rest. But we are not left without the promise of a new and better faith, and the evidence of the awakening of a noble and higher life.

She believed that the Gladstonian Liberal Party would soon be entirely shattered by the question of Irish home rule on the one side, and the growth of 'the English democratic party' on the other. She evidently had no time for revolutionary socialism, but she was eventually to follow the Pankhursts together with her husband into the Independent Labour Party, albeit somewhat reluctantly.[39] She remained always an idealist and a utopian who placed her faith in human perfectibility through reason and moral example, rather than the pragmatic tacking of party politics.

Rollit's bill in its turn failed to win a majority in the House of Commons, but the following year brought an advance which paved the way for the reunification of the women's suffrage movement, for it resolved once and for all the question of the inclusion of married women in the demand. The Liberal Party was briefly back in power, and introduced the new Local Government Bill. Under pressure from women's suffragists, and against the wishes of the government, Walter McLaren and other suffragist MPs won support from the House for a significant amendment to the Bill. An Instruction was passed which required the government to consider further extending the rights of married women to local government franchises under the bill. Ursula Bright reported to Emmeline Pankhurst that Walter McLaren had been 'utterly astounded at his victory', and it was one which proved a considerable embarrassment to his party.[40]

Subsequently, the Women's Franchise League claimed the lion's share of honour for the victory which followed. But all the suffrage societies exerted whatever influence they could to secure a successful outcome. Elizabeth Wolstenholme Elmy, for example, recorded that she had organised pressure from the constituencies of over 400 MPs to secure a majority for the instruction, and succeeded in raising a special fund to pursue this opportunity. She wrote after these efforts: 'I am so tired, but so happy.' In her view, the significance of the vote lay in the fact that Conservative suffragists 'now accepted the married women and we shall have that trouble the less in our fight next session for the Parliamentary Franchise'.[41]

Correspondence between Millicent Garrett Fawcett and Walter McLaren suggests that both the Parliament Street and Great College Street Societies also lobbied forcefully for the amendment. The aim was to extend all the existing local government voting rights held by women to all those married who possessed the necessary qualifications.[42] So it is not clear why Ursula Bright claimed all the glory for this campaign. Nor does it seem likely that the Parliament Street Society was 'simply mad at our success. They never calculated on such a decisive victory.' Emmeline and Richard Pankhurst had by this time returned to Manchester to live, and were evidently taking an active part in the Manchester Society for Women's Suffrage, alongside Alice Scatcherd. Ursula Bright relied on them to ensure that the Manchester Society gave this new opportunity its fullest support, declaring: 'It would make so great a difference to my whole life if the clause were passed.' She did not altogether share Harriot Stanton Blatch's hopes that a new unity might come out of such a victory, however. As yet, Helen Blackburn would give no firm commitment on the part of the Great College Street Society to abandon its pursuit of 'spinster bills' (measures of women's suffrage which excluded married women). Consequently, Ursula Bright felt the need to warn against the League's members becoming the 'cats-paws' of the larger societies, believing it unlikely that her opponents would easily abandon 'their cherished belief' in the more restricted demand, even now it had been 'so rudely smashed'. She commented, somewhat smugly: 'It is hardly in human nature that they can be delighted with what is manifestly *our* triumph.'[43]

The next few months were anxious ones for suffragists, as the government attempted to wriggle out of a commitment which the Liberal leadership found embarrassing. In the end the minister responsible for the measure negotiated a compromise whereby the rights of married women to local franchises were made equal with those of single women, but all women were excluded from the occupier qualification. Even Ursula Bright was grudgingly prepared to accept this compromise, though she hoped to defeat the added limitation by organising an additional amendment. In this she was buoyed up by the advice of Charles Dilke that the occupier qualification for women was not an issue outside London, and that the 'insane dread' of the House of Commons that women occupiers 'were all prostitutes' might be overcome. She was unusually pragmatic also in observing that success depended on the support of Conservative suffragists, 'for we cannot trust the Liberals to go against the Government'.[44] She even rejoiced in the news that Elizabeth Wolstenholme Elmy was active in the campaign, though somewhat faintly and in terms which misrepresented her former ally's commitment to the enfranchisement of married women.

The advance in the position of married women secured under the Local Government Act of 1894 paved the way for greater unity within the suffrage movement, though this possibility was only gradually realised. Ursula Bright found 'astonishing' the new possibility of cooperation between the Women's Franchise League and the Parliament Street Society evident in the preparation for a major London suffrage demonstration in May 1894. Her connection with it immediately aroused suspicions in Elizabeth Wolstenholme Elmy, however, who announced herself unwilling to attend. None the less she urged others to be there to represent the WEU, so as to ensure that Ursula Bright attempted no 'nonsense'.[45]

New realignments within the suffrage movement became evident in the period which followed the passage of the Local Government Act, and a fresh opportunity in the plans of Radical MPs to introduce a new Registration Bill. Elizabeth Wolstenholme Elmy now began to work closely with Esther Roper (1868–1938), who was appointed secretary of the Manchester Society in 1893. Like herself, Esther Roper came from a family without wealth, and of humble origins. Through the Sunday-school movement, her father had escaped the life of a factory-hand, to become a minister of the church and a missionary. His death, while serving overseas, and the family's relative poverty, had made Esther Roper eligible for scholarships which had eventually led to her studies at Manchester University. She had been prepared for a working life in the women's movement through the separate women's debating society and university settlement established there.[46] Under Esther Roper's guidance, the Manchester Society began, like the Women's Franchise League, to seek the support of women in the cooperative movement, and from the newly established Independent Labour Party.

The growing recruitment of former Radical Liberals, including Richard and Emmeline Pankhurst to the Independent Labour Party (ILP) now became a further factor for division among Radical suffragists. Ursula Bright was regretful when Emmeline Pankhurst decided to resign from the Lancashire and Cheshire Union of Women's Liberal Associations. She also expressed some doubts that the new party would ever secure electoral success as its methods to her mind were 'too violent and contemptuous of other people's methods'.[47] So while some Radical suffragists were finding it possible once more to work within the mainstream of the suffrage movement, others were breaking away altogether, and placing their hopes instead in the growing socialist movement.

Meanwhile, some of her oldest friends among WEU supporters continued to worry over the ever-deepening financial plight of the Elmys. During these years, Harriet McIlquham kept up a regular supply of game, poultry, fruit and preserves for the Elmys' table, while she, Harriot Stanton Blatch, Anna Maria Priestman and other old friends gathered together a Christmas gift of £9 in 1895. This evidence of 'sympathy and very practical support' was gratefully accepted by Elizabeth Wolstenholme Elmy, but it was necessarily only a stop-gap solution. She was now in her sixties, and her friends began to explore the possibility of financing an annuity for her old age. A 'Grateful Fund' was established, though this required a degree of circumspection, given the sometimes controversial nature of her role within the women's movement, and her own constant reminders to them of 'the sensitiveness of the poor'. Thinking over possible contributors, Harriet McIlquham advised Anna Maria Priestman that she knew of no friction between their friend and the wealthy J. P. Thomasson (son-in-law of Margaret Bright Lucas, and husband of Kate Thomasson), but that since the breach within the Women's Franchise League 'I should say Mrs Jacob Bright and Mrs Elmy have decidedly not been friendly'.[48] Other wealthy Liberal women, like Mary Illingworth, did support the Grateful Fund, however, and another old friend, Mary Martindale was still managing its affairs a decade later.

The splits and divisions which followed the defeat of women's suffrage hopes in 1884, and the political and social turmoil of the late 1880s, has generally been seen only in terms of setbacks which served to fragment the suffrage movement. Such an interpretation has recently been challenged with considerable effect by David Rubinstein, who argues that in this decade 'patterns and trends were established' on which the twentieth-century movement was to build. In consequence, he questions the 'exaggeratedly sharp break' with the past which is generally assumed in histories of the twentieth-century suffrage campaigns.[49] The evidence presented here suggests that this argument can be taken further still: the activities of the Women's Franchise League and the WEU reflected the new organisational directions which suffragists had begun to explore, and the consolidation of those new constituencies that they had begun to establish, during the agitation which had preceded the 1884 Reform Act. Both organisations promoted also a far broader conception of women's claim to citizenship, and the League began to organise working-class support on a more continuing basis than ever before. The importance of such support had only been reinforced by the extension of the franchise to some two million more male working-class voters in 1884, and the subsequent growth of a new movement for the independent representation of labour in parliament. The significant expansion of married women's voting rights and rights to stand in elections, secured by the Local Government Act of 1894, also brought new opportunities for working-class women to become politically active. The Independent Labour Party fostered the entry into local politics of many working-class women in these years, and brought together middle-class recruits to socialism, like Emmeline Pankhurst, and working-class socialists, like Hannah Mitchell, who now enters our story.

Plate 3 Hannah Mitchell. By courtesy of Manchester Central Library.

5

AMONG THE 'INSURGENT WOMEN'

Hannah Mitchell, socialist and suffragist

In 1895, Hannah Webster, a dressmaker, married Gibbon Mitchell, a tailor's cutter. She was twenty-four years old, and her wedding arrangements reflected the standing she had achieved as an independent, self-supporting woman over the past ten years. Hannah Webster refused to marry from her parents' home, as her mother wished her to do. Instead, she chose to marry from the home of the married sister where she had lodged from time to time. Subsequently, she remembered the contribution of neighbouring women to marking the day as

> One of the loveliest things I have ever known . . . when I rose early on my wedding day I found that every neighbour had risen earlier still, cleaned her windows, and whitened her flags back and front, thus giving the whole street quite a festive appearance on that glorious September morning.[1]

Hannah Webster also organised her own wedding breakfast at her sister's home, one which they themselves prepared, 'a very modest spread' of boiled ham, a large piece of roast beef, fruit pies, sponge cakes, fruit cakes, jellies, trifles, tea and coffee with cream. A male relative provided wine, beer and cigars. The one piece of 'swank' which Hannah Webster allowed herself was the attendance of three bridesmaids, 'a novelty for working-class folk in those days'. There was no white satin or orange blossom, however: 'a simple grey frock and grey velvet hat was my choice'.[2] The wedding was unusual also in that it took place on the weekly half-day holiday which had recently been won for shop-assistants, the only free time for many apart from Sunday. A walk in the local park, and an 'ample tea', completed the festivities, before Hannah and Gibbon Mitchell returned to Bolton for work the next day.

A wedding is an important right of passage in any life. But in her autobiography, Hannah Mitchell invests hers with a range of meanings which were particular to her time, place and personal history. From the perspective of old age, Hannah Mitchell represented her wedding above all as a political act. To begin with, her decision to marry at all was a deliberate and carefully assessed choice, rather than the automatic acceptance of norms regarding the proper course of a woman's life. It was a choice which reflected a sense of new possibilities for women within marriage, without which Hannah Webster would probably have chosen to remain single. Looking back, she felt that 'Perhaps if I had really understood my own nature, as I came to do later, I should not have married.'[3]

Her own unhappy childhood had made her determined to escape the fate of her mother, a lonely, overworked, embittered farm-wife, given to violent tantrums vented on her children, and especially on Hannah, the fourth in a family of six. Growing up in the remote Peak District of Derbyshire, Hannah Webster had seen other girls of her own age become victims of 'the primitive passions of the farm lads', marrying only to avoid the ostracism that accompanied giving birth to a child out of wedlock. As a consequence, Hannah Webster acquired 'a sort of "anti-male" complex'. This later moderated under the influence of the more urbane young men and courting customs she encountered after running away from home at fourteen to work in the neighbouring mill-towns of north-east Lancashire, first as a domestic servant and later as a dressmaker.[4]

She had decided to leave home for good after a particularly violent confrontation with her mother, and in consultation with her father and uncle. The main issue in contention between the two women had been Hannah Webster's desire for an education, and her resistance to the harsh drudgery of women's work in a farming family. Because of her mother's demands on her time and labour, she had been permitted only a fortnight's 'schoolin', for the nearest school was too far away for daily attendance. Her apprenticeship to a kindly and encouraging dressmaker had also been cut short because of the domestic needs of the farm. When she left home, then, she was determined on self-cultivation and social advancement. Her ambition was to become a teacher, and she had counted herself fortunate when she found her first position as a domestic servant in the house of a schoolmaster. Though the work was long and hard, with only one free day a fortnight, and though her pay was a mere four shillings a week, she was allowed to borrow from a well-filled bookcase, a benefit in which she freely indulged. She also showed herself capable, even at the age of fourteen and in such vulnerable circumstances, of a remarkable self-assertiveness. Not only did she resolutely resist serving at table, she also refused to wear the cap and apron of the maidservant, as 'the muslin badge of servitude'. When she believed her mistress to be bent on extorting more than a fair amount of work from her, she also engaged in her 'first battle for my rights as a worker', arranging a clandestine flight from the house at the cost of her previous week's wages.[5]

In finding new work as a seamstress she increased her independence from her employer, living now as a lodger with her married sister. She also had more time for study and leisure, with Tuesday evenings and Sunday free every week. Despite having to keep herself on eight shillings a week, she managed now to subscribe to a small library and buy exercise books to improve her handwriting. Working in these small dress shops and workrooms, Hannah Webster also encountered young women better-educated than herself. From them she learnt how to adapt her dress and speech, and among them she found friendships which 'did much to lessen the inferiority complex from which I suffered badly at that time'. As her work skills improved she also found that 'something of the pride of craftsmanship was stirring in me'.[6] For a time she was engaged to a schoolteacher, though this love affair foundered. By the time she met her future husband, she was working in one of the superior workshops in Bolton, and earning 15 shillings a week, 'quite decent wages judged by the low standards of the time'.[7] She had good lodgings, too, yet managed to save a shilling each week. Hannah Webster had recently taken part in the campaign to improve the working hours of shop workers, a campaign which had won the regular, weekly, half-day holiday on which she chose to marry. She had also taken part in a successful protest against one of her employers, in the practice of fining her employees for late arrival at work. Though security of employment was always uncertain in dressmaking, Hannah Webster none the less held high hopes of continuing the path of gradual self-improvement and social advancement which she had set herself.

She came to know Gibbon Mitchell first as a fellow-boarder at her lodgings, and as a joint participant in the campaign to preserve a footpath on Kinder Scout, near her old home in the Peak District.

Richard Pankhurst was the legal adviser employed by the campaign, and also a leading figure by this time in local socialist politics. Gibbon Mitchell also was a socialist, and it was he who introduced Hannah Webster to some of the new ideas and ideals being promoted by the movement. The friendship between the two 'developed into an attachment', leading to their marriage two years later. But this was a step that Hannah Webster did not take lightly. Married life, as she observed it among her own friends and family, held 'no great attraction' for her. But both she and Gibbon Mitchell were tired of living in lodgings, and Hannah inclined to think that a home of her own might be preferable. She wrote later:

> probably I should have hesitated, even then, but for the newer ideas which were being propounded by the Socialists. Men and women were talking of marriage as comradeship, rather than a state where the woman was subservient to, and dependent on the man.[8]

She married, then, with expectations of a life quite different from that of her mother, who had scoffed at Hannah's bookishness, and insisted on the right of menfolk to leisure, recreation and personal service afforded by the domestic labours of the women of a household: 'Even my mother, who quite definitely ruled the roost in our home, paid lip service to the idea of the dominant male.'[9]

So, the marriage of Hannah Webster and Gibbon Mitchell reflected the hopes and ideals of the socialist movement for new forms of relationships between men and women, where the equal standing of each found acknowledgment. The way Hannah Webster chose to organise her wedding made manifest such a view of marriage in the way it deliberately broke with custom and convention so as to emphasise her sense of being a fully independent and autonomous person. Looking back in later life, she felt her hopes to have been misjudged, 'for I soon realised that married life, as men understand it, calls for a degree of self-abnegation which was impossible for me. I needed solitude, time for study, and the opportunity for a wider life.'[10] Her memoirs testify to 'the problems working-class women faced when they became involved in political campaigns'.[11] And she also soon came to realise that 'Socialists are not necessarily feminists'. It proved uphill work, making do for two on one wage, a task for which her husband would assume no responsibility, 'just handing over his wages and leaving all the worry to me'.[12]

From the socialist movement she had learnt also that there were ways of limiting the size of a family, another factor in her decision to give up her single life. She explained the harshness of her own mother in terms of the strain and overwork of caring for a large family on a small income. She had also seen many 'pretty, merry girls . . . turn into slatternly and prematurely aged women'. The alternative promised by birth control she believed all her life to be 'the simplest way at present for the poor to help themselves, and by far the surest way for women to obtain some measure of freedom'. This possibility was another factor in her decision to marry.[13]

Her anxiety and discontent in her position as wife only grew, therefore, when she realised she was pregnant: 'at first I was desperate and wept many bitter tears'. Her husband seemed not to understand 'that money is not elastic'. In order to provide for the needs of the coming child she had to undertake dressmaking from home, as well as her domestic work. The birth itself proved traumatic, for her son was delivered by forceps and without an anaesthetic. She never forgot the 'sheer barbarism' and 'wilful cruelty' of this experience. Her baby was cross, fretful and difficult to feed:

> only one thing emerged clearly from much bitter thinking at that time, the fixed resolve to bring no more babies into the world. I felt it impossible to face again either the personal suffering, or the part of bringing a second child up in poverty.

On this point, at least, she found her husband 'had the courage of his Socialist convictions'.[14] She gave birth to no more children, though she did later adopt a niece, an example of the mutual aid among working-class families and communities which provides some of the happiest memories in her autobiography.

At this time Hannah Mitchell's life was a constant round of 'wash days, cleaning days, cooking and serving meals'. The 'tyranny of meals' she found the greatest burden on the housewife:

> Her life is bounded on the North by breakfast, South by dinner, East by tea, and on the West by supper, and the most sympathetic man can never be made to understand that meals do not come up through the tablecloth, but have to be planned, bought and cooked.

In her experience, then, marriage might prove 'fatal to ambition', even in a woman as determined as herself. She noticed that most women gave up forever their own aspirations under the burdens of family life, settling for 'a vicarious satisfaction out of their children'.[15] For a time, she herself had to abandon her plans for study and intellectual development as there was no library in Newhall, the village where the couple then lived. But she was able to keep up her active participation in the socialist movement, joining the local branch of the Independent Labour Party, providing hospitality for speakers on the socialist lecture circuit. For many socialists in this period, Robert Blatchford's *Clarion* was essential reading, and for Hannah Mitchell another pleasure in these years was the visits of the Clarion van and the Clarion cyclists, who toured the smaller towns and villages in the summer spreading the socialist message.

An even greater level of political activity was possible for Hannah Mitchell when the couple moved to Ashton-under-Lyme in 1900. Gibbon Mitchell had obtained work there in the cooperative society, work which was better paid, more secure, and more in keeping with their political and social ideals. Here she was able also to join the Labour Church, working alongside others committed to the kind of socialism promoted by William Morris and his followers. This was a socialism which acknowledged the cultural and aesthetic, as well as material, needs of working people: 'not just bread, but roses, too' was a motto which appealed especially to Hannah Mitchell. In her new home she was also able to join a branch of the Women's Cooperative Guild, an organisation devoted to helping working-class women take a larger part in public life. Alongside its social functions, it also provided opportunities to learn about the political issues of the day, about the growing opportunities for women in local government, and to learn the skills of committee participation and public speaking. Very soon Hannah Mitchell took over from her husband as secretary of the local Labour Church, and so was brought into personal contact with many of the leading figures within the socialist movement, including Keir Hardie, Bruce Glasier, and Richard and Emmeline Pankhurst. It was through her participation in these social- ist and labour movement bodies that Hannah Mitchell first encount- ered women public speakers. And it was a speech by Katharine St. John Conway (afterwards, Katharine Bruce Glasier) which provided her with an inspiration that later sent her 'out to the street corners with the same message'.[16]

She first found a public voice of her own after sitting 'in silent rage' while a member of the local debating society discoursed on 'women and politics' in terms which 'ranged from the frankly con- temptuous to the sloppily sentimental'. Offering a comment from the floor she congratulated him on his 'intimate knowledge of the Almighty's intention regarding the status of women', and capped his quotation from Milton with one from Tennyson: 'the woman's cause is man's; they rise or fall together'.[17] She made her first full speech, and learnt how to chair a meeting, when she was persuaded to undertake both these new roles during the regular annual visit of the Clarion van. Very shortly, she became in demand locally as a public speaker, and in 1904 she was invited to become an ILP candidate for the Poor Law Board elections. It was also through the socialist movement that she learned more of the demand of votes for women, when Emmeline Pankhurst's eldest daughter, Christabel, came to speak on the topic.

Christabel Pankhurst came into the suffrage movement under the influence of Esther Roper, the secretary of the North of England Society for Women's Suffrage in Manchester. Emmeline Pankhurst had taken little part in this organisation after she and Richard Pankhurst had joined the Independent Labour Party. When her husband died suddenly in 1898, Emmeline Pankhurst confronted the task of rearing their four children with very little means, for Richard Pankhurst's law practice had been adversely affected by his association with radical causes. In the early years of the twentieth century, then, Emmeline Pankurst was supporting her family as an assistant registrar of births and deaths in Manchester. As a member of the Independent Labour Party, she also stood and was elected to the board of Poor Law guardians in Manchester. Christabel Pankhurst at this time worked in a small business established by Emmeline Pankhurst, selling fashionable furnishings. Under Esther Roper's guidance, however, she enrolled to study law.

As secretary of the Manchester suffrage society, Esther Roper had continued to develop the approach taken by Radical suffragists, in attempting to win the support of working-class women through local socialist and Labour movement organisations, most especially the Women's Cooperative Guild, and branches of the textile workers' unions. Her lifetime companion, Eva Gore Booth, was secretary of the Manchester and Salford Women's Trades Council, consolidating further the links between suffragists and the Labour movement. Together they helped organise the large textile petitions which became such a colourful feature of suffrage campaign in the early years of the twentieth century. It was in this campaign that Christabel Pankhurst first gained experience as a public speaker and political organiser. It was also through such links, as we have seen, that

Hannah Mitchell first encountered women's suffragists. For the time being, however, her sympathies remained with those within the Labour and socialist movements who saw the demand for sexual equality in the franchise as a purely middle-class demand, given the property qualifications which remained in place. At this time she lent her support to the call for an extension of the franchise in the form of adult suffrage, believing this to represent the best interests of both her class and her sex.

Between 1894 and 1896 all the various suffrage societies had worked together to help collect another major petition, the Special Appeal, in the management of which Esther Roper had worked alongside the two secretaries of the Parliament Street and Great College Street Societies. It was this enterprise which first prompted her focus on the women textile workers in the Manchester area. This cooperation also paved the way for a reunification of the movement, promoted by the Manchester Society at a conference which it organised in 1896. Out of this came, the following year, the National Union of Women's Suffrage Societies (NUWSS), formed under the leadership of Millicent Garrett Fawcett. The suffrage movement enjoyed its first success for many years when, supported by the Special Appeal petition, Faithfull Begg's bill of 1897 gained a majority on its second reading in the House of Commons. Once again, this was a private member bill, and could go no further without government backing, but the victory provided, none the less, an enormous fillip for the suffrage movement.

Neither the Women's Franchise League nor the Women's Emancipation Union were absorbed into the NUWSS, for both had objects wider than winning the vote, and were not willing to abandon these as membership of the new national organisation would have required. The NUWSS continued, with the notable exception of the Manchester branch, with the more conventional approach which had marked both the Parliament Street and Great College Street Societies. Alice Scatcherd had advised the joint suffrage convention which preceded the formation of the NUWSS:

> The day of the average public meeting, which we have been holding for the past fifteen years is practically over; and the drawing meeting is also becoming a thing of the past. What is needed now is conviction. Conviction leads to action.[18]

Radical suffragists remained impatient of the caution and moderation which continued to characterise the NUWSS under Millicent Garrett Fawcett.

In 1897, for example, Alice Scatcherd and Florence Fenwick Miller, both of the Women's Franchise League, and the latter also editor of the *Women's Signal*, organised a memorial of 3000 'representative women' to Queen Victoria on the occasion of her fiftieth jubilee in 1897. Radical suffragists were to the fore among the signatories, including 'our revered friend and "Mother of Israel" ', Priscilla Bright McLaren, alongside Ursula Bright and Margaret Tanner. The terms of the memorial itself were admonitory, asking for:

> One royal word of sympathy with the progress which women have achieved during your Majesty's illustrious reign, one expression of gracious confidence and hope in the happy results which may be expected to follow from still further enlarging the area brought under the influence of women.[19]

Some commentators were critical of this 'cool request', judging it an 'unfair attempt to trade on a national occasion'.[20] Millicent Garrett Fawcett hastily organised an alternative, and much more respectful, address from among moderate suffragists which acknowledged the Queen's own 'exalted example' in showing women how to harmonise 'the claims of the public weal with the claims of home affection'.[21]

Radical suffragists were more surprised, and therefore even more disillusioned, when Sir Charles Dilke failed to unite his campaign for a new Registration Bill with the enfranchisement of women. Ursula Bright at this time confessed her despair to Emmeline Pankhurst, recording 'the awful difficulty of getting all our friends up to scratch at the right moment. . . . First one then another jibs till I get so disgusted, I only lose heart.' She hoped Emmeline Pankhurst might be able to advise her on how best to mobilise new political forces: 'Think for me what can be done for this meeting. If we could only get the working men to move in a body to the hall with banners and music!' But Ursula Bright was also to be found in an altogether unusual role, urging greater moderation on her friends in Manchester, among whom a certain disunity was evident. Alice Scatcherd was adopting an 'irreconcilable attitude' in urging suffragist MPs to vote against the Registration Bill if the women's suffrage amendments failed. Ursula Bright considered such intransigence unwise, and advised Emmeline Pankhurst: 'We must consider their party sympathies', urging her 'Be wise as a serpent and as gentle as a dove.'[22] The Pankhursts evidently shared her view of the matter, urging Manchester suffragists not to follow Alice Scatcherd's direction, but to adopt the Registration Bill being promoted by Charles Dilke, rather than a separate women's suffrage measure. In this they appear to have failed.

For her part, Ursula Bright understood the impatience of Alice Scatcherd as a consequence of the long, wearying, experience of the older generation, who had 'borne the brunt of these widows and spinsters' and did not yet trust that a great change was at hand. She also confided that some of Alice Scatcherd's abrasiveness was a consequence of her time of life which 'makes her irritable and weary at times', and maintained that she remained none the less 'a very fine woman and a most valuable worker'.[23] Ursula Bright was also herself under strain in these years. Jacob Bright was seriously ill with the disease which eventually took his life in 1899, and much of her energies were devoted to his care. Through her daughter, Esther Bright, and their mutual friend, Annie Besant, she had been introduced to theosophy which also took her further away from her previous political interests. Sylvia Pankhurst recalled her in after years: 'very gentle, very remote. We seemed to be conversing through a veil.'[24] So Alice Scatcherd was keeping the Women's Franchise League alive almost single-handedly in 1897, and it seems to have faded away in the years that followed. The *Women's Signal*, which became the voice of Radical suffragism after Florence Fenwick Miller took over as editor, also struggled to survive in these years, despite the efforts of Priscilla Bright McLaren to find further funding for it.[25]

Like Alice Scatcherd, Elizabeth Wolstenholme Elmy was impatient with the approach of the national leadership within the NUWSS. The Women's Emancipation Union evidently also believed that it continued to have a distinctive role to play in the suffrage movement. In these years Elizabeth Wolstenholme Elmy still resisted well-meaning efforts to provide her with a salary, as her colleagues became increasingly anxious about the heavy workload she now carried, which included all her own housework, alongside her voluntary labour for the WEU. She insisted that to accept such payment would be 'altogether to change my position and so tie my hands in many ways'. Once again, she had recently confronted a threat to her position among its leadership by discontents within the WEU who sought to appoint as joint secretary a Liberal MP, Atherley Jones. This recalled her experience a few years before with the Women's

Franchise League and so she insisted 'To take one penny would destroy my position certainly. . . . Mrs Fenwick Miller would never have dared her insolence and wrong-doing but for the pretence that I was a paid agent. Never again will I risk such insult.' Instead, she recorded, the Elmys mortgaged their house so that she might be able to go on working for two, possibly three years more, without pay. Under continuing pressure from her friends she agreed that some kind of testimonial further in the future might prove acceptable, provided it was offered 'not on the grounds of my poverty, but of the successful work done'. The continuing decline in the Elmys' fortunes during these years was made worse by Ben Elmy's 'illness almost unto death' early in 1895, through which he was nursed by his wife. His growing frailty remained a constant source of anxiety for her thereafter.[26]

Mary Cozens and Atherley Jones subsequently broke away to form a 'little separate society' after failing to oust Elizabeth Wolstenholme Elmy as secretary of the WEU. In consequence, the annual income of the WEU halved. This new organisation – whose name does not even appear to have survived – became an increasing embarrassment to the suffrage movement in general for the next few years. After one particularly ill-conceived intervention, Frances Power Cobbe wrote dryly to Millicent Garrett Fawcett: 'Miss Cozens should be scraped to death with oyster shells.'[27] For the time being the WEU continued to find supporters among the generation of provincial Radical suffragists, especially in the Manchester and Bristol regions, who had helped found the women's movement in Britain: Mrs Pochin, Maria Colby, Mrs J. G. Grenfell were all on its committee, alongside Agnes Sunley, who appears to have shifted her allegiance from the Women's Franchise League after many years of campaigning alongside Alice Scatcherd. The WEU continued to argue 'slavery of sex is the root of all slavery' and that injustice to women, especially within the family, was 'the perennial source of all other injustice'. It remained emphatically non-partisan, declaring that the emancipation of women should be 'paramount to all personal, sectional, or party considerations whatever'.[28] Its terms of membership continued to require 'Personal Effort' on behalf of the society's objects, not merely financial support.

The publication and distribution of a series of sex education books for young people by 'Ellis Ethelmer' became one of its last major undertakings, a series which attracted a significant level of interest beyond its own membership. The year 1895 also saw Elizabeth

Wolstenholme Elmy re-establishing working relationships with former colleagues in the Women's Franchise League. She and Harriot Stanton Blatch organised, for example, an informal deputation to discuss with the government minister concerned 'the dangers and wrongs of restrictive legislation', that is legislation which limited the conditions of women's work. Emmeline Pankhurst, for her part, provided a paper for the WEU's annual conference which Elizabeth Wolstenholme Elmy considered 'capital'. In this period, though, the WEU concentrated most of its resources and energies on monitoring and encouraging women's participation in local government, both as voters and candidates for election. One hundred and ten of its supporters were elected onto local councils in the year after the passage of the 1894 Local Government Act. Here, Elizabeth Wolstenholme Elmy was glad of 'the hearty help' she anticipated from members of the Women's Cooperative Guild and the Independent Labour Party, as well as the Women's Liberal and Radical Union, women Fabians, the society for Women Poor Law Guardians, the Pioneer Club and the Somerville Club.[29]

Though the WEU was also consulted on arrangements for the 1896 conference of suffrage societies which brought the reunification of the movement, Elizabeth Wolstenholme Elmy declined to take any part in its proceedings.[30] She always doubted the capacity for 'prompt and vigorous action' of large and far-flung organisations. She remained committed to the pressure-group tactics by which she had secured her earlier advances for women. Strong, independent branch societies for her always proved 'sources of division and weakness', as Mary Cozens' role in the WEU had shown, and so generally meant 'more labour to the real workers. . . . One or two good earnest workers do more in every way than any of our local societies of 50 or more.'[31]

Elizabeth Wolstenholme Elmy was also greatly dismayed that the 'foul and degrading barbarism' of coverture had only just received fresh endorsement from the judiciary. The decision in the recent Clarence divorce case served to maintain the 'hideous claim' of husbands to conjugal rights over wives. While Elizabeth Wolstenholme Elmy believed any further progress to be quite hopeless 'till we are free citizens and help to make the laws', she resisted any narrowing of the objects of the WEU and its 'absorption into servile dependence' within the NUWSS, where she feared a partisan spirit continued to hold sway. Nor did she have great faith in the leadership which was emerging for this unified suffrage body, or the emphasis which was being placed on 'organisation', that is in the gradual building of a solid network of suffrage societies. She asked 'What on earth have the large Suffrage Societies done with their money?', suggesting that the WEU had accomplished as much, if not more, with far fewer resources. She put her alternative perspective on these matters before the Manchester Society, where she evidently met with a great deal of sympathy and support, and was made 'quite tired of shaking hands and being thanked.' But her views did not prevail, so for the time being the WEU maintained an independent existence, while the main body of the suffrage movement continued to consolidate.[32]

It was clear, however, that the days of useful work for the WEU were numbered. Funds proved an ever increasing difficulty. Elizabeth Wolstenholme Elmy reported her hopes that among the Bright family circle, the wealthy Radical suffragist MP, J. P. Thomasson, might support the activities of the WEU 'though I am never sanguine as to what rich men will do, or for that matter rich women either. It is always the men and women to whom to give costs something, who give the most steadily and liberally.'[33] But it proved impossible any longer to win sufficient financial support to maintain a separate organisation, and the Women's Emancipation Union wound itself up at a final celebratory meeting in 1899. Her friends had by this time succeeded in establishing the Grateful Fund on an ongoing basis, and it continued to provide Elizabeth Wolstenholme Elmy with a small regular income. For the time being she focused her hopes on the work of Esther Roper in organising suffrage support among the textile workers, and in the one remaining organisation which provided expression for the Radical suffragist perspective, the Union of Practical Suffragists.

This body was established in 1898 as a ginger-group within the Women's Liberal Federation, and as Elizabeth Wolstenholme Elmy preferred to maintain her distance from party organisations, she did not herself join it. But she continued to uphold the efforts of its founder, Anna Maria Priestman, her old friend from the campaign against the Contagious Diseases Acts, founder of one of the first Women's Liberal Associations in Bristol, and a promoter of the Grateful Fund. After the local WLAs joined together to form the Women's Liberal Federation in 1886, those Radical suffragists who had so far dominated its councils gradually found themselves ousted as office-holders and policy-makers by women whose loyalties to Gladstone and the Liberal Party took priority over support for women's suffrage.

Radical Liberals, like Anna Maria Priestman, Ursula Bright and Harriot Stanton Blatch, sought, through the Union of Practical Suffragists, to make women's suffrage a test question for Liberal candidates wanting the support of the WLF, by now a major part of the Liberal Party's election machinery. For a few years, it became the only surviving separate organisation fully sympathetic to the Radical suffragist perspective.[34] And their dedication to women's suffrage was not general within the WLF. Elizabeth Wolstenholme Elmy complained: 'These Liberal women who put party first are heart- breaking. It needs such noble souls as the Priestmans who put justice first, to keep one from loathing party as an unmixed evil.'[35]

Though the National Union gradually displaced the variety of Radical suffrage groups which had grown up in the early 1890s, their perspective was not altogether lost. Indeed, it could be argued that it re-emerged in the early twentieth century, when Emmeline Pankhurst formed the Women's Social and Political Union (WSPU) in Manchester in 1903, the organisation which was to stir up the suffrage 'militancy' which has been the most remarked-upon aspect of the twentieth-century campaigns. Though it seems to have ended with a whimper, Harriot Stanton Blatch, looking back, saw the origins of militancy in both Britain and the United States in the work of the Women's Franchise League during the 1890s.[36] Such a claim appears startling in terms of standard accounts of the British suffrage movement in the nineteenth century, accounts which emphasise its moderation, even conservatism. It is startling also in terms of current understandings of suffrage militancy, which is still usually discussed in terms of the extreme violence of militant demonstrations in the 1912–14 period.[37] Undoubtedly, the Women's Franchise League had helped pioneer new methods of agitation, and had developed new sources of suffrage support among organised, working-class women, both important factors in the early years of militancy. And it had also provided Emmeline Pankhurst with her apprenticeship as a suffrage leader. But it is probably more accurate to think of the continuities between twentieth-century suffrage militancy and the nineteenth-century campaigns in terms of Radical suffragism, for past members from a range of Radical suffragist organisations were among the earliest supporters of the new 'militant' stance on votes for women. Elizabeth Wolstenholme Elmy, along with Priscilla Bright McLaren, Anna Maria Priestman, Ursula Bright and Harriot Stanton Blatch, all lent their support to the WSPU.

The memoirs of another early member of the WSPU, Dora

Montefiore, also clearly situate the origins of militancy among circles of Radical suffragists, in both London and in Manchester. They suggest, too, that Elizabeth Wolstenholme Elmy was closer to the centre of this new development in suffrage organisation and movement strategy than most other accounts acknowledge. Dora Montefiore had returned to Britain from Australia where she had also been active in the suffrage movement in the late 1890s. She recognised Elizabeth Wolstenholme Elmy as someone who might sympathise with her own heterodox outlook on life, and who was among the most able of the campaigners on behalf of women's rights. She also found 'continuous signs that a breaking away of more urgent spirits was imminent', and here she singled out the Union of Practical Suffragists, which she joined, for special mention. It was through this body that Dora Montefiore first sought to revive the tactic of tax-resistance among suffragists, a tactic she said she had been introduced to by Quaker friends, almost certainly the Priestman sisters, who had themselves first attempted to introduce this long-standing Quaker method of protest to the broader women's movement a generation before. When Dora Montefiore helped form the London WSPU such methods were central to her conception of militancy as passive resistance and civil disobedience. What distinguished these 'urgent spirits', then, was an impatience with the approach and outlook of the NUWSS, a desire to adopt more confrontational methods, and a disillusion with the Liberal Party, where there was not already an active or growing adherence to socialist politics. Dora Montefiore, for example, departed the Women's Liberal Federation and joined the Social Democratic Federation in these years.[38]

The campaigns among the textile workers promoted by Esther Roper and the Manchester Society were clearly the other major influence in the formation of the Women's Social and Political Union, for this is where Christabel Pankhurst served her suffrage apprenticeship. But Esther Roper found it increasingly difficult to pursue this approach within a branch society of the National Union, for reasons which are not entirely clear, but which almost certainly reflect the continuing dominance of middle-class, Liberal Party women within that body. In 1903, then, Esther Roper, established the Lancashire and Cheshire Textile and Other Workers' Representation Committee (LCTOWRC). The aim was to use the power of women textile workers within their unions to secure the election of Labour MPs committed to women's suffrage. Its 1904 manifesto declared: 'The one all-absorbing and vital political question for labouring women is to force an entrance into the ranks of responsible citizens, in whose hands lie the solution of the problems which are at present convulsing the industrial world.'[39] The LCTOWRC also supported womanhood suffrage – the vote for all women, irrespective of property qualification – a formula which went beyond the demand for equal rights under existing franchise laws. Emmeline Pankhurst's object in forming the Women's Social and Political Union around the same time appears to have been somewhat different. Initially, the WSPU was conceived as a ginger-group within the Independent Labour Party, where support for women's suffrage was not by any means universal. The WSPU held to the formulation of the suffrage demand in terms of sexual equality, and many socialists, including Hannah Mitchell, still preferred to seek women's enfranchisement through a demand for a universal suffrage – the vote for all adults, men and women.

Elizabeth Wolstenholme Elmy lent her support to the LCTWORC and also became among Emmeline Pankhurst's closest colleagues in the early years of the WSPU. It was her firm conviction by this time that 'the best work for women's suffrage is being done by the splendid women workers outside the National Union which seems quite incapable of rising to the greatness of the question.'[40]She declared that the work of the LCTOWRC was 'of more value to our cause than all the work of the National Union put together'.[41] So she did her best to use her long-established contacts with members of the Bright circle to bring funds to the new body. And once again she also lent her support to those Liberal women who sought to strengthen the women's suffrage commitment of the WLF. In 1905 she recorded that 'a great fight' was going on within that organisation, where their opponents were intent on 'undoing all the work of the Practical suffragists'.[42] Anna Maria Priestman had wound up the Union of Practical Suffragists with some sense of gratification in 1903, having brought the WLF firmly behind the demand for women's suffrage at last. But her achievement proved short-lived, and as the Liberal Party prepared to fight a general election which it was expected to win, its women's auxiliary retreated from its earlier commitment to make women's suffrage a test question. Not surprisingly in such circumstances, Anna Maria Priestman herself became an ardent supporter of militancy in the years that followed.

In these years, then, Elizabeth Wolstenholme Elmy celebrated the emergence of those she characterised as 'insurgent women', a new breed who were the heirs, where they were not the survivors, of Radical suffragism.[43] Elizabeth Cady Stanton had noted some years before that Radical suffragism might well take a different course in the future. At the first international gathering of suffragists in Washington in 1888, she had declared: 'It requires no prophet to foretell the revolution ahead when women strike hands with Nihilists, Socialists, Communists, and Anarchists, in defence of the most enlarged liberties of the people.'[44] And again, in the following year, she had warned that her generation had been

> bred in the pacific school of the old Abolitionists, dominated by the non-resistance ideas of Garrison, and where the presence of so many Quakers spread about an atmosphere of brotherly love. But we are passing away, and the new American woman is coming to the front. Cave Canis.[45]

In this way, then, Elizabeth Cady Stanton had 'prophesied and in anticipation, welcomed the militant suffrage movement'.[46] Though she died in 1902, before the formation of the first 'militant' suffrage society in Britain, her daughter, Harriot Stanton Blatch, was among those who took the militant approach to suffrage campaigning back to the United States in the years that followed.

In 1904 Elizabeth Wolstenholme Elmy helped Emmeline Pankhurst secure a place for a women's suffrage bill in the forthcoming session of Parliament, expressing the new impatience represented by militancy: 'I think it is time to demand and not to sue!'[47] Hannah Mitchell, along with a number of other working-class socialist women, joined the WSPU that year. This decision reflected her growing disillusion with the Independent Labour Party, for she had come to realise that many socialists 'would be quite content to accept Manhood Suffrage in spite of all their talk about equality'. She recalled: 'We heard a lot about adult suffrage at this time from men who never seemed to have thought about it before.'[48] It was at Emmeline Pankhurst's house that she met two other early recruits, Annie and Jessie Kenney, both of whom she found 'fine examples of the self-respecting Lancashire mill girl, intellectual and independent'. The WSPU at this time focused its attention on local trades councils, debating societies and branches of the Women's Cooperative Guild, while 'quite often', Hannah Mitchell recalled, 'one of us would take the ILP meeting' in Manchester on Sunday nights. In the summer of 1905, she, together with Emmeline Pankhurst and her three daughters, Christabel, Sylvia and Adela, held outdoor meetings all around Lancashire and much of Yorkshire. ILP men, including Gibbon Mitchell, formed 'a sort of bodyguard' for them among the crowds who came to watch, and 'kept the worst elements in pretty good order'. But Hannah Mitchell also recorded how many of the men 'became "anti" if their wives were out too often', and how 'public disapproval could be faced and borne, but domestic unhappiness, the price many of us paid for our opinions and activities, was a very bitter thing'.[49]

Emmeline Pankhurst later dated the onset of militancy from the protest she and Elizabeth Wolstenholme Elmy staged outside the House of Commons when a women's suffrage bill was talked out, in the spring of 1905.[50] Her account added a new dimension to militancy, one which associated this new current within the suffrage movement with a readiness to disrupt public order. In the following October, during the run-up to the general election at which a Liberal government was expected to be returned, Emmeline Pankhurst decided that the strategy of the WSPU should be to focus on 'would-be' Cabinet members among the Liberal leadership. From this time on, 'militancy' involved a distinctive political strategy, as well as more challenging methods of protest. Whereas the NUWSS's policy during elections was one of studied neutrality, the WSPU began an aggressive assault on the Liberal Party. When Sir Edward Grey came to address a pre-election rally in the Free Trade Hall, Manchester, Christabel Pankhurst and Annie Kenney were present in the audience, and challenged him on whether his party would bring in votes for women. Ejected from the meeting, they were arrested outside when they attempted to maintain their protest, and Christabel Pankhurst deliberately committed a technical assault on a policeman. The two women were sent to gaol when they refused to pay a fine for these offences, the first prisoners for the cause, and, as they had hoped, this ploy brought the press attention which the movement had failed to secure by more routine and orderly methods.

Hannah Mitchell declared that it was after this event that 'the smouldering resentment in women's hearts burst into a flame of revolt. There began one of the strongest battles in all our English history. It was fitting indeed that it began at the site of Peterloo.' She was among those at the gates of the prison to greet Christabel Pankhurst and Annie Kenney on their release, alongside Eva Gore Booth, and members of the Manchester Society and the ILP.[51]

Shortly afterwards, she followed their example, attending one of Winston Churchill's election meetings in Manchester equipped with two 'votes-for-women' banners. Here again, she asked 'Will the Liberal Government give the Vote to Women?', brandishing the first of her banners, and bringing forth the second when that was removed.[52] In this instance, she was invited on to the platform, and there repeated the demand. She was more fortunate than other such suffrage demonstrators in escaping without any further rough handling by stewards or crowd. Shortly after, she repeated the exercise at one of Lloyd George's meetings.

Here again, suffragists found themselves confronted with the issue of adult suffrage, a cause which had gained a fresh popularity with Liberal candidates as well as socialists. Hannah Mitchell's response was: 'Let those who want votes work for them', she and other militants 'having no mind to get our heads broken, as women did at Peterloo, in order to get more votes for men.'[53] This harassment of leading Liberals continued after their 'landslide' election victory early in 1906, and the numerous by-elections which in those days followed the appointment of a new Cabinet minister provided ample opportunities. Hannah Mitchell's own first arrest occurred at this time, along with that of Adela Pankhurst and some other WSPU members, after they had staged a succession of interruptions at a meeting addressed by Winston Churchill and John Burns. When she refused to pay her fine, she was given a short prison sentence, but found herself released within a matter of hours. Angrily she remembered how her husband had come to the prison and paid her fine: 'Most of us who were married found that Votes for Women were of less interest to our husbands than their own dinners. They simply could not understand why we made so much fuss about it.'[54] A celebration meeting was subsequently held to mark the release of the prisoners, but increasingly the militants found themselves confronting hostile crowds. On this occasion 'the mob played a sort of Rugby football' with Hannah Mitchell and her colleagues. Being 'strong i' th'arm' she managed to fell two of her younger assailants. An older man, who was yelling obscene suggestions from the side-lines, she set about with her umbrella.[55] It was in such circumstances that militancy first departed from the practices of civil disobedience with which it had begun.

While such methods gradually came to dominate militant agitation in the years that followed, Dora Montefiore, in London, kept alive the practice of civil disobedience for a while longer. After she had refused to pay her taxes her London house came under a state of siege in 1906, as the bailiffs surrounded it.[56] The WSPU received further valuable press coverage from such tactics and their adoption was endorsed by the WSPU's recently appointed organiser, Teresa Billington, when she came to London to help organise support for the WSPU there.

On this occasion Teresa Billington shared the Chelsea lodgings of Sylvia Pankhurst, the second daughter of Emmeline Pankurst, who was at this time an art student in London, and also secretary of the WSPU. Teresa Billington was another larger-than-life figure: 'Her lips curled perhaps rather too much, and, like many other bright young people, perhaps she pushed her arguments rather too crudely.'[57] The unhappy marriage of her parents had made for a home life full of conflict and tension. She had rebelled against the prudish and repressive outlook of her mother, especially with regard to the body, and to sexual relations, while holding her father in scant respect. As Sylvia Pankhurst recalled:

> She was not afraid to be considered unconventional; on the contrary, she sought so to be regarded. . . . She was one of the 'new' young women, who refused to make any pretence of subordinating themselves to others, in thought or deed.[58]

She impressed other young women among the WSPU by her open adoption of a self-consciously challenging outlook as she 'declaimed on the virtue of flouting Mrs Grundy, and expatiated with youthful excitement on the joys of her love affair with the worthy Scotsman' whom, in fact, she was later to marry.[59]

Early on, she had determined to establish herself as an independent woman with a career. The pupil-teacher system had provided her with the opportunity to fulfil this goal. Through the women's settlement attached to Manchester University she had met both Esther Roper and Emmeline Pankhurst. The latter had helped extricate her from a professional dispute over her unwillingness to provide the religious instruction which was part of her duties as a teacher. Emmeline Pankhurst also helped secure her subsequent appointment as the first women organiser for the ILP. Strong convictions and an assertive personality, which some found egocentric and overbearing, led Teresa Billington into frequent conflict with colleagues in the women's movement. In 1906, however, she was one of the WSPU's chief assets as a speaker and organiser, one able to appeal to the unity of socialist, Labour and suffrage sympathies which was at this time bringing increasing numbers of working-class women into the campaign for votes for women.

Plate 4 Mary Gawthorpe, *c.* 1909. By courtesy of the Mary Evans/ Fawcett Library.

6

'A MERRY, MILITANT SAINT'
Mary Gawthorpe and the argument of the stone

Mary Gawthorpe (1881–1973) was 'Yorkshire born'. Like Hannah
Mitchell, she was a woman of working-class background who joined
the suffrage movement by way of socialist and labour politics in the
early years of this century. But, again like Hannah Mitchell, when
she looked back upon her militant suffragism, she located its origins
within the context of domestic life, and the oppression of women
within the family. Mary Gawthorpe grew up among the back-to-
back houses of Meanwood in Leeds where her father worked in the
local tannery. Before marriage, her mother had escaped from work
in the mill by helping with a home dressmaking business established
by a sister. Though the family was poor, it was one which, during
her early childhood, enjoyed a certain standing in the local community. Mary attended the local Church of England school. Her
father was choirmaster, superintendent of the Sunday school and lay
official of the church. He was also captain of the cricket team, a
'good lodge man', and honorary secretary of the local Conservative
Party branch. In the days of Lord Randolph Churchill's 'Tory
democracy' there had even been some talk of his standing for Parliament. But instead he had to be content with acting as the political
agent for his employer, who was also the local Conservative Member
of Parliament. John Gawthorpe loved books, read widely, and
enjoyed some success in literary competitions. Looking back from a
new life she later established for herself in America, Mary Gawthorpe
identified her father as a victim of 'the caste system of England', 'an
intellectual soul who would have done brilliantly in an intellectual
profession' if the social system had allowed him such opportunity.[1]

The family's stability and social position proved vulnerable to the
many hazards of working-class life, however. The Gawthorpes lived

in housing which was common in working-class districts of Leeds at this time, but which Mary Gawthorpe recalled as a slum, with no inside sanitation, and with one privy shared between several houses. She believed it was poverty, poor housing and insanitary conditions which accounted for the deaths, within a single year, of two of her sisters, alongside the serious illness of her mother. After these trials, by the time Mary was ten or eleven years old 'the family pattern was already breaking up'. Now, she increasingly saw her father through her mother's eyes. The family had been left in debt by its considerable medical expenses, and the de-moralisation of her father also began to become evident. This was a de-moralisation which Mary Gawthorpe associated at least in part with his having now become a political agent part-time: 'There was much unhappiness, spasmodic intemperance on the part of Father and many other symptoms that are better understood in this psychological age and country [that is, the United States] than in those days in England.' Her father's decline intensified the material privations of the family, and began, too, the domestic disharmony which Mary Gawthorpe presented as such a potent influence upon her own development. Annie Gawthorpe was hostile to her husband's new activities because of the 'instability threatened by the fruits of this alternative career' – political agents were paid according to results in those days. It seems she also disliked the associated life style. Annie Gawthorpe soon became known among her husband's new associates as 'the Puritan'.[2]

Education was an important part of the Gawthorpe family's strategy for maintaining its worth and respectable identity, and Mary was a bright child who received every encouragement to do well at school. But the economic pressures on the family also meant that child labour remained an important additional source of income. Mary's schooling was undertaken alongside helping her father run a newsagency by which he supplemented his declining wages, together with second-hand book dealing and local sports journalism. In this last endeavour Mary was the messenger who ran his copy from sportsground to the newspaper offices. She noted that Annie Gawthorpe's contribution to the family's economic survival was also significant, especially in terms of making, mending and adapting clothing. But her mother's rigid notions of respectability did not allow the taking in of additional sewing for payment, something to which Hannah Mitchell had resorted, however grudgingly, when she found herself in difficult financial circumstances.

The economic contribution of the children became essential as John Gawthorpe's feckless ways worsened. When Mary reached school-leaving age, her headmaster entered her for an examination for a scholarship to the local high school in which she was successful. But the need for her to earn was too pressing, so instead her father arranged for her to stay on at her old school as a pupil-teacher. And so, still only thirteen years old, she began on the career which she hoped would eventually free her from the trials of working-class life, and set her on the road to personal advancement. Mary Gawthorpe coped with the increasing unhappiness of her home life by a promise she made to herself – that she would work towards becoming an independent woman, one able to maintain a household of her own. 'When I am twenty-one' was her secret motto from the age of ten years or so. Teaching offered her, as it did many young women in similar circumstances, the opportunity to become that new phenomenon, a woman professional. Though her family could not afford to support her education as a full-time student, the pupil-teacher scheme did make it possible, by exceedingly hard work, to combine professional training with further education. It meant working all day in the classroom, and studying at night and weekends. Mary Gawthorpe did well in the successive examinations, and once again won a scholarship to go away to attend college full-time for the final stage of her training. But she decided against taking up this opportunity, unwilling to leave her mother dependent on the uncertain earnings of her father. With even greater determination, she set out to finish her apprenticeship, become a fully certificated teacher and by that means achieved her goal of personal autonomy.[3]

This protective stance towards her mother had grown as Mary Gawthorpe had become increasingly aware of another, more hidden aspect of the tensions between Annie and John Gawthorpe. It was now quite common for her father to come home late after an evening of drinking, and for such returns to be followed by noisy disturbances from her parents' bedroom. Without understanding quite why, Mary felt she should intervene and offer her mother the sanctuary of her own room. From that point mother and daughter shared the same bed increasingly often, until one night brought 'the battle of the beds'. John Gawthorpe insisted that his wife return to his bed. Recalling his semi-dressed and 'un-Puritan appearance' on that occasion, Mary Gawthorpe concluded that her mother had reluctantly complied to spare her daughter any more disturbing spectacle. Experiences of this kind only further confirmed her in her determination to escape her father's house.[4]

Mary Gawthorpe became a fully qualified primary school teacher shortly before her twenty-first birthday. She then sought a better post some way from her home, in pursuit of her advancement towards the life of an independent woman. By this time, she and her younger brother were the main breadwinners in the family, and on her insistence the whole family moved, both to be nearer to her new school, and to find improved housing. In her memoirs, Mary Gawthorpe presents this move in terms of an assertion of her new sense of authority within the family, and her desire to retrieve and advance its social standing. Her father soon missed his old haunts, however, becoming restless in their new environment, and seeking a return to their previous situation. His continuing ravages on the family finances were by now threatening their continued ownership of a piano, that symbol of social advancement, and an important aid in having found her brother a congenial post in a music shop. At this point Mary determined on a final break with her father. But she also felt unable to abandon her mother and her brother to the vagaries of life with John Gawthorpe. So, having first explained the problem to the vicar of the church school in which she taught, she organised their secret flight to a new address. In this way, she at last established herself as an independent woman, head of her own household – and also for the first time a voter on the local government register. None of the family ever returned to live with John Gawthorpe. After sending a policeman to talk to his wife without success, he at last left them in peace. Annie Gawthorpe became 'distinctly younger looking', while Mary Gawthorpe, having for a while not liked 'the look of the marriage business at all', now began to look forward to her own marriage as 'a culminating fact' in a woman's life.[5]

She became engaged to a typesetter on the *Yorkshire Post*, only ever referred to in her memoirs as 'FL'. Tom Steele suggests that these initials probably stand for 'first love', and has identified the young man concerned as T. B. Garrs.[6] In her pursuit of professional advancement and improved circumstances for her family, Mary Gawthorpe changed jobs again, and moved her household out to Bramley, which was then still a semi-rural area. She continued with a programme of self-improvement which included training in singing, at which she excelled, elocution classes, and study for a university degree. It was through T. B. Garrs that Mary was introduced to the local socialist movement, and soon discovered that she was not the Conservative in politics she had always unthinkingly assumed herself to be. She recalled in later years that T. B. Garrs was an avid reader of the Australian socialist weekly, the *Bulletin*, and that together they took an active part in the local Labour Church. It was here that Mary Gawthorpe gained her first experience of journalism, editing the women's page of its local paper, *Labour News*. It was also in the Labour Church that she began to develop the powers of public speaking so long remembered among suffrage colleagues.

Through one of the sub-editors on the *Yorkshire Post*, the couple also gained membership of the Leeds Arts Club. Here they encountered some of the most radical thinkers of the day, men like Edward Carpenter and George Bernard Shaw, and had access to the library gathered together by the three organisations which shared this building, the Fabian Society, the Theosophical Society, and the Arts Club. They also came to know A. R. Orage, one of the charismatic local figures who had founded the club. He was soon to leave for London, to take over as editor of the *New Age*, a weekly that addressed itself to the avant garde in art, literature and politics. She later remembered how: 'It was stimulating, refreshing and nourishing' to be a member of such circles as a young woman intent on going places.[7]

Mary Gawthorpe's participation in local socialist circles led to her becoming the Labour Church delegate to the local Labour Representation Committee (forerunner of the Labour Party), Labour delegate to the University Extension Committee, and also Vice President of the Leeds Independent Labour Party. Professionally, she was coming to the fore in the local National Union of Teachers, and the National Federation of Assistant Teachers. Her experience of working and living in the poorer districts of Leeds also led her to take a prominent part in the campaign for school meals. This came to a head in the winter of 1904–5, when severe unemployment exacerbated the problem of hunger in the classroom. As a member of the Lord Mayor's Children's Relief Committee she found herself alone as a Labourite among a group of local dignitaries. When this committee was wound up in October 1905 because of the lack of an enabling act, Mary Gawthorpe found that 'the relation of the Vote to Acts of Parliament was thrown into distinct relief'. The need for the enfranchisement of women now became for her 'a burning issue'.[8]

As we have seen, it was impossible to be active in socialist and Labour movement politics in these years and remain unaware of the revival of interest in women's suffrage. Mary Gawthorpe first heard

Christabel Pankhurst speak on the demand for the vote at her local Labour Church some time before her name figured in newspaper headlines, or militancy had been established as an alternative approach to suffrage campaigning. Many socialists viewed the Women's Social and Political Union 'as a branch of the Labour movement', though subsequently it was to draw away 'certain forces which never returned'.[9] Mary Gawthorpe was to become one of those lost by the British labour movement to the WSPU, for by the time she returned to organising on behalf of labour a decade or so later she was living in the United States. The arrest and imprisonment of Christabel Pankhurst and Annie Kenney in October 1905, after their demonstration at the Manchester Free Trade Hall, first drew Mary Gawthorpe into the suffrage movement. She wrote immediately to Christabel Pankhurst to say she too was ready to go to prison, if that was what was needed to win the vote. In response, she was showered with press cuttings, some reporting subsequent protests, and one of a letter from Elizabeth Wolstenholme Elmy to the *Labour Leader* on the issue. Mary Gawthorpe is somewhat apologetic in her memoirs about how she contented herself at this time with a series of letters to the local press defending the new tactics. She explains:

> I was deeply in love with labour politics, with none of the long years of suffrage experience which was the background of the Pankhursts as a family; experience which was also the very heart of that long suffrage life which was Mrs Elmy's.[10]

Despite her continuing commitment to socialist politics, however, she began her own single-handed harassment of politicians during election meetings in Leeds and its environs, earning a burlesque of herself from 'Buff', the local cartoonist, Anton Wilson.

Alice Scatcherd was no longer a presence in women's suffrage circles in Leeds by this period, though her previous record might make her appear a likely sympathiser with the new militancy. She died at the end of 1906, and her absence may reflect simply her old age or ill health. Closer participation in the WSPU was not anyway a practical possibility in late 1905–early 1906 for someone living in Leeds, as its organisation still centred on Lancashire and London. Instead, Mary Gawthorpe joined the Leeds branch of the NUWSS, itself led by a pioneer of women's trade unionism and one of the founders of the Independent Labour Party, Isabella O. Ford. Isabella Ford was an old and close friend of Millicent Garrett Fawcett, and her mother, Hannah Ford, had earlier been one of the circle of Quaker women who had helped mount the campaign against the Contagious Diseases Acts. Also prominent in the Leeds Society at this time was Mary Gawthorpe's old friend from teaching college days, Ethel Annakin, who had recently married the future Labour MP and cabinet minister, Philip Snowden. Relations between the WSPU and the NUWSS remained cooperative at this time, and many in the older societies, like Isabella Ford, were openly sympathetic to the new campaign methods and strategies, and to the association of suffrage with labour campaigning. It is not surprising, then, to find that Christabel Pankhurst was a guest of the Ford sisters at their home, Adel Grange, in February 1906, or that she spoke to the Leeds Women's Suffrage Society. Even at this stage, however, Christabel Pankhurst expressed to Mary Gawthorpe the growing impatience of the WSPU with the Labour Party in the House of Commons: 'From what I have heard it is quite necessary to keep an eye on them. . . . The further one goes the plainer one sees that men (even Labour men) think more of their own interests than of ours.'[11]

Mary Gawthorpe records that in the first part of 1906 her diary was filled by engagements to speak at a 'mass of meetings' for local branches of teachers' organisations, trade unions, and socialist and suffrage societies. By the middle of the year, her name was becoming sufficiently well-known to bring invitations to speak outside the Leeds area. She had also published her first paid contribution to a newspaper, one which led Isabella Ford and Ethel Snowden to summon her to 'an otherwise innocent tea'. Here they sought to make it clear that she should first seek the permission of the Leeds branch of the NUWSS, before publishing her personal views on suffrage movement questions. The exact nature of their dispute with Mary Gawthorpe remains unclear, but her account suggests that it reflected increasing anxieties among the NUWSS leadership concerning the growing prominence of the WSPU. Both Isabella Ford and Ethel Snowden had just taken part in a major suffrage deputation to the Prime Minister, Campbell Bannerman, one at which some of the WSPU members were thought by many to have behaved in an unhelpful manner. Elizabeth Wolstenholme Elmy was present on this occasion, and certainly she had forcefully rejected the Prime Minister's admonition to be patient, declaring that she had already passed a long life-time waiting for politicians to live up to the principles they claimed to hold.[12]

The growing tensions between militants and constitutional suffragists at leadership level were, as yet, of little practical significance at the local level. Mary Gawthorpe was invited on to the executive committee of the Leeds branch society of the NUWSS, despite her 'blind resistance' to any attempt to curb her freedom to offer public support to the militants. Isabella Ford and Ethel Snowden also sought her help with a series of 'camp stool' meetings in the Leeds public parks on the question of women's suffrage. These meetings appear to have been organised under the aegis of the ILP, and involved both NUWSS and WSPU supporters, illustrating once more how close the suffrage and socialist movements might be at a branch level, and how constitutionalists and militants might still cooperate locally. It was in the course of these meetings that Mary Gawthorpe first came to meet Teresa Billington, and Emmeline and Frederick Pethick Lawrence. The Pethick Lawrences had only been newly recruited to the London leadership of the WSPU through the good offices of Keir Hardie, among the most staunch of the ILP's leadership in his sympathy with the cause of women's suffrage. This couple were wealthy supporters of the labour movement, with a background in the settlement movement which had sought to bring the working class and middle class together in urban communities dedicated to a moral and cultural uplift.

In mid-1906 Mary Gawthorpe was among those who helped form a Leeds branch of a new organisation, the Women's Labour League (WLL). This had been established by Margaret Macdonald, wife of James Ramsay Macdonald, one of the leaders of the ILP, ostensibly as a women's auxiliary to that party, though many believed its main purpose was to stem the flow of women out of socialist ranks into the women's suffrage movement. Shortly after its formation, Mary Gawthorpe was chosen to represent her local branch at a Labour Representation Conference. By the following month she was on the executive committee of the WLL, and was invited to London to join Margaret Macdonald in informal talks at the Board of Education on the question of school meals for children. On this occasion she enjoyed her first lunch with a Cabinet Minister, receiving 'authentic instruction on how bills came to be nourished and brought into fruitful being' while doing her best 'to deal effectively with the lobster mayonnaise'.[13] During this visit, too, she met some of the leaders of the women's trade union movement, including Mary Macarthur and Gertrude Tuckwell.

All this activity was only possible because Mary Gawthorpe had resigned from her teaching post sometime between March and June 1906. Though an account from around this time suggests that her position as secretary of the Women's Labour League was paid, such a step must surely have endangered the independent life which she had established through her teaching career.[14] Her memoir offers no explanation, though in this context she does mention the disturbing theft of her week's wages from the staff cloakroom at her school during March 1906, and her belief that as such a prominent and vocal socialist she had made enemies among her colleagues.

In her new role, she was sent by the WLL to campaign for the Labour candidate, Robert Smillie, in the by-election in Cockermouth in August 1906. This turned out to be 'a hot spot', 'a seething cauldron' for Mary Gawthorpe. It was during this campaign that the WSPU extended its election policy beyond opposition to government candidates, to reflect a new 'independent' stance in relation to the ILP and the labour movement. Labour candidates could no longer expect support from the suffrage militants during elections. In these circumstances, Mary Gawthorpe found the campaign 'running fire, outwardly and inwardly'. With this change of policy, it appeared most likely that the Conservative, and not the Labour candidate would benefit from WSPU attacks on the Liberal Party. At the same time labour women were beginning to strike from campaigning for their party's candidates because of its wavering position on women's suffrage. The annual conference of the Labour Party had only that year passed an adult suffrage resolution in preference to one supporting sexual equality in the franchise. During this election the WSPU tried to win Mary Gawthorpe away from her work for the WLL, a move she resisted for the time being. As she explained it, she 'had not yet grasped either the virtue or value of the tactics: "Keep the Liberal out" if it meant – *at any cost*' that is, if it helped a Conservative candidate to win.[15]

The re-emergence of the demand for adult suffrage provided fresh ground for disunity among suffragists. The Women's Cooperative Guild, for example, shifted toward this formulation of the demand for franchise reform at this time. Radical suffragists had always favoured universal suffrage in principle, and, as we have seen, Ursula Bright and Emmeline Pankhurst had advocated the pursuit of women's enfranchisement through a general overhaul of the Registration laws in the later 1890s. Now, Dora Montefiore took a similar stand when she reported to an international conference that the WSPU stood for adult suffrage. In doing so, she both read 'universal suffrage' into the more ambiguous demand for 'adult suffrage', and altogether ignored the formal object of the WSPU, which was the narrower one of sexual equality in the franchise laws.

A similar confusion and lack of unity of view emerged during Emmeline Pankhurst's appearance at a by-election campaign in Aberdeen in January 1907. Here, the two local WSPU members who proposed and seconded the women's suffrage resolution at the meeting each used a different formulation of the demand, – 'one referring to adult women and the other to the woman taxpayers' – here again, neither speaker held to the WSPU's official formulation of the demand, which remained sexual equality in the franchise laws. The WSPU's organiser in Aberdeen, Helen Fraser, had earlier sought to clarify the situation by denying that her organisation was 'working for indiscriminate votes for all women', and Isabella Mayo, who chaired Emmeline Pankhurst's meeting, similarly articulated the demand in terms of the existing qualifications for men. But Emmeline Pankhurst herself insisted that the resolution be allowed to stand in the form of a demand for adult suffrage. Isabella Mayo accepted 'Mrs Pankhurst's dictum under protest'. Perhaps the WSPU leader had been primarily concerned with distinguishing her society clearly from the long-established Aberdeen branch of the NUWSS. After years of bowing to the anti-suffrage views of the Liberal MP there, this society had at last agreed to take a slightly less supine position. It had persuaded the new local Liberal candidate to support the parliamentary vote for women municipal voters – something short both of sexual equality, and of adult suffrage – in return for its support during his election campaign.[16]

Though the official object of both the NUWSS and the WSPU was sexual equality in the franchise laws, both Liberal and Labour suffragists were susceptible to the argument that such a measure was far more likely to work in the interest of the Conservative Party, given the continuing property basis of the vote. On the other hand, suffragists of all shades of opinion suspected, with some justification, that many 'adultists' would be quite satisfied with an extension of the franchise only to all adult men, ignoring the sexual disqualification in existing laws. Formulating the demand in terms of adult suffrage was conveniently ambiguous in a political system where men alone presently voted, and it is noteworthy that few 'adultists' in these years chose to formulate their demand in terms of universal suffrage. The matter became a divisive one among suffragists. The main body of the suffrage movement very shortly retreated from any association with the demand for adult suffrage, while those like Dora Montefiore who sought to unite the two met with increasingly stern opposition from suffrage colleagues.

From 1906 on, many socialist and labour movement suffragists like Mary Gawthorpe found their pre-existing political commitments undermined by a growing sense of sexual solidarity with women of other parties and classes. Shortly after the Cockermouth by-election, when she had worked on behalf of the Labour candidate, she was invited to London to spend a week with the Pethick Lawrences. During this visit she was introduced to Emmeline Pankhurst, and spoke alongside Annie Kenney, who had just been released from another term of imprisonment in Holloway gaol. She was also offered, and accepted an appointment as a WSPU organiser, at a salary of £2 a week, somewhat more than a school teacher of her age might expect to earn. A post as a WSPU organiser involved a demanding and itinerant life away from her home and established friends, but, she recalled, 'My own engagement had not matured to the point of marriage and now it was having to take care of itself.' She undertook to send her mother half her wages each week to maintain the family home. For his part, 'FL' was 'uneasy and approving, all at the same time'. Soon she found herself 'a wanderer, sans home, and only the Movement was stable'. Her personal life she left 'to get on as best it may', as she became one of the WSPU's most popular and effective speakers. Emmeline Pethick Lawrence offered this personal testimony: 'All who have ever heard her speak realise the immense influence which she brings to bear upon the electors. Her power over great audiences is something to be wondered at.'[17]

She joined an organisation dominated, then, by socialist suffragists, but one in which the national leadership was undoubtedly more determined on a separation from its socialist origins than many of its members or local societies. Elizabeth Wolstenholme Elmy, for example, was increasingly dismissive of certain ILP leaders, most especially Bruce Glasier, in whom she saw 'a great desire to use women as mere tools like the other political parties'. She herself had overcome her dislike of party organisations, and had joined the Manchester ILP in 1904 with the hope of strengthening its commitment to women's suffrage. She regarded as a 'silly impertinence' the Manchester ILP's unsuccessful attempt to secure the resignation of Teresa Billington and Christabel Pankhurst in the summer of 1906, after the change in WSPU policy that had been announced with the Cockermouth by-election. In her view 'women everywhere are staunch and true, and we can better afford to dispense with the ILP then they to dispense with us'.[18] For her part Teresa Billington had said she would be prepared to resign from the ILP if in that way she might further 'true socialism.' But she was less easy with the cult of leadership which was emerging in the WSPU, and with its lack of any democratic structures for decision-making. Equally, Emmeline and Christabel Pankhurst became increasingly anxious as new figures moved to the fore, once the focus of WSPU activities shifted to London. These anxieties increased when Sylvia Pankhurst resigned as secretary of the WSPU in the summer of 1906 while her elder sister was still completing her law degree, and not yet free to step into her shoes. This key position was now filled jointly by Charlotte Despard and Edith How-Martyn, both socialist suffragists.

It was hoped that some of these tensions would be eased by a general meeting of the WSPU called in London in October 1906. Teresa Billington had drafted a formal constitution and rules for the militant organisation for the consideration of its branch societies. Elizabeth Wolstenholme Elmy travelled to London for an eight-day round of activities, meeting up with Dora Montefiore and together visiting another old friend who had helped establish the WSPU in London, W. T. Stead. The two women joined other WSPU speakers including Teresa Billington, Annie Kenney and Irene Fenwick Miller in a series of meetings in London halls and parks. Hannah Mitchell also travelled south for the event, enjoying both her 'first real sight of London' and the 'Cockney idea of wit' evident in her hecklers: 'They did not show the sullen hostility of the "yahoos" in the North; they seemed more like a crowd of chattering monkeys, who regarded the Suffragettes as a sort of show, got up for their amusement.' She found herself 'feeling very shabby in my old brown costume' when she attended a reception at WSPU headquarters, and saw 'the smart frocks' of the London women. But she also recalled that at this time there still remained 'a unity of purpose in the suffrage movement, which made social distinction seem of little importance'.[19]

Sixty-four branches sent delegates to the conference itself, an indication of how rapidly the WSPU had grown in the previous year. These local representatives heard reports of recent activities from the five organisers now employed by the WSPU, including Mary Gawthorpe. She had just returned from her campaign alongside Christabel Pankhurst in the Mid-Glamorgan by-election. Here she had broken up the meetings of the sitting Labour candidate, Samuel

Evans, 'as a protest against his talking out the Women's Suffrage resolution' in the House of Commons the previous spring. According to Elizabeth Wolstenholme Elmy, she delivered a 'lively report' of these events 'and set herself to relieve the heavy tensions of the day by her wit and humour'.[20] For the time being the question of the WSPU's constitution seemed settled.

The conference had been timed to precede the opening of Parliament on 23 October, and a deputation of WSPU supporters attended on that day. While members from the provinces sought interviews with their MPs, Emmeline Pankhurst and Emmeline Pethick Lawrence attempted to gain an audience with the Prime Minister. Sylvia Pankhurst had also organised a contingent of women from London's East End. Elizabeth Wolstenholme Elmy reported that an official had asked her how 'ladies' could associate with 'women from the slums'. With a 'curl of the lip and flash of scorn' she had responded 'Why not, they are our sisters.'[21] When the news came that the Prime Minister still refused to make women's suffrage a government measure, Mary Gawthorpe 'sprang on one of the sacred velvet chairs, and began to speak'. Hannah Mitchell spread a 'Votes for Women' banner on the base of one of the statues with the help of Elizabeth Wolstenholme Elmy, so enraging one of the policeman present that 'in a fit of berserk frenzy he seized it, and tore it to shreds'. In the confusion, Emmeline Pankhurst fell, and many of the MPs who had rushed in to watch events were seen 'guffawing loudly' at the spectacle.[22]

Hannah Mitchell and her host in London, Louise Cullen, broke through the police cordon and so escaped arrest. Others among the WSPU demonstrators were not so lucky. Mary Gawthorpe remembered these events as her 'baptism of fire', and subsequently she and Annie Kenney, Annie Cobden Sanderson, Adela Pankhurst, Teresa Billington, Dora Montefiore, Emmeline Pethick Lawrence, Irene Fenwick Miller, Charlotte Despard, and Minnie Baldock each received a two-month prison sentence. Sylvia Pankhurst was also gaoled for a subsequent protest over the event. Noting in her memoirs that all but one of those imprisoned were 'Labour women', Mary Gawthorpe commented:

The time had not yet arrived in the militant movement for the tide of conservative women, whose coming denoted the beginning of the end, though there were many conservative women in the National Union of Women's Suffrage Societies at that time.[23]

While in Holloway, Mary Gawthorpe was visited by both her mother, staying in London as a guest of Charlotte Despard, and 'FL'.

Her published account of her imprisonment is restrained: 'I pass over the unpleasantness of what appeared to us semi-filthy conditions.'[24] In an earlier, unpublished memoir, she could not forebear to mention one detail: 'The nauseating undergarment tried me severely, stained as it was in a revolting and suggestive manner in spite of whatever sanitary precautions may or may not have been taken in those days.'[25] Subsequently, another suffragist prisoner in Holloway, Constance Lytton, took up the lack of provision of sanitary napkins with the prison authorities, one of the many improvements in prison conditions for which suffragists campaigned. All the prisoners were unexpectedly released after little more than a month. The government was defending yet another seat, in a by-election in Huddersfield, and the Liberal candidate there had found the issue of suffragists in prison an embarrassing one.

Hannah Mitchell organised the WSPU's campaign on this occasion, and recalled how it had been 'like putting a match to a ready-built fire. The Yorkshire women rose to the call and followed us in hundreds.' The released prisoners hurried from gaol to Huddersfield, parading through the streets on the eve of the poll. It was during this parade that Mary Gawthorpe encountered her father once more, among the crowd of spectators. He tipped his hat and bowed low to her:

> eyes gleaming a trifle sardonically for all the respect in the gesture, as who should say: 'The author of your being', or with an amending eye on mine, 'Well, co-author at least'. All this in a flash. I ignored him completely. But I knew he was proud of his belligerent offspring.[26]

One of the released prisoners, Annie Cobden Sanderson, was also a longstanding friend of Millicent Garrett Fawcett. Though the head of the NUWSS disagreed with militancy as a tactic, she frequently acknowledged her admiration for the women who embarked upon it and made this public declaration: 'Let me counsel all friends of women's suffrage not to denounce the flag-waving women who ask questions about women's suffrage at meetings, even at the risk of rough-handling and jeers.' She argued that such demonstrations had proved women were now in earnest about the vote.[27] In this instance she responded to the courage of the militants by organising a banquet at the Savoy to celebrate their release. Among the committee who had joined her in this project were many long-time stalwarts of the suffrage movement, including another old friend, Lilias Ashworth Hallett. Among the planned speakers were Isabella Ford, while the toast was to be given by Sir Charles McLaren, whose mother, Priscilla Bright McLaren had recently died without seeing the successful outcome of the cause to which she had devoted so much of her life. Neither Sylvia nor Christabel Pankhurst accepted their invitation to attend.[28] This event provides the final episode in Mary Gawthorpe's memoirs, suggesting its special significance for her as the culmination of an uphill struggle from working-class Leeds to national recognition as a leading figure in the suffrage movement.

From this point, it is necessary to reconstruct Mary Gawthorpe's work in the suffrage movement from other records and other memoirs. By this time she was the WSPU's National Organiser, and a member of its central committee, though the function of this group appears to have been no more than to endorse and legitimise the leadership of the Pankhursts and Pethick Lawrences. The pace of her work was intense, for she remained one of the WSPU's most popular organisers and speakers. Only a few days' rest were permitted at Christmas, and she celebrated the holiday with Emmeline Pankhurst and her family in lodgings in Teignmouth, in the neighbourhood of their next by-election campaign. Sylvia Pankhurst drew a pastel portrait of her at this time, though its whereabouts are no longer known, and she also later provided another of her vivid, written sketches. It recalls Mary Gawthorpe at this time as:

> a winsome, merry little creature, with bright hair and laughing hazel eyes, a face fresh and sweet as a flower, the dainty ways of a little bird, and having with all a shrewd tongue and so sparkling a fund of repartee, that she held dumb with astonished admiration, vast crowds of big, slow-thinking workmen and succeeded in winning to good-tempered appreciation the stubbornist opponents.[29]

She won friends equally among members of the NUWSS. Helena Swanwick, another Manchester suffragist who subsequently came to prominence as editor of the NUWSS's paper, the *Common Cause*, recalled her 'big "fog-and-frost" voice ruined by over-strain; with a daring, a good fellowship and a sense of good humour beyond all praise'.[30] Rebecca West, who was still a schoolgirl when she began to take an interest in the suffrage movement and encountered Mary Gawthorpe, recalled 'a merry militant saint' who travelled the country

> suffering fools gladly (which I think she found the hardest job of all).... Occasionally she had a rest in prison, which she always faced with a sparrow-like perkiness. She had wit and common sense and courage, and each to the point of genius.[31]

The Rutland by-election campaign in the spring of 1907 tested Mary Gawthorpe's daring and speaking powers to the full. She had to face down threatening crowds, and generally managed to win their tolerance, if nothing more. On one occasion, however, her wit only brought a greater wrath down on her head. While being pelted with bullseyes, she responded by quoting from Shakespeare, declaring them 'Sweets to the sweet.' A pot-egg was added to the barrage, struck her on the head and left her unconscious. Undaunted, she returned to the campaign the next day, becoming the heroine of the election. In the first half of 1907, Mary Gawthorpe took part in seven election campaigns. The constant pressures on organisers from WSPU headquarters in London are revealed in some of the correspondence of Jennie Baines, another working-class organiser remembered fondly by both Mary Gawthorpe and Hannah Mitchell. During 1907 she was constantly bombarded with letters from Emmeline Pankhurst, Christabel Pankhurst and Emmeline Pethick Lawrence, with suggestions and directions for further work. A strict accountability on even the smallest sums was required, for as Emmeline Pethick Lawrence revealed to Jennie Baines: 'We are spending an awful lot of money just now, and your poor Treasurer has sleepless nights.'[32]

Hannah Mitchell was also at full-stretch, and she and Mary Gawthorpe were among those who campaigned in the particularly strenuous by-election in Jarrow. By this time Hannah Mitchell was suffering from severe insomnia: 'Exciting days and sleepless nights are not conducive to good health.' WSPU activists such as these had now endured several years of occasional violence and imprisonment, sometimes painful breaches with old friends and political loyalties, as well as constant travel, and continual overwork. After one further rigorous campaign in the Colne Valley, Hannah Mitchell's health began to give out, and she collapsed on reaching home. She recalled how during the weeks of mental breakdown that followed, 'I wandered mentally in a strange world, all sorts of delusions passing through my disordered mind. . . . "Overwork and underfeeding" was the doctor's blunt diagnosis.' Charlotte Despard visited her, and when she heard of the doctor's assessment, sent money to help buy the nourishment he recommended to aid recovery. Another socialist suffragist, Marion Coates-Hanson, also provided the funds for Hannah Mitchell to take a holiday by the sea.[33]

Mary Gawthorpe also became seriously ill with appendicitis at this time. She was treated by the surgeon, Louisa Garrett Anderson, daughter of Elizabeth, and niece of Millicent Garrett Fawcett, and convalesced at the country retreat of the Pethick Lawrences. They also took her away to Italy, along with Annie Kenney. But Mary Gawthorpe's recovery was slow, and the WSPU was reporting in late September that it would be some little time yet before she would be able to return to active campaigning. Mary Gawthorpe recalled that she never fully regained her good health afterwards, and though she continued to work as an organiser she was frequently ill in the years that followed, and 'old in exhaustion and overstrain'.[34] As a consequence of ill health, both Mary Gawthorpe and Hannah Mitchell were out of the fray when a split among the WSPU leadership occurred in the autumn of 1907.

The WSPU leadership became aware of discontent among some of its supporters in the summer of 1907. Christabel Pankhurst replied to a letter from Jennie Baines that she was 'very sad that such a spirit as you tell me of should be growing up in the Union, but as you say the oldest and best members are sound and true'.[35] This was not an altogether accurate assessment of the matter. Since her marriage, Teresa Billington Greig had moved to Scotland, and had begun to build a network of branches there in which she sought to establish greater autonomy from London, and through which she sought to push for greater democracy in the WSPU. Once again, she and others of like mind sought to raise these issues at the WSPU's annual conference, due to be held under the new constitution in the autumn of 1907. Emmeline and Christine Pankhurst sought to block this development by cancelling the annual meeting, but the dissidents went ahead by organising one of their own. The outcome was the formation of a breakaway militant organisation, the Women's Freedom League (WFL), in which socialist suffragists like Charlotte Despard and Teresa Billington Greig were to the fore.

Elizabeth Wolstenholme Elmy was of the opinion that Charlotte Despard had joined the WSPU 'resolved to dominate'. She herself stayed loyal to the Pankhursts and the WSPU, believing 'each party will work better independently'.[36] Hannah Mitchell, in contrast, had good reason to lend her support to the WFL, because of the pulls of personal loyalty she felt towards Charlotte Despard, as well as her continuing socialist sympathies. Thereafter, her suffrage activities were undertaken as a member of the WFL. Concern over her health, and the demands of her continuing involvement in the labour and socialist movement, reduced, however, the scale of her participation in the suffrage movement from this time.

Mary Gawthorpe left no record of her views on the issues raised by the split. Though clearly she could not have been unaware of the controversy, her actions suggest that loyalty to the Pankhursts weighed more heavily with her than concerns over the autocratic nature of the WSPU leadership, or its increasing distance from the ILP. Personal friendship, gratitude, and possibly even economic dependence consequent on her long illness, would have made it even more difficult for her to depart from the WSPU at this time. Instead, Mary Gawthorpe emerged from the dispute a member of the new committee of the WSPU, clearly, now, accepted among the leadership. By the end of her convalescence, she was appearing as a main speaker at some of the major London meetings of the WSPU. During her period of recovery she had also written a new pamphlet, putting the militant position, and entitled 'Votes for Men'. Here she took a historical approach to the question of franchise reform, and pointed out that men had engaged in riot and bloodshed to win extensions of the suffrage.[37] By the end of November 1907, she was once more on the campaign trail and organising militant interventions in by-elections. She seems to have lost none of her high spirits and enthusiasm. On one occasion, for example, she and Jennie Baines hid in the flies of the Oldham Theatre in order to be able to heckle undisturbed John Burns, a member of the Liberal government. Emmeline Pankhurst recalled especially vividly the by-election at South Leeds early in 1908, where Mary Gawthorpe found herself campaigning in her home town:

> The throngs of mill women kept up the chorus in broad Yorkshire: 'Shall us win? Shall us have the vote? We shall!' No wonder the old people shook their heads and declared that 'there had never been owt like it'.[38]

Such enthusiasm extended equally to the constitutionalists involved in the by-election, and Isabella Ford reported to Millicent Garrett Fawcett:

The WSPU behaved splendidly – and there were no rows. I see more and more their policy is far more workable than ours: but we never clashed . . . Mrs Pankhurst's procession was fine and we cheered and waved as they passed our rooms – and they did too.[39]

She also told of the growing disaffection among women Liberals, some of whom were refusing to work for their own candidate during this by-election. Like them, Isabella Ford 'longed to "go for" the Liberal and had to hold myself down'.

Whereas the WSPU's by-election policy was directed at opposing government candidates, the NUWSS offered support for 'the best friend' to women's suffrage among the candidates, and took a neutral position where no such distinction could be operated. Many, like Isabella Ford, wanted to see a more aggressive policy in place, and believed that support of Labour candidates offered the best means of realising this. At Jarrow the previous year, for example, the local constitutionalists in fact ran a campaign in favour of the Labour Party candidate, Pete Curran, on the grounds that they found him the 'best friend' to their cause among all the three candidates. Here were the first signs of the NUWSS's gradual shift toward a working alliance with the Labour Party in order to attack the Liberal government. At Colne Valley the NUWSS once again campaigned on behalf of the Labour candidate, Victor Grayson.

Mary Gawthorpe continued as one of the WSPU's main speakers at major rallies and demonstrations up and down the country. Her activities were recorded regularly in *Votes for Women*, the paper begun by the Pethick Lawrences in 1907 to provide militant commentary on the campaigns. In one such report she was described as 'small, brisk and dainty', a speaker whose 'descriptive charm and racy humour' was especially popular with audiences. She continued, despite her poor health, 'one of the most indefatigable' of organisers, who 'lived a life crowded with work'.[40] She was also one of the main organisers of, and speakers at, the massive demonstration staged by the WSPU in Hyde Park in June 1908. Some estimates put the crowds which attended at a quarter of a million. Elizabeth Wolstenholme Elmy made one of her last prominent public appearances here, leading the procession. She was now in her mid-seventies, and was finding the travelling to and from London increasingly difficult. For the WSPU it marked a watershed in the development of militancy, for the new Prime Minister, the anti-suffragist Herbert

Asquith, remained unmoved by this large-scale, peaceable demonstration of support for the suffragist demand. It was from this time that militancy, conceived as civil disobedience, verbal harassment of representatives of the Liberal government, and peaceful demonstration, was gradually replaced by the organisation of more threatening demonstrations and acts of deliberate violence, initially in the form of undirected and uncoordinated individual acts of windowbreaking.

The reports of Mary Gawthorpe's activities in the summer of 1908 show that the pace remained hectic. She also underwent further arrests, although in her case no periods of imprisonment appear to have followed. At this time she was still used by the WSPU as a kind of roaming representative of the London leadership, a star attraction at major meetings around the country in her own right, and an acceptable surrogate when the top leaders were unable to fulfil their engagements. As yet she appears to have had no routine responsibilities for the organisation of any one city or district. This changed in the last half of 1908, when she became the WSPU's organiser in Manchester. She had already spent a large part of June and July in Lancashire helping Annot Robinson, like herself a former teacher and ILP member, to organise support for the Hyde Park rally, together with a follow-up demonstration in Manchester. Annot Robinson received a three-week prison sentence during this campaign for her part in a 'spontaneous demonstration' that the pair had led in that city. The police estimated that they had drawn a crowd of 150,00 in Heaton Park, Manchester on 19 July. Mary Gawthorpe was one of the main speakers at a similar demonstration on Woodhouse Moor in Leeds, near her childhood home.[41]

By the end of August 1908, Mary Gawthorpe's base had become Manchester, but she continued to move about constantly between WSPU branches elsewhere in the area, notably in Liverpool, Rochdale, Preston and Stockport, and did this despite her commitments elsewhere. Not surprisingly, the Lancashire report in *Votes for Women* at the end of December had to record another bout of ill-health for Mary Gawthorpe. But by the middle of January 1909 she was back on the speaking circuit at as great a pace as ever. The next six months saw a series of major WSPU rallies in Manchester and Liverpool where the London-based leadership made appearances. Equally, Mary Gawthorpe continued to be in demand for WSPU events in the capital, like the breakfast organised at the Criterion to welcome WSPU prisoners on their release from Holloway, a breakfast attended by a number of delegates from the International Women's Suffrage Alliance then meeting in London. She also undertook a campaign among women teachers meeting in Morecambe for the annual conference of the National Union of Teachers, a group she continued to be especially interested in organising.

Under her leadership the Manchester WSPU showed considerable ingenuity in publicising their activities. On one occasion posters were pasted in the small hours of the morning on 'Government pillar-boxes, barrack and prison walls', presumably as a symbolic act of defiance, as well as a means of advertisement, and the press responded well to the ploy. On another occasion, when the continual winter rain of Manchester threatened to dampen proceedings, members turned themselves into human billboards, each bearing a letter of Christabel Pankhurst's name. In this guise they marched abreast to spell it out, while distributing leaflets advertising her imminent arrival. A 'slight collision with the police' occurred when they stopped to oblige the press photographers, 'giving a greater advertisement than ever'.[42]

In these years, then, Mary Gawthorpe became a national figure to followers of the suffrage cause, and her popularity among rank-and-file supporters was testified to even by constitutionalist organisers. The NUWSS caravan was travelling around Yorkshire in the summer of 1909, and as it entered Harrogate 'members of the ILP came up to us and rendered all assistance in their power', while making many inquiries after Mary Gawthorpe. The NUWSS's organiser reported how Mary Gawthorpe had 'created a lasting impression' when she had visited the area as a WSPU speaker the previous year. Evidence of this kind illustrates both how persistent was the link between socialist and suffrage organisation in many localities, and how shared was the goodwill on which organisers of both wings of the movement might draw. Rank-and-file suffragists were often either oblivious of, or indifferent to, the divisions among the national leadership, or between that leadership and the leadership of the labour movement.[43]

In May 1909, Mary Gawthorpe came back to London briefly to help organise the WSPU's major effort that summer, a 'Women's Exhibition'. There she featured alongside Emmeline Pankhurst, Emmeline Pethick Lawrence, Christabel Pankhurst, Annie Kenney and Flora Drummond as an attraction of the exhibition. Further engagements in London followed, where she enhanced her popularity as a speaker by her usual means of keeping the audience 'convulsed'. By this time Mary Gawthorpe clearly had a considerable personal following, for a group of WSPU supporters established a fund to commission a bust of her, as a sign of their admiration. Organising this fund was Rose Lamartine Yates, who became a longstanding friend to Mary Gawthorpe. It is possible that the growth of such a personal following became something of a cause for concern among the national leadership, for her name all but disappears from the pages of *Votes for Women* for a few months after the exhibition.

It was in this period, too, that Mary Gawthorpe, speaking for the WSPU, and Helena Swanwick, for the NUWSS, organised a debate on the relative merits of the tactics of the two organisations. Helena Swanwick recalled how she found to her own amusement 'that I did not want to beat her before that particular audience, which was obviously anti-militant from the start'. So they took no vote, and at the end of the debate 'came away arm in arm, she snuggling up and remarking, "You *are* a brick, aren't you!" '.[44] But such comradeship and cooperation between militants and constitutionalists became increasingly difficult as WSPU demonstrators turned to more violent protest, and met, in their turn, ever greater government repression and personal assault, of which Mary Gawthorpe herself eventually became a victim.

Plate 5 Laurence Housman speaking in Trafalgar Square on the Census boycott of 1911. By courtesy of the Museum of London.

7

WOMEN'S SUFFRAGE AMONG THE BOHEMIANS

Laurence Housman joins the movement

Lulworth Cove provided the camping ground for a party of artists and writers in the summer of 1905. Among this group was Laurence Housman (1865–1959), an illustrator, art critic and writer. His conversion to 'that will-o'-the-wisp, the simple life', as well as to naturism, was of a piece with the general rebellion against Victorian prudery which marked his life.[1] Mixed camping and nude bathing were part of this rebellion, and after one swim Laurence Housman reported that 'I was scraped and pounded by the shingle till I felt like an Indian curry come to life.' The local vicar continued to call on the campers, although the party had tried 'to shock him off: but all the shock has been taken out of him . . . there is no more Grundy left in him'.[2]

In such ways, Laurence Housman displayed his rejection of 'the savage imposition of ignorance under the Victorian code' which had meant that 'the language of life in their own bodies' was excluded from the education of both boys and girls. Looking back, he recalled how such a 'cruel stitching-up of minds' and 'monstrous perversion of modesty' had rendered even a visit to the lavatory an act of tortuous discretion in his youth. Laurence Housman later believed that it was his resistance to this code which made him a feminist and a suffragist 'long before the day of battle actually arrived'.[3]

He had been born in 1865, the seventh child in a family of eight, and had recently enjoyed his first popular success as an author at the time of his stay at Lulworth. His novel, *An Englishwoman's Love Letters*, had been published anonymously to begin with, and before his authorship was revealed, speculation about the authorship of this mawkish account of blighted love and death had included the names of many notable women of the day, including Queen Victoria. His eldest brother, Alfred Edward Housman, was the noted classical scholar and poet, whose literary standing increasingly overshadowed his own popular achievements in this period. The two brothers kept up a wry correspondence about their competing reputations, and the frequent confusion in the public mind over the authorship of their two very different kinds of literary work. As his elder brother wrote to Laurence Housman: 'if I bring you money, you bring me fame'.[4]

Their mother had died when Laurence Housman was 5 years old, 'worn out with child-bearing', and it has been suggested that his 'later prejudices against procreation and his earnest advocacy of birth control' stemmed from this family tragedy. Before her death, his mother had entrusted his care to an older sister, Clemence. Together they had fled the increasingly sombre and rigid family home when Laurence was eighteen, to remain life-time companions.[5] Their flight had been made possible by a legacy to each of £500. This they used to establish themselves in cheap lodgings in London, where Laurence began his studies at Lambeth School of Art while Clemence began her noted career as a wood-engraver and illustrator. A second legacy enabled Clemence Housman to support her brother in further studies in South Kensington, when he came under the influence of John Ruskin and the Pre-Raphaelites. Both also began to write. Laurence Housman's autobiography tells little of this period in his life, a period marked by frustration at not finding his own artistic vision, by religious turmoil, and by the trials of coming to terms with his own homosexuality in a society which outlawed sexual relationships between men.[6]

Professional recognition eventually began to grow in his late twenties, when Laurence Housman became one of the 'nest of singing birds' of the publisher, John Lane, initially as an illustrator like his sister.[7] In the 1890s, he became one of the contributors to the *Yellow Book*, and was appointed the art critic of the *Manchester Guardian*, with a regular weekly column. His book of poems, *The Green Arras*, was also published (in the same period, A. E. Housman published *A Shropshire Lad* privately). This period also saw the beginning of one of the few long-term, close relationships with men which he acknowledges in his autobiography, though only hinting at its sexual nature. This was also the time of Oscar Wilde's trial and imprisonment for homosexuality, and Laurence Housman was among those who kept up their friendship with the ostracised writer after his release from prison and exile in Paris.

In 1902, Laurence Housman had the first of what was to become many encounters with the Lord Chamberlain. His nativity play, *Bethlehem*, was forbidden public performance on the grounds that it breached censorship rules in representing the holy family on stage. On other occasions his plays were censored because of their representation of long-dead members of the royal family. By this time his regular literary associates were figures like George Bernard Shaw, Somerset Maugham, G. K. Chesterton, Havelock Ellis, Thomas Hardy, John Masefield, James Barrie and Harley Granville Barker, and in 1909 he joined an inconclusive campaign against the current practices of the Lord Chamberlain. In that year, too, his play *The Chinese Lantern* was put on at the Haymarket with Shaw's *Getting Married*, but the programme proved a failure, and for many years afterwards he abandoned the commercial theatre. He had, none the less, arrived as a contemporary man of letters, and together with Clemence Housman had made the move from Battersea to Kensington.[8]

The nature of male sexuality and a masculine identity, and how these might or might not be brought into fuller harmony with female sexuality and a feminine identity, remained a constant interest for him throughout his life. It is a topic which crops up time and again in his letters, including those to some of his closest female friends. On one occasion, for example, he told Janet Ashbee how he had been set thinking 'more than ever on the social problem generally, and the sex problem in particular and the comparative obsession . . . of the male instinct and the female'.[9] And these concerns found political expression in his growing involvement in the suffrage movement, which he begins to mention in his letters in 1908. That summer he took part in the Hyde Park demonstration which Mary Gawthorpe had helped organise. He watched the procession which Elizabeth Wolstenholme Elmy had headed, alongside other leaders of the WSPU, reporting how it had taken forty minutes to pass from beginning to end. He was especially impressed by the contingent of 500 women university graduates: 'One felt happy and hopeful seeing such a large number of beautiful and noble types among them.'[10]

His growing involvement in suffrage campaigning increasingly interrupted his writing career for the next few years.[11] Looking back, Laurence Housman credited the votes-for-women campaigns as having 'first brought me into active sympathy with the aims and doings of my own generation'. One of the first political meetings he ever attended was to hear Millicent Garrett Fawcett speak on women's suffrage. But he dated his increasing interest 'in the political problems and controversies of the present day' from when he first heard Emmeline Pankhurst speak on votes for women at a meeting in Chelsea: 'Until that time I had made rather a cult of being much more interested in things of the past than of the present.'[12] He himself suggested that his involvement in the suffrage movement was probably a result of sharing a house with his sister, for Clemence Housman was a committed supporter of the WSPU. Shortly, he too was taking part in suffrage demonstrations and processions. Looking back in his old age, Laurence Housman felt:

> The winning of Woman Suffrage has, in some of its results, disappointed me; but it was not a waste of time. It pulled me up from my roots, uncomfortably, but very effectively; I was never able to set them back in their old ground.[13]

Both Clemence and Laurence Housman were active in a number of suffrage organisations, and their Kensington cottage became a manufactory for the banners which were so important a part of the adoption of spectacle on the part of suffragists to attract public attention to their cause. The banner he made for the Kensington WSPU to carry to the Hyde Park demonstration in 1908 'really did arouse enthusiasm', and he wondered whether perhaps 'I am destined to end as a poster-artist!'[14] Brother and sister also became leading members of the Suffrage Atelier, and Laurence Housman chaired its first public meeting in June 1909. This was one of a number of groups formed by writers, artists and theatricals seeking to put their various skills and crafts to the service of votes for women. Members of London's Bohemia provided a most valuable contribution to the campaigns, especially in terms of providing counter-representations of women which not only mocked suffrage opponents but also helped form the new and challenging identities which suffragists had to build for themselves throughout these campaigns. As Lisa Tickner has demonstrated so effectively, ' "Art" was itself complicit in the regulation of sexualities, and in the constructions of femininity which underpinned the identity of the woman artist.'[15] There was also the practical, everyday help of banner-making, poster-printing, and pageant-staging. The Suffrage Atelier put a special emphasis on teaching cheap, immediate skills useful in propaganda, for example cartoon illustrating and poster and banner making. Pageantry and spectacle became a particularly effective part of the twentieth-century suffrage campaigns, and this aspect depended to a considerable extent on the support which the movement was able to attract among London's Bohemia.

Laurence Housman, for example, used his language and writing skills to provide a translation of *Lysistrata*, 'discreetly worded' so as to pass the censor. The play was performed by Miss Kingston's Little Theatre, and published by the Women's Press. He also wrote his own feminist play, *Alice in Ganderland*, as well as a suffragist penny pamphlet, 'Bawling Brotherhood', which he later proudly remembered could still fetch five shillings years afterwards in the old-book trade. His 1912 novel, *John of Jingalo*, was a social and political satire which he described as being 'prompted by the Liberal Government's hanky-panky manipulation of King and Constitution, and its dishonest treatment of the Woman Suffrage Movement'. His experiences as a suffragist also created in him 'a political antipathy' which enabled him to write the satire *Trimblerigg* some years later. Even so, he claimed that by creating in him 'that most uncomfortable thing, a social conscience', the suffrage movement in these years 'got badly in the way of my book-work'. He believed he might have written at least one additional novel without the demands it made on his time and energy. When a colleague happened to regret the effect on his literary output, he recalled how another suffragist present had responded: 'What does his silly old work matter? Votes for Women is far more important', an assessment which he shared.[16]

These years also saw the formation of various men's auxiliaries to the suffrage movement, especially among those who sympathised with militancy, for membership of both the WSPU and the WFL was restricted to women. Laurence Housman was active in both the Men's League for Women's Suffrage, which had especially close links with the Women's Freedom League, and the Men's Social and Political Union, which, as its name suggests, was closer to the WSPU. Members of such essentially auxiliary organisations often felt a greater personal affinity with the outlook and methods of the militant wing. Like the various writers', artists' and actresses' suffrage organisations, however, they generally took a neutral position on questions of method and policy, and assisted with both constitutional and militant agitation. They provided, too, a further useful mediating presence between the two wings. Laurence Housman recalled how his membership of such a range of suffrage organisations had meant a regular grind of speaking at Sunday meetings, meetings which eventually came to require police protection from the opponents who sought to break them up. He, along with the radical journalists Henry Nevinson and H. M. Brailsford, also endured the ordeal of parading London's West End in top hats and sandwich boards, in order to advertise the cause. On one occasion, Laurence Housman recalled, the sporting hero Jack Hobbs 'startled the clubs of Piccadilly' by joining one of the men's sections in a London suffrage procession: 'When the hated cause had enlisted the support of a famous cricketer, matters were becoming serious.'[17]

The question of violence was one which increasingly worried Laurence Housman as the WSPU campaign progressed. Window-breaking, which had become a routine part of militant demonstrations from 1908 onwards, did not perturb him, for he saw it as a relatively harmless but meaningful protest. The existence of glass windows he saw as a symbol of the consent of the governed, and 'if consent was withdrawn on a large scale, glass would become an expensive luxury and shutters a necessary substitute'.[18] He was able to cite Millicent Fawcett in support of his contention that such methods had 'brought the movement to life, and made it practical politics'.[19] He also repeated the view, commonplace throughout the suffrage movement, that the responsibility for the growth of a militant temper lay with the authorities: 'the illegal use of violence began with the police'. By their actions in preventing WSPU marches on Whitehall and Downing Street, the authorities had overturned 'the Constitutional right of the voteless to petition to Parliament'.

This right was subsequently reaffirmed in the courts, but the WSPU leadership no longer had any faith in the power of such constitutional proceedings to advance their cause.[20] In contrast, the leadership of the Women's Freedom League, and most notably Teresa Billington Greig, believed that the most effective expression of militancy lay in a forceful, unbending but essentially reasoned appeal to abstract principles and established constitutional precedent. Significantly, as Laurence Housman records, it was the Women's Freedom League which made the most consistent use of the reaffirmed right to petition, with one of its deputations waiting doggedly to be received for almost four months. Such an approach to militancy was one with which Laurence Housman found himself in increasing sympathy, as his unease with the methods of the WSPU grew.

From 1909 there was a spiralling descent into government barbarity and militant recklessness, which brought suffering and injury to individuals, mostly the suffragists themselves, alongside growing levels of damage and destruction to property. For as the militant sense of injustice began to burn ever more fiercely, militancy increasingly moved beyond symbolic acts of defiance, and the authorities responded with greater and greater repression. In the autumn of 1909, the campaign had taken perhaps its most serious turn with the forcible feeding of WSPU prisoners who adopted the hunger strike. This was a new tactic introduced on her own initiative by Marion Wallace Dunlop, in prison after protesting the government's denial of the right of petition. As a consequence of refusing all food, she was released after only 91 hours in prison. Her aim was to force the government to acknowledge suffragists as political prisoners, whose sentences should be served in the first division of the prison system. There, prisoners were allowed to retain their own clothing and were permitted other privileges such as writing and reading materials. Following her release, another group of WSPU members, in prison for window-breaking, announced their intention of also adopting the hunger strike, alongside refusing to cooperate with the prison authorities in terms of freely changing into the prison clothes required of second- and third-division prisoners. A rapid release again followed from these protests.

Though the leaders had not initiated such developments, their advantages were quickly realised. Window-breaking became more than a symbolic protest – it was now deliberately encouraged as a speedy and effective way of ensuring arrest without the prior battering which was becoming a customary part of WSPU demonstrations. Similarly, the rapid release which followed the hunger strike both returned militants to action and embarrassed the authorities by circumventing their powers to detain. But such developments rested more on independent initiative, courage and commitment than they did on the organisational activities and inspirational speaking of the leaders. It required authentic acts of will from heroic individuals, and threatened to leave the leadership in the role of powerless spectators, who had either to applaud and emulate, or openly reject such actions. Support for window-breaking threatened both to increase the wrath of the government and to undermine leadership control over militant policy-making. Similarly, the hunger strike endangered the remaining authority and legitimacy of the WSPU leadership, in the face of spontaneous acts of heroism from the rank-and-file.

In fact, the WSPU leadership had little choice but to endorse these new developments in militant methods, methods which had moved still further beyond the tactics of civil disobedience and passive resistance with which militancy had begun. Unsurprisingly, a certain ambivalence is evident in a letter Christabel Pankhurst wrote to Jennie Baines as a further group of WSPU prisoners in Birmingham refused food. She begins positively: 'Thank goodness for the hunger strike. But for that the women sentenced at Birmingham would, in view of the long sentences with hard labour, have to undergo a very severe punishment for their brave action.' Such equanimity reflected the WSPU's legal advice that any resort to forcible feeding by the prison authorities would be illegal. This advice proved sadly mistaken, as did Christabel Pankhurst's belief that forcible feeding could not be carried out 'with any real effect if the prisoners make a resistance'.[21]

It is noteworthy, however, that in this same letter, Christabel Pankhurst attempted to exert some discipline in the matter of window-breaking. She insisted that no such protest be undertaken at the police court or police station should demonstrators find, as was sometimes the case after arrest, that they were to be released without charge. Christabel Pankhurst urged that windows should only be broken as part of 'a protest against the Government', and not deliberately so as to bring about a charge and imprisonment: 'If it should happen that protesters are not sent to prison it is rather an advantage than otherwise because they are able to go somewhere else and make another protest.'[22]

Very shortly, however, the authorities responded by forcibly feeding the hunger-striking prisoners in Birmingham. This only added further fuel to the burning anger and sense of injustice felt by many militants. It strengthened a sense of solidarity among those who decided they must follow the militant path to whatever bitter end. Militant campaigning now entered a phase even more personally dangerous and demanding for those at the forefront. Male sympathisers like Laurence Housman experienced growing despair at the suffering they saw among their WSPU friends.

Mary Gawthorpe was one of the earliest victims, and her experience exemplified the dangers and confusion which arose from the new militancy. Under her leadership, Manchester militants had undergone their own share of arrests and imprisonments, and a core of intransigents was created in the region which proved continually troublesome to the London leadership of the WSPU. Among Mary Gawthorpe's closest colleagues in Lancashire at this time were Dora Marsden and Rona Robinson. Like her, both had been teachers, and Dora Marsden had followed a similar route through the pupil-teacher system. Unlike Mary Gawthorpe, Dora Marsden had been fortunate enough to be able to take up a place at Victoria University in Manchester, after which she had enjoyed a rapid promotion to become head of a training school. Her career was halted, however, when she became a suffrage militant.

To Mary Gawthorpe, such supporters became her Lancashire 'warriors', and she ensured that those who went to prison were greeted with processions and receptions on their release. The new tenor to her campaigning was evident also when she introduced Christabel Pankhurst at a demonstration in Liverpool: 'We have come to tell you something about a war – a war against a Government which resolutely refuses to do justice to women.'[23] She also organised a protest outside Walton Gaol in Liverpool against the forcible feeding of WSPU prisoners. It led to several more arrests, including that of Dora Marsden and one of the movement's most courageous 'irregulars', Emily Wilding Davison, who, during her suffrage career, underwent many forcible feedings, and considerable violence at the hands of prison authorities. In October 1909, Mary Gawthorpe herself confronted the possibility of such treatment. Together with Dora Marsden and Rona Robinson she was arrested after disrupting a ceremony at the Victoria University in Manchester, and wrote to Marion Wallace Dunlop that, if sentenced, they would go to gaol 'determined to resist forcible feeding with our lives'.[24] In the event the charges were dropped, and she contented herself with a 'spirited address' to the Manchester WSPU, promising trouble at Strangeways Gaol if forcible feeding should be attempted there. Speaking alongside Emmeline Pethick Lawrence at a meeting in London, she repeated her support for the new militancy: 'I am so glad that the stones have been thrown . . . the question is not now one of morality but of war.' When it was learned that Emily Wilding Davison was being forcibly fed in Strangeways, she organised the threatened demonstration, though she also reportedly 'marshalled the crowd away' when the police became intimidatory.[25]

In November she organised a rally in Stevenson Square from which several thousand again marched on Strangeways, and hosted a reception to greet Emily Wilding Davison and other released prisoners at the Free Trade Hall. Arrests and imprisonments continued among the Lancashire WSPU. Mary Gawthorpe herself successfully avoided such punishment, and this may possibly have been on instructions from London. The WSPU leadership there saw no advantage in its best agitators wasting, both literally and figuratively, in gaol. Emmeline Pethick Lawrence wrote to Dora Marsden in this vein, insisting that she should not seek arrest during a forthcoming demonstration:

> We simply cannot afford to lose our organisers in this way. The movement cannot go on and grow without effective and constant leadership in every part of the country. It is not only that imprisonment robs us of the organiser's services, it is the undermining of her health, and the impossibility of getting into any regular fruitful line of action.[26]

She concluded: 'I assure you that you are not serving the best interests of the Union in exposing yourself to more imprisonment. It is far better that there should be no arrests than that there should be these sacrifices of organisers.' Nor would she countenance the re-arrest of Emily Wilding Davison, at least until after the hearing of a previous charge which was still pending against her. Over the next few years, the WSPU leadership attempted to reinforce its control over members by marginalising all those intransigents and irregulars who appeared of too independent a mind, those authentics dedicated to expressing their own rightful wrath against a tyrannous government, at whatever cost to themselves or the movement. But they were powerless to stop them.

The end of 1909 was a difficult period for the leadership of the suffrage movement for other reasons too. Herbert Asquith, the Prime Minister and noted anti-suffragist, announced that *adult* suffrage was now part of his government's long-term goals. A People's Suffrage Federation was formed by leading Labour and Liberal figures to create popular pressure behind the demand. Among them was the head of the Women's Cooperative Guild, Margaret Llewellyn Davies. The women's suffrage organisations responded with a certain suspicion, even hostility to this development. They believed the government had raised the matter to deflect support from the campaign for sexual equality in the franchise, and feared that its goal was merely manhood, not universal suffrage. Margaret Llewellyn Davies and the People's Suffrage Federation sought to disarm their suffrage critics by a clear statement of their own commitment to universal suffrage. They knew that many in the suffrage movement were universal suffragists who had been driven to focus on women's exclusion from the franchise because of the luke-warm commitment to sexual equality they had encountered in Labour, socialist and

Liberal circles. So Margaret Llewellyn Davies made an appeal to those she termed 'democratic suffragists' in the following terms:

> To combine the splendid uprising of women against their subordinate position with the democratic demand that the suffrage should be placed on a human and not a property basis is the way to secure the passing of a great Reform Bill.[27]

It needed several years of cooperating with and campaigning alongside the People's Suffrage Federation to ease suspicions of the adult suffrage demands among suffragists, however. But such democratic opinion extended throughout the movement, and was to be found among members of all its organisations, constitutionalist and militant. At the same time, democratic suffragists were moving to the fore of the NUWSS, and there was growing pressure for the constitutionalists to adopt a more aggressive stance towards the Liberal government, most especially by seeking greater cooperation with the labour and socialist movements.

For the time being, however, the suffrage movement turned its attention to the general election called at the end of 1909. This campaign saw Mary Gawthorpe sustain injuries which, added to exhaustion and overwork, left her a partial invalid for some time, unable any longer to be at the forefront of militant direct action. The incident occurred when, together with Dora Marsden, she attempted to break up one of Winston Churchill's election meetings in Southport. Rebecca West was an observer of this campaign. She subsequently recalled how 'great physical violence' was commonly used by stewards at such meetings, and that on this occasion Mary Gawthorpe had sustained 'grave internal injuries' and became 'an invalid for many years as a result of a blow received in this way'.[28] Afterwards, the two women brought charges against a local councillor, Dr Arthur Limont, involved in the assault, but these were dismissed in court and it proved necessary to make an appeal to *Votes for Women* readers for help with the legal costs.

Reflecting on these events, Rebecca West declared Mary Gawthorpe 'the most brilliant organiser' ever employed by the WSPU, but believed on this occasion the militants 'made a most disastrous hash of a great opportunity'. In consequence, 'Mr Churchill had a triumphant passage through Lancashire, at what time his supporters, in the ecstasies of political hysteria, mauled the suffragists in the street or sentenced them to stiff terms of imprisonment from the Bench.' This failure, she believed, reflected the lack of any popular base for such a campaign:

> If in every mill half the women workers had been ramming the truths of feminism into the heads of the men workers, there might have been a public in the right frame of mind to put the fear of death into Mr Churchill.

As it was, 'not even Miss Gawthorpe's genius could avail against the fact that she was creating revolt from without and not from within'.[29]

Mary Gawthorpe's capacities as a public speaker do not appear to have waned, however. After her appearance at a subsequent suffrage demonstration in Belfast, one member of the audience declared:

> It will be a very long time before the impression left by Miss Gawthorpe's personality and eloquence will fade from the memories of those privileged to come in contact with her. . . . I never saw a speaker receive greater respect and attention than she did.

She had even disarmed a body of students, who had attended bent on breaking up the meeting. In such ways she proved 'rather a shock to the nerves of those (and there are many here) who think that "Suffragette" is another word for hooligan'.[30] But Mary Gawthorpe herself recalled this as a period when 'the strain became unbearable and I was beginning to feel and fear I could not last'. Rebecca West remembered her as 'sick unto death' in the months that followed.[31]

It was at this time that Lady Constance Lytton first met Mary Gawthorpe, and became inspired by her to undertake one of the best-remembered protests against forcible feeding. Constance Lytton was the daughter of a former Viceroy of India, whose family had faced financial difficulties after his death. For a time, her mother had taken a post as lady-in-waiting to the Queen, while she herself had found occasional secretarial employment among family members. It had taken some months of acquaintance with the leaders of the WSPU for her to become convinced of the rightness of their militant approach to the question of votes for women, but by the time she met Mary Gawthorpe she had served prison sentences in both Holloway and Newcastle gaols. She had also recently been taken by Emmeline Pankhurst to a nursing home in Birmingham to see one of the first of the WSPU prisoners to have endured forcible feeding. The experience led to a new determination: 'I would take the very next opportunity of making my protest with a stone.' That opportunity came during a demonstration in Newcastle, in which Christabel Pankhurst also took part. Constance Lytton's companion for the task of window-breaking was Emily Wilding Davison.

Once arrested, Constance Lytton held to her determination to join with the other WSPU prisoners in a hunger strike, even though she knew her heart to have been weakened by a childhood illness. But here again she met the differential treatment she had already experienced in Holloway. On each occasion the prison authorities had justified their privileged treatment of her on medical grounds, because of the heart condition which had both times been detected during the routine medical inspection that occurred before each imprisonment. But Constance Lytton had also observed that other prisoners with equally serious medical problems, but less elevated connections, received no such consideration. On this occasion, she was not only given a lighter sentence than the other WSPU members arrested, but she was also released a day earlier than the others, and without having been forcibly fed. So, too, was Jane Brailsford, the wife of one of the leading Liberal journalists of the day, Henry Brailsford. Again, Constance Lytton suspected that influential connections explained their privileged treatment, for it was something neither had personally sought.

Constance Lytton now became another of the WSPU's roving attractions, and it was as a visiting speaker at Lancashire meetings in early 1910 that she met Mary Gawthorpe. Her recollections of this meeting confirm both Mary Gawthorpe's failing health in this period, and the overwrought responses which were the outcome of constant exposure to government brutality. Both were distressed at hearing details of the ill-treatment of two more hunger strikers. Constance Lytton recalled:

> Mary Gawthorpe said, with tears in her eyes, as she threw her arms around me "Oh, and these are women quite unknown – nobody knows or cares about them except their own friends. They go to prison again and again to be treated like this, until it kills them."

Reflecting on the 'shameless way' she herself had been 'preferred against others' at Newcastle, Constance Lytton determined 'to try whether they would recognise my need for exceptional favours without my name'.[32]

Disguised as a working-class seamstress, she secured arrest during a demonstration outside Walton Gaol. Once in prison she received only the most cursory of medical examinations, and was forcibly fed over several days, until the authorities were alerted to her real identity, and a rapid release was arranged. It took many months of convalescence for her to recover from the ordeal, after which she was offered a permanent position as an organiser for the WSPU. With her earnings she was able for the first time to establish herself as an independent woman, with a flat of her own. This independence was to be short-lived, however, for the following year she suffered a stroke from which she never fully recovered, and she died prematurely a few years after.

Constance Lytton's story is instructive both in terms of how militants were made, and how an individual might be drawn into ever more extreme forms of protest. The Liberal government denied a demand couched in terms of the very principles for which it was supposed to stand. It also abused the powers of the state, in a cynically calculated exercise of those powers against the weakest among its suffrage opponents. Such actions created a burning sense of injustice in those whose backgrounds had perhaps protected them from the harsh nature of the society in which they had previously led such conventional and upright lives. In this way a mild, highly moral, vegetarian, animal-rights advocate and philanthropist from a leading Conservative family, like Lady Constance Lytton, was led to the argument of the stone. The illegitimate use of the law by the government had made her, in response, lawless. This was an analysis of militancy which Millicent Garrett Fawcett did not tire of making, even long after militancy itself had lost her former respect and sympathy, and the NUWSS had taken the step of forbidding joint membership of the WSPU (a formal requirement it appears never to have enforced, at least at a local level). Sharing such experiences created a moral community, and a particularly intense bonding, among militants.

Perhaps because of her failing health, or possibly just simply because of the scale of work, Mary Gawthorpe was assisted in Lancashire by a growing number of organisers in 1910. This was a year which saw a general election at both its beginning and its end, and in between a new all-party initiative on women's suffrage, the Conciliation Bill. This had been devised by a committee of MPs, organised by Henry Brailsford, husband of Jane Brailsford, and headed by Lord Lytton, the brother of Lady Constance Lytton. The provisions of this bill had been precisely balanced so as to be acceptable to the large majority of Conservatives, Liberals and Labour

MPs, by enfranchising women occupiers. Though it embodied a property-based franchise, the qualification was such that its advocates could claim that a significant number of working-class women, especially widows and spinsters, would gain the vote by its passage. The WSPU thought this initiative sufficiently encouraging to call a 'truce' and suspend militancy while the bill was going through the House of Commons. In these circumstances all the main suffrage organisations were able to work much more closely together than for a number of years, and a massive nation-wide campaign in support of the bill was waged. The nature of these campaigns now pushed the NUWSS to the forefront of suffrage agitation, for it was constant pressure on MPs from the constituencies which was required. The NUWSS had put far more of its energies and resources into building an ever-growing network of branches which reached the most remote villages. Its members were also well-trained in the time-consuming methods required for parliamentary lobbying. Together both wings of the movement were able to return success-fully to staging the peaceable spectacles which drew so much more public attention.

This period saw the eclipse of Mary Gawthorpe among the WSPU leadership, however. She took prolonged leave in the summer of 1910 in an attempt to restore her health. The Manchester Society was looking forward to her return in October, but was advised that Mary Gawthorpe 'acting on medical advice, is prolonging her holiday'.[33] By the end of the month she was no longer listed as a WSPU organiser, nor was she ever again advertised as a WSPU speaker. Though ill health was undoubtedly a reason for her disap-pearance from the ranks of the WSPU leadership, other factors may also have been at work. Along with Dora Marsden and Rona Robin-son, who had increasingly stood in for her during 1910, she had shown little care for instructions from London about the avoidance of arrest and injury. These Lancashire-based militants were also evidently close to the London circle of WSPU activists around Rose Lamartine Yates, which included Emily Wilding Davison. (It will be remembered that it was Rose Lamartine Yates who had tried to organise the purchase of a bust of Mary Gawthorpe, and it was with her that Mary Gawthorpe was to leave her press cuttings and other memorabilia from suffrage days, when she later left for America.) These were among the more impatient spirits among the rank-and-file of the WSPU, given to using their own initiative in matters militant, admiring of the national leadership, but subservient to no one. For them the 'truce' of 1910 proved especially trying, while the leadership in its turn was irritated by continuing anxiety about how long it might continue to restrain them.

At the 'very kernel' of this group were those like Dora Marsden who identified themselves as 'S. O. S. – sick of Suffrage', especially 'the unending donkey work of the gutter and the pavement'.[34] They wanted a quick end to the campaigns, and sought this by maintaining the fiercer militancy which followed on from the introduction of forcible feeding. So they were doubtful of the wisdom of the truce from militancy decided on by London headquarters. Their views on sexual emancipation were also beginning to worry the central leadership. By the end of 1909 they were being seen as 'a troublesome group' of 'uncontrollable freelovers', who had ignored instructions not to seek arrest, or undertake a hunger strike during the general election campaign.[35] Their influence was also evident in Constance Lytton's protest in Liverpool. Though this had proved a propaganda success, it had been undertaken because of emotions aroused by the Lancashire militants, and again quite independently of leadership sanction.

Mary Gawthorpe's ill health not only allowed her withdrawal from activities which were making increasing physical and emotional demands on its participants, but it may also have allowed her to distance herself somewhat from the tensions which continued to grow between London headquarters and sections of the local WSPU leaderships in the provinces. Though for the earlier part of 1910 Dora Marsden continued to enjoy something of the 'star' status the WSPU allowed its most popular organisers, the internal conflicts were steadily deepening. She was refused permission to participate in the demonstration in November which marked a brief cessation of the WSPU truce, and which became known as 'Black Friday' because of the deliberately orchestrated police brutality which met the protesters. The leadership also stalled, and eventually cancelled a major local event which she had been planning for several months, and in January 1911 Dora Marsden finally resigned from the WSPU.

Yet it was the intrepid courage displayed in such militant activity which continued to provoke public sympathy and support. Laurence Housman was himself becoming something of a star speaker for the WSPU in this period, and recalled many stories to illustrate the 'nice personal touches of courage and quaint humour' he encountered among women suffragists. Such characteristics, together with the resourcefulness with which 'the rank and file played their pranks on the enemy', won his continuing admiration. One of his anecdotes from this time concerned the American suffragist, Alice Paul, who was eventually to return to the United States to lead some of the more militant among the movement there. She came to one demonstration so padded out to protect herself against manhandling by the police that she was not at first recognised by her accomplices. Laurence Housman records how, when 'the rough handling began, the buttons (strained beyond endurance) broke from their moorings in swift succession, and the padding like the entrails of some woolly monster, emerged roll upon roll'. Such a spectacle was found highly diverting by the crowd, and ' "Oh, look at the stuffing!" was the cry; immediately she became a popular favourite . . . and cheers followed her.'[36] Laurence Housman sought to encourage the new unity made possible by the truce called by the WSPU leadership. He chaired a meeting organised by the Men's League for Women's Suffrage where Millicent Garrett Fawcett, Emmeline Pankhurst, and Charlotte Despard appeared together on the same platform. Introducing the 'militant lion' and 'constitutional lamb', he recorded that it was Millicent Garrett Fawcett who had first made him feel militant on the question of women's rights, an ironic joke she would have appreciated.[37]

Clemence and Laurence Housman were also active in the Tax-Resistance League, another organisation which served to bring together both militants and constitutionalists. Indeed, this tactic was often advocated as a method which combined the best of both approaches. Laurence Housman became a popular speaker for this group, touring around the country to speak on its behalf, often at the expense of his professional commitments as a writer. For her part, Clemence Housman actually put the principle of no taxation without representation into practice, refusing to pay the rates on a house which she rented especially in order to make such a protest, also borrowing furniture in order to avoid any option of distraint. Eventually, she was arrested for this offence, but refused to pay the cost of the taxi to take her to the prison. The arresting officers agreed to meet this expense, and were also 'most kind' in allowing Laurence Housman to accompany them for the ride, after he had undertaken to pay the extra sixpence this would entail. In this way, he recalled, they all drove to Holloway, at a net cost to the government of 4s 2d. Clemence Housman then spent six days in the gaol, before the authorities decided her presence there on such a charge was too much of an embarrassment, and released her.[38]

By this time, Dora Marsden and Mary Gawthorpe were also searching around for new roles and new methods to secure the emancipation of their sex. Their relationship was still at this time a 'close, affectionate and loving' one, despite their disagreements over the WSPU leadership, towards whom Mary Gawthorpe always retained a personal loyalty. At her suggestion, Dora Marsden approached the Women's Freedom League regarding the ideas she had for a new feminist weekly. Negotiations went well at first, but foundered on the considerable demands for resources which Dora Marsden made of her potential sponsors. It is likely, too, that the WFL was wary of the too close association with the sexual radicalism advocated among such circles. Mary Gawthorpe then directed her friend towards the women of the Fabian Society, to whom Dora Marsden argued the need for a 'really popular agitation', 'a natural movement' for the vote, which required that 'the philosophy of the women's movement will have to be worked out in terms of everyday life. . . . The Suffrage Societies are trying the short cut to women's freedom and there are no short cuts.'[39]

Such a viewpoint shared the perspective being put forward at this time by Teresa Billington Greig, whose disillusionment with the suffrage movement had led to her own recent resignation from the WFL at the beginning of 1911. There were increasing numbers of suffragists who were now questioning its concentration on the vote as the key to women's emancipation. In part this reflected a growing disillusion with militancy as a strategy, in part the effect of a revived concern with sexual liberation in radical circles, and in part the influence of a new revolutionary current within the labour movement, deriving from anarchism and syndicalism, and as such impatient of expectations of change through parliament.

Eventually, the publisher Charles Grenville agreed to back Dora Marsden. The launch of the new journal, entitled the *Freewoman*, took place in November 1911, with Mary Gawthorpe listed as a co-editor. In fact she had resisted this role for many months on the grounds of her poor health, though she was also clearly worried about the attacks on the WSPU which she anticipated the journal would contain. During the preparations for the new journal, she had urged Dora Marsden 'I want you to keep your mind free of bitterness', for she continued to respect many among the WSPU leadership, even though she felt that they had not treated her well since she had become an invalid. Though she, too, intended to resign altogether from the WSPU, she declared: 'I have something to say before I do.'[40]

Dora Marsden accused her friend of cowardice. She had been relying on Mary Gawthorpe's name to attract a readership to the new journal. Mary Gawthorpe responded by refusing the kind of 'forced giving' which her friend sought as 'another form of prostitution. I am neither prostitute nor commercial seller.' She appears to have agreed at last to become co-editor on a temporary basis, and only after receiving assurances that there would be no editorial attacks against the suffrage campaign for at least a year. She also used her new role, and the need to speak freely which it would require, as the reason for her resignation from the WSPU in September 1911. She was given a cheque to cover the costs incurred during her illness and convalescence, one which Dora Marsden thought quite inadequate thanks for her friend's years of service. For her part Mary Gawthorpe tried to dispel any further source of bitterness in Dora Marsden's mind: 'You *shall* understand me. I DO NOT MIND. THE JOY HAS BEEN MINE. THEY DO NO INJURY.'[41]

Mary Gawthorpe's role on the new paper was to be largely one of moral support, and of building contacts, despite her formal designation. It was she, for example, who introduced Rebecca West to the *Freewoman*. The young writer claimed to adore 'Lovey Mary', and wrote a portrait of her for the new Labour daily newspaper, the *Daily Herald*. The content of the new journal reflected the attitudes and concerns of the young radical intelligentsia. As such, it provided what one of its financial backers, the wealthy Fabian, Charlotte Payne Townshend Shaw, described as 'A valuable medium of self expression for a clever set of young men and women.'[42] In an interview with the *Evening Standard* in October 1912, Dora Marsden set out her manifesto, first apologising for using the term 'feminism', only just then becoming current, and one which she saw as presently wrongly restricted in its application to the demand for the vote. Instead she advocated an expanded understanding of the term, as a movement which 'would accomplish a vast revolution in the entire field of human affairs, intellectual, sexual, domestic, economic, legal and political'.[43] Above all, the new paper challenged conventional ideas on sexuality. Not only did it advocate the end of marriage in favour of free love, at least in terms of serial monogamy, but it also allowed expression to those who found celibacy a preferable option, and to explorations of the nature of homosexuality in both women and men. Its conception of emancipation rested on economic independence for women, and release from domestic ties through communal childcare and cooperative housekeeping. As such it necessarily and deliberately addressed itself to an elite among women, which it expected to form the vanguard in new patterns of sexual relations which would eventually free all women.

The *Freewoman* was impatient of any thought of change through formal, constitutional politics. Its links with anarcho-syndicalism and with the "rebel" section of the socialist movement around the *Daily Herald* were so extensive that one admiring American account referred to its position as 'Sex Syndicalism'. Many suffragists were sympathetic to its expansive conception of liberation. Ada Neild Chew, for example, a working-class organiser for the NUWSS thought it 'meat and drink to the sincere student who is out to learn the truth, however unpalatable the truth may be'.[44] It found an enthusiastic audience among some suffragists in the United States, one of whom wrote to Mary Gawthorpe: 'To us all, it seems almost too good to be true, because none of us felt that we had got far enough to enable such a journal to be born, much less to live.' She doubted that it could have been produced in her country, but believed that its distribution would prove invaluable there:

> I personally feel grateful to it because it came just at the right moment to put new blood into my enthusiasm for the work we are doing here for suffrage by reviving my vision of the greater things beyond – a vision that had suffered somewhat from the tarnishing effects of the routine business of promoting a cause.[45]

Others were alienated, most especially by its sexual radicalism. Maude Royden, at this time editor of the *Common Cause*, referred to it as a 'nauseous publication', while Millicent Garrett Fawcett regarded it as mischievous.[46] Anti-suffragists were not slow, also, to use its reputation against the demand for votes for women. They issued a call for its suppression, attempting to smear the suffrage movement by association by presenting its appearance as 'the dark and dangerous side of the "Woman Movement" '.[47] But as Mary Gawthorpe had feared, it was not long before Dora Marsden began to use its columns not only to attack the narrowness of the suffrage campaign as such, but also the personalities of the WSPU leadership.

Plate 6 Alice Clark, *c.* 1908. By courtesy of the Clark Archive.

8

'ON THE HORNS OF A DILEMMA'

Alice Clark, liberal Quaker and democratic suffragist

While some close to the centre of the WSPU became increasingly disillusioned with militancy from 1910, for other suffragists it still offered the best hope for their cause. Alice Clark (1874–1934) was beginning her slow recovery from the tuberculosis of the throat and lungs which had threatened her life the previous year. She was still largely bed-ridden at her family home in Street, Somerset, and remained speechless, under medical advice, until the latter months of 1910. It was a tedious and frustrating time, observing from a distance events in which she wished urgently to play a part. She wrote to her great-aunts, Anna Maria and Mary Priestman: 'I rather long to go and break some windows. I am not sure whose but I think any liberal offices would answer the purpose.'[1]

This is an unexpected sentiment to find in a woman in her mid-thirties, with a position of considerable standing in her local community as a major employer, a pillar of the local temperance and other reform and philanthropic societies, and a member of the Society of Friends. She was also a Liberal by birth and upbringing, the granddaughter of John Bright, and daughter of Helen Priestman Bright Clark. During Alice Clark's childhood her mother had confronted John Bright over women's suffrage at the great Reform convention at Leeds in 1883, and pushed forward the need for greater sexual equality in the governing bodies of the Society of Friends. As a young woman Alice Clark herself had given over a considerable amount of her time to 'political work among women' in the neighbourhood of Street: 'She thought that by such means women would come to understand the importance of the vote, and that they would strengthen their position for winning it by working for Liberalism.'[2] This was a common approach among politically progressive, middle-class suffragists in the 1890s, despite the disappointments surrounding Liberal Party policies on the issue. Such an outlook was undoubtedly a product of heightened loyalties provoked by the Home Rule–Unionist split within the party, and its loss of office for such a prolonged period. Once the Liberal Party regained power in 1906, however, that loyalty was increasingly tested by the failure of the government to take up the demand to extend the parliamentary franchise to women. Only a few weeks before declaring her desire to break windows, Alice Clark had told Mary Priestman: 'I have given up on the Women's Liberal Federation' and 'very much prefer the methods of the WSPU'.[3]

Alice Clark had been brought up with the longstanding ideals of middle-class radicalism. Another great-aunt, Priscilla Bright McLaren, regularly reminded her, for example, that she had been born on the anniversary of the emancipation of slaves in the British colonies. Some of her favourite reading in adolescence was *United Ireland* and the history of the Anti-Corn Law League, in which John Bright had played such a prominent role. Through the friendships of her mother and her great-aunts she came to know many other pioneers of the women's movement in Britain and America, including Josephine Butler, Millicent Garrett Fawcett and Elizabeth Cady Stanton. The progressive girls' school in Southport, where she spent her only year or so of formal education in the early 1890s, allowed, where it did not encourage, attendance at trade union demonstrations, and at meetings addressed by Annie Besant and Charles Dilke. Her Latin teacher passed on ideas then current about the 'matriarchate' at an earlier stage of civilisation.[4]

Alice Clark's parents had done much to promote women's opportunities for advanced and higher education. All her sisters undertook some course of university study after school, and her American sister-in-law had first come to England on a postgraduate scholarship from Swarthmore. But Helen and William Clark also hoped to see one of their daughters, as well as their two sons, enter the family firm, and in this way pioneer a further field as a woman industrialist. Alice Clark appears readily to have chosen this alternative course, in the face of some perplexity from teachers and friends at school, for she had proved an able student, and had gained good results in the Cambridge matriculation examinations.

Shoe-making was an industry in which women had found an increasing role with industrialisation. By the time Alice Clark entered her family's factory, the lighter processes, and those requiring machine top-stitching were all undertaken in departments staffed by women. In her late teens she herself began learning each of these processes on the shop floor, moving on subsequently to the heavier men's processes in the cutting and bottoming rooms. Though this meant standing all day, she reported that she found it easier work than that she had undertaken in the women's room. Subsequently, she spent some months as a shop assistant in Edinburgh, learning the retail and customer-relations side of her family's business. For part of this time she lived with Priscilla Bright McLaren, helping her great-aunt in her efforts to keep the *Women's Signal* afloat a while longer as the voice of Radical suffragists like the women of the Bright circle.

Back at home in Somerset, she was introduced into public life and gradually learned community leadership roles through the temperance movement, and the local Women's Liberal Association, which she helped found in 1890, and of which she remained secretary for eleven years, when the office passed to her youngest sister, Hilda Clark. She learned how to run a society, chair a meeting, speak in public, canvass electors. In these years, too, she faced up to hostile audiences as the member of an actively pro-Boer family, and controlled the jubilant celebrations of the jingoistic members of the Clark's workforce after Mafeking. She also saw at first hand the practice of tax-resistance adopted by her brothers in protest at the South African war.

By 1906, when the WSPU first became a national organisation, Alice Clark was already an experienced suffrage campaigner. Her earliest recorded efforts for this cause took place in 1890 when only just sixteen. She set about providing a column on the course of the women's movement, by collecting news from around the country. It was this undertaking which brought her to the notice of suffragists beyond her immediate home circle, including Alice Scatcherd and Elizabeth Cady Stanton, who subsequently sought to uphold the young recruit's enthusiasm with news from the United States' movement. A year or so later, and now at school, Alice Clark took part in a debate on women's suffrage, writing to her mother for material to use in her contribution, just as one of her older brothers had done a year or so before.

On her return home she began to speak on the question, most generally at meetings of local Women's Liberal Associations. She was soon acting as delegate from these local societies to the regional and national conventions of the Women's Liberal Federation. None of her immediate family circle appear to have taken a major role in any of the suffrage societies in the years following the NSWS split in 1888, unlike other members of the Bright circle. Eva and Walter McLaren, for example, played a leading role in the Parliament Street Society and remained an important channel of communication between that society and the Great College Street Society, in which their cousin, Lilias Ashworth Hallett, worked alongside her long-standing friend, Millicent Garrett Fawcett. Ursula Bright, as we have seen, turned her back on the national organisations, and pursued her perspective on women's suffrage through the Women's Franchise League.

In the west of England, however, the women of the Clark family, together with their favourite aunts, the Priestmans, chose to channel their suffrage energies through the Women's Liberal Federation. For these Radical suffragists, their own party continued to seem the best hope for their cause, while their approach to women's suffrage had always been one which saw it as part of a larger programme of social advancement. For them, the most pressing imperative was to bring their own party to a proper view of the question, so as to strengthen also the cause of reform more broadly. Anna Maria Priestman, as we have already seen, formed the Union of Practical Suffragists in the latter 1890s to secure just this end, work to which both Ursula Bright and Alice Clark lent their support. Such an approach did not mean putting women's suffrage second to Liberal politics, but rather pushing suffrage to the fore of reform politics. When Alice Clark made a visit to the Priestman sisters in Bristol in November 1893, for example, she wrote home asking for permission to attend four suffrage meetings that were to be held during her short stay there. Alice Clark and other members of her family also took an active part in the collection, during the mid-1890s, of the Special Appeal, the petition which was presented with seemingly good effect prior to the successful second reading of Faithfull Begg's women's suffrage bill in 1897. And by the end of the decade, they believed they were at last in sight of their goal of committing the Women's Liberal Federation (WLF) to making women's suffrage a test question for those candidates seeking its support during elections.

After attending the 1898 WLF annual meeting with the Priestman sisters, Alice Clark reported to Priscilla Bright McLaren that they were all feeling 'most jubilant', having only narrowly failed to carry their resolution on the test question. She herself felt confident it would be carried the following year, though 'the Aunts won't confess to being quite so sanguine'. All the existing Union of Practical Suffragist members on the WLF executive committee had been re-elected, while Lady Carlisle, the President of the Federation had been so conciliatory that 'even Aunt Annie [Anna Maria Priestman] has quite softened . . . and there has been a great lying down of the lion and lamb'. She reported, too, how one of the women speakers had appealed in these terms to the leading Liberal politician, John Morley, at a public meeting held to coincide with the convention: 'She said we were loyal workers to the Liberal Party but that also we were loyal to our womanhood.' The leadership of the party was put on notice not to place these Liberal suffragists 'on the horns of a dilemma'.[5]

It was a warning that was to go unheeded, however. The Union of Practical Suffragists did eventually succeed in having women's suffrage made a test question for WLF support in 1903, as we have seen, and, somewhat over-optimistically, wound up its campaign. Alice Clark was already out canvassing and campaigning in local constituencies with a view to the next general election. When she surveyed local Liberal candidates she found 'a considerable strengthening of their sentiments in favour of the Suffrage', for they very much wanted the kind of practical support which the local Women's Liberal Associations could provide. She saw local party agents, too, to ensure they also understood that such support would depend on a candidate's stand on votes for women. But it was not long before their opponents organised a counter-offensive within the WLF. By the 1905 annual meeting the issue was back on the agenda and Alice Clark anticipated a 'stormy time'. On this occasion she was able to report that the policy had been protected by Lady Carlisle speaking 'with much fervour and imploring for unity and goodwill'. But afterwards the battleground simply shifted to the local branches, where their opponents attempted to build opposition to the test-question policy. Anna Maria Priestman was ousted as President of her own local WLA, the formation of which had marked the beginnings of the present national body. She was replaced by the wife of the local Liberal MP, who with her supporters then set about reversing the branch's position on the test question.[6]

This was the context, then, which gave rise to Alice Clark's preference for the policies of the militants – a longstanding disaffection among her circle of Radical suffragists from the national suffrage societies, equivocal and insecure support from the Women's Liberal Federation on which the political strategies of such Radical suffragists had depended, and an ever-deepening disillusion with the Liberal Party, on which their hopes for this and other reforms had rested during a decade and more of Conservative government. It was a disillusion Alice Clark shared with other suffragists among her family circle, including those great-aunts who had helped initiate the demand of votes for women over fifty years before, Ursula Bright, Mary Priestman and Anna Maria Priestman. Her own three sisters, Esther Bright Clothier, Margaret Clark (subsequently, Gillett), Hilda Clark, and her American sister-in-law, Sarah Bancroft Clark, were all of like mind.

If Alice Clark's commitment to militancy marked a deliberate rejection of the political legacy of her upbringing, it drew some strength from her religious inheritance. Membership of the Society of Friends coloured every aspect of her life. The values of this religious community, and the 'national family' to which it had given rise, conditioned her social relations, and shaped her physical environment in the model company town which had been developed around her father's factory.[7] Any major decision, whether personal or public in its implications, was examined in terms of the leadings of conscience, and the knowledge of earlier Quaker exemplars. Such an inheritance led Alice Clark to assume a wide-ranging set of responsibilities, attached to her privileged standing as the daughter of a well-to-do industrialist and employer of labour, responsibilities which might variously require a political activism on her part, or a commitment to humanitarian causes, or to the writing of history. Her religious inheritance is evident also in the stoicism with which she coped with the grave illnesses that interrupted her life from childhood; it informed her somewhat austere manners and dress – 'Miss Alice always wore grey', one unnamed employee recalled many years later; and it helped her maintain her sometimes stiff-necked independence and self-reliance on issues of principle and personal values, while at others it informed her persistent pursuit of conciliation and consensus among divided colleagues.

The sympathy with militant policies and methods, which she was still expressing in 1910, had not been reached without considerable deliberation on her part, then, and remained always equivocal, especially with regard to their more violent forms of expression. When the WSPU had first made its presence felt in London at the opening of the new Parliament early in 1906, she had written to Priscilla Bright McLaren about these 'rather trying women'. Her concern was that they should do nothing to 'damage the cause' though, perhaps reflecting on both her great-aunt's and her own career as a suffragist, she also remarked that 'agreeableness does not seem to have helped much'.[8]

And her Quaker background also led Alice Clark to identify with militants, especially when she heard them derided as extremists. She reported responding to one critic in these terms: 'I said my Quaker descent made me feel that it was rather an admirable thing to go to prison for one's principles.'[9] Within a year she herself was participating in the WSPU's first raid on the House of Commons, in February 1907. Also present at this demonstration was her mother's cousin, Lilias Ashworth Hallett, one of the grander figures of the nineteeth-century movement, known for her stylish house, her magnificent clothes, her haughty beauty on the platform, her generally imperious manner – not a figure to be expected in a mêlée around the House of Commons. Sympathy with militancy was also publicly expressed by Priscilla Bright McLaren only shortly before her death, when she signed a letter of sympathy with those women sent to prison in October 1906. Her elder son, Charles McLaren, was a principal speaker at the Savoy banquet to welcome WSPU prisoners on their release in November 1906. Her youngest son, Walter McLaren, joined Millicent Garrett Fawcett in defending the early WSPU demonstrators against their detractors. His wife, Eva McLaren, praised the militants to an audience of WLF women, as did his sister-in-law, Laura McLaren. So Alice Clark was not alone among her family circle in her growing sympathy with militant methods.

But it was not the Pankhursts or the Pethick Lawrences but Charlotte Despard with whom Alice Clark seems mostly closely to have identified among the militant leadership. Like Ursula Bright, Charlotte Despard was a convert to theosophy. Her suffrage speeches often expressed a blend of mysticism and politics which has been described as 'theosophical feminism'. Religious faith was a factor in the making of many suffragists, in terms both of the way they conceived of their political activities, and in the form of campaigning to which they were drawn.[10] The constitutional militancy which marked much WSPU, as well as Women's Freedom League, activity in this period fitted well with Alice Clark's outlook on social protest as a Quaker. In 1907, she emulated Dora Montefiore by resisting the payment of taxes. 'New Suffragette Move by John Bright's Grand-daughter', declaimed the headline in the *Daily News*, and other newspapers around the country quickly picked up the story. Her stand brought letters of support from as far afield as New

Zealand, and from all sections of the suffrage leadership, including her mother's old friend, Millicent Garrett Fawcett.[11]

Alice Clark's letters from this period reveal the open interaction between different sections of the movement which was still possible. They contain evidence also of some of the tensions to which the advent of the WSPU, and developments in its methods and policies, were giving rise. During a visit to Millicent Garrett Fawcett, for example, she learnt of Esther Roper's bitter hostility to the Pankhursts by this time: 'She won't appear on the same platform with them.' It seems that Esther Roper also resented the resistance of women suffragists to her efforts to defend women's right to work as barmaids. For her part Alice Clark hoped to persuade her to come and speak to the conference of Somerset Women's Liberal Associations in 1907.[12]

Alice Clark's letters do not reveal directly her views on the growing tensions within the militant wing of the movement. These have to be interpreted through her actions. Though she took part in WSPU demonstrations and initiated her own militant protests, she remained a member of the NUWSS. The matter worried her: 'My heart goes out greatly to the Suffragettes and I often wonder whether it is cowardice that still keeps me from joining them.' In temperament she believed herself well-suited to the new methods:

> In some ways I skip all the decorous intervening generation of Friends and my sympathies go direct to the contemporaries of George Fox, who protested in the steeple-houses against the false teaching of the Priests and annoyed the magistrates by wearing their hats in court and using their plain language.

Yet still she held back: 'I seem to crave however some clearer sign from Heaven to tell me to go and do likewise.'[13]

Significantly, she seems to have had no such reservations about the Women's Freedom League, and did become a subscriber to that organisation. Almost certainly its continuing advocacy of methods of civil disobedience and passive resistance were a factor in this decision, together with its commitment to democratic processes of decision-making. Alice Clark reported on an international gathering of suffragists in Holland in 1908, emphasising 'the admirable way in which the suffragettes set forth their case'. But it was the leaders of the Women's Freedom League whom she singled out for individual mention: 'Mrs Despard, Mrs Billington Greig and Mrs Sanderson spoke with such skill and tact that they won the sympathy and respect of all present, although many had disapproved of their action before.'[14]

Other members of her family circle at the very least lent their moral support to the WSPU. Her eldest sister, Esther Bright Clothier, took part, for example, in the Hyde Park demonstration in the summer of 1908. Militancy seems also to have re-awakened Ursula Bright's interest in the movement, after the withdrawal which followed her husband's death, and despite her own crippling illness. Alice Clark recorded:

> She sits in a wheel chair, but seems very bright and cheerful mentally, and her mind seems rather more open to this world's interests. At least she has much sympathy with the Suffragettes. She knew the Pankhursts when they were little more than babies.[15]

When the WSPU staged one of its major London exhibitions, it was able to advertise it with messages of support from Ursula Bright, Anna Maria Priestman, Eva McLaren, Laura McLaren and Lilias Ashworth Hallett.

If Alice Clark felt unable to join the WSPU, or to adopt the increasingly violent methods which marked its campaign from mid-1908, she was prepared to act as an apologist for such methods: 'While I absolutely disapprove and lament over their offensive tactics, such as throwing tiles and stones, we may hope that good may still be done.' She compared the militants with Garibaldi and his followers, who had fought for Italian unity the century before:

> Without defending such things or thinking them necessary I think where there is an overwhelming moral force at work it does bend all things to good. That is the divine power to bring good out of evil. It is the willingness to sacrifice everything to the cause that is the attractive power of the suffragettes. The way they sacrifice is sometimes wrong. My heart goes out to them all the same.[16]

This letter was written to her Priestman aunts, perhaps suggesting a wish to comfort some unease of their own at the most recent turn in militant tactics which had brought in its train the hunger strike and forcible feeding. Alice Clark had received the confirmation of her own serious illness only some weeks before, and faced a long period of enforced inactivity, if not death. But she was kept in touch with happenings in the suffrage movement through her closest female kin. Her younger sister, Margaret, was among those, for example, who picketed Downing Street early in September and had written that the sentences passed against those arrested during the demonstration had been quite unwarranted: 'It was absolutely peaceable, such as any member of the Society of Friends might have done.'[17]

Such sympathy was only reaffirmed with the announcement of a militant truce during the introduction of the first Conciliation Bill. Alice Clark 'felt very dull' because she was unable to join Margaret Clark Gillett and their sister-in-law, Sarah Bancroft Clark, marching in the WSPU's coronation procession that summer. She regretted that the National Union of Women's Suffrage Societies had not seen fit to join it, commenting: 'It is wonderful what a change has come over public opinion' as a consequence of such peaceable pageantry. Her sisters and sister-in-law worked hard for the NUWSS during the first general election campaign of 1910, collecting signatures for the Voters' Petition. A local branch of the NUWSS was established in Street itself shortly afterwards, and plans to appoint a secretary were discussed at one of the regular regional Quaker gatherings which provided an opportunity to meet with other like-minded women.

Sarah Bancroft Clark had a young family to care for at this time, and explained to Alice some of the tensions this created for her:

I should like to do much more myself, but I don't feel very clear how much I ought to do. I can't altogether neglect the children and what with them and a few domestic cares and occasional visitors . . . it seems as though nothing but little bits of time are left, nothing consecutive.[18]

Alice Clark was at this time in a local tuberculosis sanatorium, so her sister-in-law wrote to tell her about the first meeting of the new society. Esther Clothier 'gave a good account of our reason for starting the new society. I thought she couldn't have spoken better.' The Voter's Petition was collected outside the Clark factory itself by other members of the society, while Sarah Bancroft Clark had undertaken to visit works in nearby towns, and another family member planned to canvass local quarry workers: 'When Pris [Sarah's infant daughter] goes for her nap presently I am going to take a few forms to Glastonbury. . . . There is so much to do and one wishes constantly for more workers.'[19] For the time being, Alice Clark's own sympathies remained with those who doubted the wisdom of the militant truce. The first Conciliation Bill failed to get beyond its second reading in 1910 because of the lack of any government support. In her view: 'It all justifies the WSPU very fully. I wish they were just a little different. I should like a society between them and the National Union.'[20]

As we have seen, she had now changed her own position on window-breaking. Her sister, Margaret Clark Gillett, also wrote at this time:

> I do not see why we need not all of us be quite free in our minds to break government windows – if that will do any good. There is no wrong in doing that as far as I can see. There seems to me a great distinction between damaging government and private property – we should not need to do it with any risk of injuring persons, and damage to property and to persons are absolutely different – aren't they?

Again, outrage at the conduct of the Liberal government was the main prompt to such thoughts, and Margaret Clark Gillett was beginning to believe that if all suffragists started breaking windows 'it would bring the government to a stop'.[21]

Alice Clark remained largely bedridden throughout 1910, and was forbidden speech until late in the year. By this time she had returned home and was undergoing tuberculin treatment under the direction of her youngest sister, Dr Hilda Clark, just beginning a career in public health, and later to work in humanitarian medical aid. Hilda Clark, and her life-time companion, Edith Pye, were also WSPU sympathisers at this time. But Alice Clark continued to direct her own moral and financial support, the only practical help she could offer presently, to Charlotte Despard and the Women's Freedom League. Black Friday, when WSPU demonstrators suffered severely at the hands of both police and spectators, proved 'a moment of rather overwhelming emotions' for her. She wrote to her great-aunts:

> I wonder a great deal if I should have been in that company of noble women if I had been well. I think I should. We four sisters are drawn very near together because I think each one of us feels as keenly as the others – and dear Sarah [her sister-in-law] too.[22]

Looking back, Laurence Housman suggested that one of the most remarkable aspects of the militant campaign was the effect that it had not just on the young and adventurous, but also on older, and formerly staid women. He remarked especially on how he had seen 'women of meek and retiring character' exhibit 'extraordinary personal courage and determination, carried to the nth degree by women who had never done anything daring before, not even to the extent of being unconventional'.[23] He and Clemence Housman came to know the Clark family in this period and through a series of anecdotes, he tried to convey something of the unexpected spirit which he found among otherwise mild women. He recalled, for example, a story he had heard told to a mother's meeting 'with the measured precision of a sewing machine' by one of two friends who had pledged themselves to take part in a large-scale window-smashing raid in Oxford Street. The speaker had recalled how;

> All at once my friend said to me 'I can't do it! I can't do it!'. I said: 'Do you mean to say you are going to break your word to Mrs Pankhurst?' 'Yes', she said: 'I can't help it, I am'. 'Then I shall never speak to you again', I said; and I left her and went straight on, for I didn't wish to be seen with her any more.

Then, suddenly, behind her, the narrator had heard a sound of breaking glass: 'I'm doing it! I'm doing it' her friend had cried, whereupon she herself hurried on to Bond Street and began her own appointed task there.[24]

In similar vein, Laurence Housman told of an elderly, retiring woman who had rebuffed his attempts at a suffrage meeting to sell her campaign literature, saying:

> 'I've read everything; a great deal has been written, and a great deal has been said, and it's no good. Something has got to be *done!* My daughter and I are both tingling to do something. I just want to go out into the street, and smash, and smash, and smash – *everything.*' Then she added in a still small voice, 'And nobody, looking at me, would suspect it.'[25]

Laurence Housman explained such unexpected steeliness in other-wise mild and conventional women by 'the repressions of their Victorian training which – when they did break out – made these women so aboundingly brave, while remaining so collected and self-possessed'. He also found that such rebellion was infectious: 'There was something in the air', producing 'instantaneous conversion' akin to a religious revival. The victims of this infection often became themselves 'terrific engines of war; once started there was no stopping them'.[26]

Though there is no evidence that any of the Clark sisters ever resorted to the argument of the stone, Laurence Housman noted with approval and some surprise their clear sympathy with militancy. Writing to Sarah Bancroft Clark after a visit to Street, he also commented: 'I found Roger's mother [Helen Priestman Bright Clark] more sympathetic to militancy than I could have expected. She is at all events satisfactorily anti-government in her feelings. *So are you.*' He hoped that Sarah Bancroft Clark would be able to stir her husband, Roger, to greater activity on behalf of the Men's League for Women's Suffrage, of which both men were members: 'Keep that dear man of yours in a proper perturbation of spirit over the half-heartedness of men in general and of himself in particular: for the better a man is in heart the more his indignation should be stirred.' Laurence Housman had just visited the area, speaking on behalf of the Men's League, and Roger Clark was able to report eight new members afterwards.[27] But Laurence Housman continued to be surprised by the hypocrisy he saw among many other Liberal men on the issue of women's enfranchisement: 'It is wonderful too how, in otherwise good men, the hidden fundamental belief in woman's inferiority and lesser rights crops up.'[28]

Laurence Housman experienced growing unease at the suffering which militancy increasingly brought to the women who adopted the methods of the WSPU. For himself, he always expressed a decided preference for the tactics of civil disobedience and passive resistance. So he took particular glee in the organisation of resistance to the 1911 Census. The WSPU had rejected a scheme he had put up to them, but he had been able to work closely instead with the Women's Freedom League, the outlook of which was much more sympathetic to such work. The tactic, he found, met with favour also among many members of the NUWSS who, he reported, 'broke away from their leaders and came in by the thousand'. He recalled: 'Census-resistance was well-suited to the mentality of the non-heroic many; thus it ensured numbers. It was also good principle, and as such could not be despised by the heroic ones who preferred to get their shock of battle in more active form.' In the event the WSPU leadership also found itself forced to participate in this protest by the 'restiveness of its own rank and file' on the issue.[29]

Laurence Housman had no idea how many women slept in his own house on Census night – with his concurrence the door was barred against him, and when he regained entry in the morning his guests had all decamped 'leaving by way of recompense a nicely prepared breakfast'. The census official recorded his responses without protest, entering 'A quantity of females, names, numbers and ages unknown' on his return. Afterwards, Laurence Housman assessed the protest as 'a useful bit of peaceful penetration into skulls which had hitherto remained offensively impervious to argument'. He believed it had served, too, to hearten the suffrage movement with a sense of its own numbers and solidarity, while the WSPU had been forced to see the value of at least one instance of cooperation 'versus the splendid isolation on which they usually prided themselves'. Above all, 'it gave all concerned in it a good time and a good laugh'. Afterwards his unknown guests presented Laurence Housman with a library chair bearing a brass plate commemorating the event, from which he later wrote his reminiscences of the campaign. The experience only served to confirm his conviction that effective, united, large-scale passive resistance was within the capabilities of the suffrage organisations, while it was a strategy which would have entailed far less individual suffering and evoked far more general sympathy than the violence of later militancy.[30]

Thereafter, Laurence Housman concentrated his efforts on the associated line of tax-resistance. He acknowledged, however, that in comparison to census-resistance it took far more trouble, entailed much greater risk of personal loss, and required much longer to bring the issue to a head. When Clemence Housman was arrested for non-payment of rates on 30 September 1911, her elder brother, A. E. Housman, was able to announce to a friend: 'there is a lovely picture of my two disreputable relatives in yesterday's *Standard*'.[31] But it had taken eighteen months for her to establish the tenancy of the house concerned, and she was released from gaol after only a week, 'looking the picture of health after having Hampdened the Government to her heart's content'.[32] For this reason, the WSPU leadership did not incorporate such tactics into militant strategy, though they never formally discountenanced them either. The NUWSS leadership similarly remained wary of such methods. Though many among its membership felt that tax-resistance offered a constitutional way of taking a more militant stance against the government, the leadership feared it was too time-consuming and too uncertain in its outcomes.

In the summer of 1911 the prospects for women's suffrage looked good. The majority secured for a second Conciliation Bill had forced from the Liberal government a promise of full facilities next session. This presented the Liberal leadership with a problem. If franchise reform was to be undertaken in that Parliament, long-term party interests dictated that it be as broad a reform as possible. A measure limited to women's suffrage also threatened to split the Liberal Cabinet, which included unbending anti-suffragists, as well as others who opposed such a measure on the grounds it was likely to increase the Tory vote, given the existing property qualifications.

It was in this context that, in the summer of 1911, Lloyd George opened negotiations with Henry Brailsford, as a prominent figure in the Conciliation Committee, and with the NUWSS leadership. His go-between was C. P. Scott, editor of the *Manchester Guardian*, and an old friend and adviser of Helena Swanwick, editor of the NUWSS's *Common Cause*. He proposed as a preferable way of enfranchising women a new Reform Bill to give the vote to all householders, with husbands and wives able to qualify jointly on the family home. He had calculated correctly on democratic suffragist support for such a measure. Henry Brailsford also proved sympathetic to such an advance towards universal suffrage, and so did Kathleen Courtney, the NUWSS's secretary, and Helena Swanwick. According to C. P. Scott's notes of his discussions, both women 'hailed the proposal as opening up a new and far better prospect of success'. They also correctly foresaw that it would be equally acceptable to Millicent Garrett Fawcett, 'her principle being "the more suffrage for women the better" '.[33] In return for such support, Lloyd George promised to back the third Conciliation Bill which, under these proposals, was to be held in reserve in case the Reform Bill failed, or women were excluded from its provisions in the course of its passage through Parliament.

The announcement in November 1911 of government plans for a new Reform Bill did not take the NUWSS unawares, then, as it had the WSPU, and many among its democratic suffragist leadership favoured in principle as broad a reform as possible. But the announcement of a general measure of suffrage reform effectively destroyed the all-party support which had been so painstakingly built up for the more limited Conciliation Bill. Moreover, Lloyd George's support for this purely women's suffrage measure proved decidedly erratic in the months that followed, and Cabinet disunity so delayed plans for the new Reform Bill that it was not introduced until *after* the third Conciliation Bill was heard in 1912. This put the two measures in a quite different relation to each other than had been the case in the original proposal, for the Conciliation Bill could no longer serve as a fallback measure, should the Reform Bill fail. Suffragists from all sections of the movement were incensed, then, at the way the announcement of a new Reform Bill effectively negated the concession of full facilities for the Conciliation Bill which had been won the previous summer. Lloyd George merely compounded suffragist distrust of the government when he provocatively referred in a major speech to the Conciliation Bill having been 'torpedoed' by the announcement of the Reform Bill.[34]

This situation caused the NUWSS to rethink its political strategies completely at the beginning of 1912. Though the constitutionalists did not completely reject the now undermined Conciliation Bill which was introduced in April of that year, it mounted no campaign of any significance on its behalf. All faith in its longstanding tactic of proceeding by private member bills had now been destroyed. Instead, NUWSS energies and resources were focused on securing a women's suffrage amendment to the government's forthcoming Reform Bill, and to strengthening the hand of suffragists within the leadership of the Liberal Party. Two additional new factors had to be taken into account in its policy-making. First, there was the growing commitment of the Labour Party to women's suffrage, evident both in the increasingly consistent support offered by Labour MPs to the Conciliation Bill, and more significantly still in the women's suffrage resolution passed at the Labour Party conference at the beginning of 1912. Afterwards, Millicent Garrett Fawcett had written to the Labour Party leader, James Ramsay Macdonald: 'I wish you were double your strength in the House of Commons', and from this time she became openly sympathetic to democratic suffragist pressure for an electoral alliance between the NUWSS and the Labour Party.[35] Second, there had been a marked decline in the support of Irish Nationalists for the Conciliation Bill in 1912, for they feared the disunity that women's suffrage might bring to the Liberal government, from which they hoped to win Irish Home Rule. Since the 1910 elections, the Liberal government had been kept in power only by the combined votes of its own members and those of the Irish Nationalists and the Labour Party. If part of this informal coalition was weakening in its support for women's suffrage, it became imperative that the advance in Labour sympathy be held and strengthened.

In the spring of 1912, therefore, with Henry Brailsford once again acting as a mediator, the leaderships of the NUWSS and the

Labour Party held delicate negotiations over the provision of suffragist support for Labour candidates in three-cornered elections. The
aim was to strengthen the threat which Labour candidates increasingly posed to the Liberal Party, both by encouraging more of such
contests, and by helping build the Labour vote where they occurred.
In this way, the NUWSS hoped both to hold the Labour Party
to its new commitment on women's suffrage, and to demonstrate to
the Liberal Party that it could not afford the active opposition
of the suffrage movement, especially from that section where Liberal
women remained a significant presence. This new strategy, known
as the Election Fighting Fund policy, had the support of those
democratic suffragists now prominent in the NUWSS, including its
national secretary, Kathleen Courtney, its acting parliamentary
secretary, Catherine Marshall, and many of its executive committee,
including Helena Swanwick, Isabella Ford, Maude Royden and
Margaret Ashton. It was endorsed by the rank-and-file at a general
meeting of the NUWSS in May 1912. The new policy involved the
collection of a special fund for the support of Labour candidates in
three-cornered elections, and help with building Labour Party election machinery in selected constituencies which the NUWSS hoped
to persuade Labour to fight. These were the constituencies held by
leading Liberals, especially those who were anti-suffragist.

For the WSPU, the announcement of the forthcoming Reform
Bill had served only to confirm its worst fears of a government
betrayal, and the unwisdom of the truce. It reiterated its longstanding
demand for a government women's suffrage measure, and extended
its policy of attack to the Labour leaders also, arguing that the
Labour Party was in effect part of an informal coalition with
the Liberals. Militancy began again, and on an ever larger and more
destructive scale. The first window-smashing raids in London's West
End occurred within weeks, and militant freelancers increasingly
turned to arson and bombs in their attacks on property. Mary
Gawthorpe was still an invalid at the time of these developments,
and she had never given up on the suffrage movement in the way
that Dora Marsden had. She remained sympathetic to militancy,
and supportive of old friends and colleagues in the WSPU like
Emily Wilding Davison. She was distressed both by the *Freewoman's*
continuing attacks on them, and by the sufferings which
accompanied the renewed cycle of arrests, hunger strikes and forcible
feeding.

This new turn was especially bewildering for the male

sympathisers of the WSPU, some of whom sought to share the martyrdom of women militants. Many now themselves risked imprisonment and adopted the hunger strike. Several endured a quite horrendous record of forcible feeding. Hugh Franklin, a member of the Men's Political Union and a nephew of a Liberal cabinet minister, was forcibly fed over one hundred times, eventually escaping to France to avoid re-arrest. Prior to this, however, he took up the case of William Ball, 'an older comrade, a workman', who himself had been arrested after protesting the forcible feeding of another member of the Men's Social and Political Union.[36] Undergoing imprisonment, the hunger strike and forcible feeding in his turn, William Ball lost his mind, was certified as a lunatic, and released into the care of Colney Hatch Hospital. Hugh Franklin wrote to his uncle, Herbert Samuel, asking 'I wonder what would be said in England if a Russian were treated like this.' He asked how this member of a Liberal government could condone such atrocities, and declared that to find 'one's own uncle is an accomplice and an active sympathiser, entirely breaks one's faith in the sincerity of his professed ideals'.[37] A subsequent government white paper found that William Ball's temporary insanity had not been caused by his treatment in prison. William Ball continued to claim during subsequent investigations, and after his return to health, that he had been subjected to electric shocks while strapped down for forcible feeding. His testimony was dismissed, however, by the medical experts who investigated his claims, as that of someone 'not strong intellectually', 'defective' in general knowledge, and illiterate.[38]

These were the circumstances which caused Mary Gawthorpe, herself still unwell, to return to the argument of the stone, though she was no longer a member of the WSPU. She was arrested among those who broke windows at the Home Office in February 1912, during a protest against the mistreatment of William Ball. Sylvia Pankhurst's account of these events suggests that Mary Gawthorpe was in prison on remand for a week, and was discharged 'on account of her chronic condition of serious ill-health'.[39] Mary Gawthorpe later claimed she had undergone both a hunger and thirst strike to achieve this release. Evidently, there followed yet again 'a trying period of a prolonged struggle for health', during which, she later recalled, old colleagues from the WSPU like Rose Lamartine Yates proved outstanding friends. Her frail health meant that she took no further active part in the suffrage movement in Britain, and provided the public grounds for her withdrawal as joint-editor of the *Free-woman*. She wrote to an enthusiastic reader in the United States:

> You may have heard a whisper of my long and tedious illness mainly induced by too strenuous militancy in the past six years? 'Repairs' are not yet complete and since throwing everything over, I have made more encouraging prodigies on the whole.[40]

In this same letter she expressed hopes of being able to contribute to the paper when she was again well, emphasising as her own main concern:

> The artistic and intellectual forces must not be permitted to degenerate during the years of 'open warfare' and I know of no better way of keeping hearts and minds fresh and clear (in contrast to 'touchiness' and 'acidity') than a fair, independent and uncompromising journal like this.[41]

But her letters to Dora Marsden show that privately Mary Gaw-thorpe had by now lost all patience with the *Freewoman*'s continual assaults on 'the Pankhurst Party'.[42] She expressed her 'sheer anger' at this, and requested that her old friend not write back, as her letters now brought on 'acute heart attacks'.[43] She found the extreme individualism now espoused by the paper to be elitist, and charged her former colleague with seeking to create a 'new aristocracy', while imitating the autocracy she claimed to find so distasteful among the WSPU leaders.[44] She was not convinced by what she interpreted as an anarchist rejection of the suffrage movement, and continued to defend the hunger strike by upholding 'the rebel and his defiance of government' against 'the anarchist and his denial of government'.[45] Yet she also continued to solicit material for the paper, and to do what she could to help with its distribution in the United States, through a married sister then living in New Jersey.

The greater violence attaching to WSPU actions from 1912 gradu-ally undermined much of the sympathy which it had previously found among non-members, like the women of the Clark family. They maintained their support of non-violent militant methods such as tax-resistance, and continued to exhibit a certain equivocation over other forms of militancy that gave Laurence Housman an opportunity for friendly leg-pulling from time to time. After some 'outrage' by the WSPU in late 1913 in which Sarah Clark had evidently taken some pleasure, Laurence Housman wrote: 'This is where your "non-militancy" finds you out: you disapprove of militancy but enjoy every defeat for "law and order" that militancy is able to pull off.'[46] But the NUWSS, together with the Men's League for Women's Suffrage and the Tax-Resistance League, remained the organisations in which the Clarks channelled their efforts on behalf of votes for women. In the summer of 1912 Sarah Bancroft Clark was able to report to Alice Clark that 'the Cause seems pretty popular in Street at present'. She had organised a women's suffrage fête at her home, the kind of low-key, highly localised community activity at which the NUWSS excelled:

> Everyone was so nice and kind and helpful. And we liked feeling that our big house was useful for once! Bancroft [her young son] was very useful selling tea tickets. I think he sold over £1 worth. The other children all enjoyed it too I think.[47]

By this time Alice Clark had left the 'dismal world' of the sick-room, sufficiently recovered by the summer of 1911 to take a part in distributing suffrage literature around the nearby towns and villages. In November she saw her London specialist who pronounced 'all signs of disease are quite gone', though a further test would be needed nine months later to confirm her cure. 'In the meantime' she told her great-aunts, 'I am to live an ordinary, wholesome life and may play tennis or row.' But she was not yet fit to return to work, and she was advised not to strain her voice by anything other than quiet conversation. She kept up-to-date with suffrage politics, none the less, and had shared in the general outrage felt by suffragists when that 'despicable person', Lloyd George, victoriously declared the Conciliation Bill 'torpedoed'.[48]

In the autumn of 1912, Alice Clark's return to health seemed secure, but her prolonged illness had brought about a complete change of direction in her life. She did not return to the factory to work for another ten years, though she did remain on its board of directors. Instead, she moved away from her family home to an independent life in London. Here she began work on the historical research which was to lead eventually to the publication of her book, *The Working Life of Women in the Seventeenth Century*. Despite her lack of any formal higher-education qualifications, she had been granted a fellowship at the London School of Economics. This was a fellowship open only to women, with the aim of allowing the holder to 'perfect themselves in the methods of investigation and research'. An earlier holder had been Eileen Power, another pioneer among economic historians.[49] Alice Clark worked under the direction of Dr Lilian Knowles, also a path-breaker in the fields of economic and social history. The fellowship she held had been established by Charlotte Payne Townshend Shaw, the wealthy Fabian wife of George Bernard Shaw, and Alice Clark's own research almost certainly reflects the influence of Fabian women on historical and social research at this time. Later she herself acknowledged Olive Schreiner's *Women and Labour* (1908) as a particular influence on her decision to undertake this research.[50]

The new democratic suffragist direction of NUWSS policy in 1912 fitted both with her political outlook, and with her desire for a more aggressive policy against the government. Her family's links with the NUWSS were extensive, and went back to its beginnings in the late 1860s. With this background, and from the basis of her new career in London, Alice Clark was able to move rapidly into a leadership role within the constitutional wing of the movement. Together with her brother, Roger Clark, she also helped to establish a friends' League for Women's Suffrage in 1912. Hers had been a complex journey, from Radical suffragist roots, via 'constitutional militancy', to the democratic suffragism which marked NUWSS policy from 1912 on. It was a journey which took her away from her Liberal Party affiliations for ever, and for a substantial period from her original career as an industrialist. The next ten years she devoted to new fields of labour, as political organiser, historian, and subsequently as a war- and famine-relief worker.

9

MEN, WOMEN'S SUFFRAGE AND SEXUAL RADICALISM, 1912–14

The policies and methods of the WSPU and the NUWSS were irreconcilable from the spring of 1912. Yet, though the affiliations of the Clarks and the Housmans were each with a different wing of the movement, they were still able to share some suffrage activities over the next two years or so. The Men's League for Women's Suffrage and the Tax-Resistance League remained organisations where militant and constitutionalist might work together. To these now was now added the Election Fighting Fund (EFF) of the NUWSS, in which both Alice Clark and Laurence Housman played a prominent role. The correspondence between the Housmans and the Clarks in these years casts fresh light both on the internal politics of the movement, and on new meanings attaching to suffragism in these years. It also reveals some of the exasperation which members of each wing of the movement felt with their respective leaderships.

Sarah Clark's expressed desire for 'some work disagreeable and difficult' was widespread within the movement, and Clemence Housman took it to indicate 'a real gain in additional force that must tell in unknown directions'. One of these directions, she noted, was the pillar-box 'outrages' of this time, when militants first began to set light to the Royal Mail.[1] Neither of the Housmans appear to have taken an active role in this escalation of militant violence. But both they and members of the Clark family continued to attend major WSPU rallies. In this regard, then, while they were formally affiliated to separate wings of the movement, both the Housmans and the Clarks might be counted amongst 'the clapping militants' whose presence within the NUWSS was such an irritant to those, like Helena Swanwick, for whom the WSPU was now a danger to their cause.[2]

From this time, however, Laurence Housman noticed a growing hostility to the presence of men in WSPU leadership circles. Male sympathisers had taken a leading role in negotiating the militants' truce during 1910 and 1911, and in the introduction of the Conciliation Bills which had since proved a failure. Moreover, Henry Brailsford, Laurence Housman and other men formerly associated with the WSPU, were beginning to work more closely with the democratic suffragists of the NUWSS in pursuit of the EFF policy. And there was a fear that some members of the men's organisations were beginning themselves to resort to methods of extreme violence. Though many male militants 'died without telling their story', it has since emerged, for example, that Harold Laski made an attempt to destroy a railway station in these years.[3] Such developments threatened to undermine the original meaning of militancy as a dramatisation of women's wrongs, and as an appeal to an essentially chivalrous conception of male–female relations.

In consequence, relations between the WSPU leadership and its male sympathisers deteriorated rapidly from the end of 1911. When the Liberal government 'torpedoed' the Conciliation Bill with the announcement of a forthcoming manhood suffrage measure, they also undermined the credibility of Henry Brailsford and other men associated with him, who had previously been close to the WSPU's inner circle. Laurence Housman recalled that most of the leading male suffragists found the militant leadership

> at times exceedingly trying; they went their own way, they did not try to please, or even to conciliate; they would take no advice. On all these points I think they were generally right: to be a real Movement the Movement had to think, and be, independently.

What alienated him was not such independence but the 'increasing incivilities' to which he and other male sympathisers were subjected from this time, leading him to betray a continuing bitterness even some decades afterwards: 'the outstanding reason why women should have the vote for themselves is that even with the utmost goodwill, men cannot understand them'.[4]

The Men's League found that the 'WSPU was persistently belittling our efforts, and occasionally resenting our aid'. When its intervention persuaded the government to receive a joint deputation from all the women's suffrage societies after the WSPU had been refused, they found the militants were furious: 'We, poor innocents, had entirely spoiled their pitch for them.'[5] Even so, Laurence Housman's sympathies, like those of Clemence, remained with the WSPU. During Emmeline Pankhurst's trial in 1912, after which she received a particularly severe prison sentence, he wrote to Sarah Clark: 'Have you read the full report of Mrs Pankhurst's speech at her trial? I think it a most convincing and moving document: it made my heart ache more than any other speech I have ever read on the suffrage.'[6]

But such militant sympathies did not stop Laurence Housman from cooperating with constitutionalists through the work of the EFF. He agreed to join its committee, along with other well-known militant supporters like Israel Zangwill and Muriel, Countess de la Warr. His hope was that they might be able to use their influence with the WSPU leadership to bring about a united suffrage effort in a policy which, it could be argued, was both militant and constitutional – it directly attacked the government, and insisted that women's suffrage become part of Liberal Party policy, but used the constitutional machinery of elections to secure this end, not threats to public order, property and persons.[7] It was his involvement with the EFF committee which first put Laurence Housman out of favour with the militant leaders. He recalled: 'My letters ceased to be answered, and presently I was no longer allowed to speak at WSPU meetings.'[8] Looking back, he felt this had been just as well, for he was unable to approve of the extension of militant methods which brought the destruction of works of art, and the firing of ancient buildings. For a time, he suspended his subscription to the WSPU. But he resumed it publicly, despite continuing to be *persona non grata* with that organisation, when he received the formal threat made by the office of the Public Prosecutor against all subscribers to the WSPU early in 1913.[9]

At this time he also publicly defended militant actions in the correspondence columns of the *Manchester Guardian*, while admitting privately to Sarah Clark that he was going through 'a period of much doubt' on the issue on grounds of pragmatism. He feared that the WSPU did not have enough members 'with their heads screwed on the right way' to make its increasingly clandestine operations successful. His 'moral approbation' of militancy remained unaltered, however, 'for I know if I were a woman I should be one of them'.[10] He also believed that the press was greatly exaggerating public hostility to such methods, and that they were not as harmful to the cause as some argued. He suggested that the firing of pillar-boxes was only regarded as so outrageous because the protesters were generally managing to escape undetected, and therefore to go unpunished. It was this fact, he punned, which was really having such 'an "arresting effect" on the public conscience'. For his part, he approved of such tactics more fully than those of window-smashing, for 'it spreads the lesson over a larger section of the community, more impartially, and not too overwhelmingly on any single individual'.[11] He publicised such views by more letters to the press, in the *Daily Telegraph*, as well as in *Votes for Women*.

Meanwhile, within the NUWSS there was growing expression of disaffection among Liberal women because of government failure to support women's suffrage. After the defeat of the third Conciliation Bill, the *Common Cause* called on Liberal Party women to resign and concentrate on suffrage work:

> Signs are not wanting that the already numerous defections of Liberal women are causing anxiety at headquarters. No party woman likes to withdraw; in fact it must always be a most painful duty. But must not non-militants use *every* means in their power at the present extreme crisis in suffrage affairs?

The EFF provided a positive direction for the expression of such alienation. One NUWSS member announced her resignation from her local WLA at this time in these terms: 'I am throwing my whole energies and substance into the support of the new development of the NUWSS policy.'[12]

The subsequent EFF campaigns offered militant sympathisers, disaffected Liberals and restless constitutionalists an opportunity to undertake together a more aggressive attack on the government, and without resort to violence. It brought a new vitality to the constitutional wing and attracted fresh supporters among working-class and Labour suffragists. Alice Clark was not directly involved in the formulation of this new direction for the NUWSS, for she was overseas, travelling around archaeological sites in Syria and Egypt during the spring and summer of 1912. But within months of settling in London the following autumn, she had been voted onto the executive of the NUWSS, and co-opted onto the EFF committee. In this capacity, she acted as the assistant to Catherine Marshall, who was both secretary of the EFF committee and parliamentary secretary of the NUWSS.

This new life allowed Alice Clark to develop friendships among members of the London intelligentsia, with whom her family already had extensive contacts. Her letters home from this period record evenings spent with the historian G. M. Trevelyan, who had recently published his life of her grandfather, John Bright, and the publisher, John Lane. She met many of the leading intellectual and artistic figures of the day, including Gertrude Stein and Roger Fry. Her youngest sister, Hilda Clark, was also now living in London at 1 Barton Street, Westminster, among neighbours who included the 'nascent Bloomsbury group'. Among this household was Marjorie Sheepshanks, a settlement worker and by this time a committed NUWSS activist, soon to become editor of the journal of the International Women's Suffrage Society, *Jus Suffragii*.[13] Another was Catherine Marshall. Perhaps it was through this household that Alice Clark was recruited into the leadership of the NUWSS. It was evidently one where active suffragist commitment became infectious. Hilda Clark reported home of her friend:

> Edie [Edith Pye] has got much taken up with the suffrage. . . .
> She came with me to an open-air meeting on Saturday night
> and got very enthusiastic. She had never been to anything of
> the sort before. She is ready to do almost anything now – and
> I think a good many are.[14]

This letter was written at a further time of turmoil for suffragists. When the Reform Bill finally came before parliament in January 1913, political excitement was high. The *Manchester Guardian* declared: 'One would have to go back nearly ten years in the history of Parliament to find its parallel.'[15] The previous months had been ones of intense activity for the NUWSS's chief organisers: series of women's suffrage amendments had been drafted, each providing for a varying degree of enfranchisement for women; negotiations had been concluded with all shades of suffrage opinion within the House of Commons; and joint lobbying had been undertaken in cooperation with the People's Suffrage Federation to ensure that women were included in some way in the reform. In the event, however, the Speaker ruled women's suffrage amendments to the Bill were out of order, and in some disarray the government withdrew the measure altogether.

The Liberal government's own ambivalence towards, and divided councils over, women's suffrage had allowed its Conservative opponents to destroy with ease this attempt to move towards universal suffrage. Another consequence was the subsequent stalemate within the Cabinet over franchise reform – suffrage ministers felt they would be compromised by any purely manhood suffrage measure, and anti–suffrage ministers would not allow the introduction of a government measure which included women. In return for this lost opportunity, suffrage leaders were offered full facilities for another private member bill. Alice Clark wrote to the Priestman sisters telling of the 'interview after interview' which the NUWSS leadership had afterwards with members of the government. She reported, too, how the Chancellor of the Exchequer, David Lloyd George 'blushed quite pink with embarrassment' when his 'bluff', the offer of full facilities for a private member bill, was rejected. It would seem that Catherine Marshall had as substantial a command of parliamentary procedure as Elizabeth Wolstenholme Elmy before her. She had pressed the government to allow a minister to speak in support of women's suffrage and, as Alice Clark reported to her great-aunts, it now appeared that 'if this had been done the Amendment would have been in order!'[16]

After these discussions with the government, the NUWSS consulted widely with leading Labour, Liberal and Conservative suffragist MPs, all of whom confirmed the rightness of its decision to reject the government's offer regarding a private member bill as 'counterfeit coin'. The view of the NUWSS towards the government was summed up by Catherine Marshall: 'If the best that the Suffrage members of the Cabinet can get for us is a worthless offer . . . we have nothing to hope for so long as the present government remain in power.'[17] She looked forward with confidence, therefore, to a strengthening of the NUWSS's anti-government policy through the work of the EFF. Once again, NUWSS leaders hoped that a change in direction on its part might make a new unity possible with the WSPU, enabling both wings to campaign together to secure a government measure. The WSPU leadership refused, however, to draw back from violence in order to make such cooperation possible.[18]

The decision now to press for a government measure of franchise reform served to confirm the commitment of the NUWSS leadership to the EFF policy. In their view, joint agitation with the Labour Party represented the most effective pressure which suffragists could exert on the Liberal government towards such a goal. Just previous to this, EFF organisers Margaret Robertson and Ada Neild Chew had successfully campaigned among the rank-and-file of the Labour Party, especially the miners' unions. Their efforts helped achieve a two-thirds majority at its annual conference for a resolution that the

Labour Party oppose any fresh extension of the franchise which did not include women. The *Common Cause* declared afterwards: 'Women know henceforth that one body of men will make a united and self-sacrificing stand on their behalf. There is the less ground for bitterness, the less excuse for the extremist tactics of anger and despair.'[19] Hilda Clark declared: 'I do really feel this will jog the Liberal women! I want to know how to join the Labour Party. I suppose to give money to them is about the best thing I can do.'[20]

In response, the NUWSS annual meeting which followed these events voted to strengthen the EFF policy along the lines already advocated by its leadership. In future, no government candidate was to receive election support however good a suffragist he might personally be, though 'tried friends' were not actively to be opposed. The EFF was now also directed to prepare particular constituencies for the next general election – either those already held by Labour suffragists, or those the NUWSS hoped to see contested by Labour. From this time, any candidate seeking NUWSS help had to include women's suffrage in his election address, agree to press the government to introduce a women's suffrage bill, and undertake to oppose any extension of the franchise which did not include women. He also had to support making women's suffrage part of his party's programme in the next election. In this way the NUWSS sought both to attack the Liberal government, and to strengthen further Labour commitment to women's suffrage.[21]

In the spring of 1913 Alice Clark took over the lease on 1 Barton Street, while Marjorie Sheepshanks was overseas. Her own accounts of her house-keeping at this time suggest a certain Spartan character. A well-to-do relative was reportedly 'rather amused', for example, by the fare he found there, which Alice Clark herself admitted was 'not very elaborate', and she asked for recipes and produce from home in Somerset. Even so, the vegetarian Catherine Marshall found the new regime at 1 Barton Street a matter for complaint, while her own untidiness, noisiness and late nights, consequent on her work in the lobbies of the House of Commons, proved a strain for others in the household. These were the unavoidable ups-and-downs of communal living among 'a vibrant group of women with changing lifestyles and priorities'.[22] But it remained a friendship circle of like-minded, middle-class, previously Liberal women whose commitment to the suffrage movement was leading them increasingly towards Labour and socialist sympathies.

Alice Clark's letters home from this period tell of hearing Laurence

Housman speak in the meetings in Hyde Park which the NUWSS organised in defence of free speech. The authorities had banned the well-established meetings of the WSPU in the park on the grounds of the threat they presented to the public order, and in standing out against such repression, NUWSS speakers, too, became subject to the kind of rowdyism which WSPU speakers had long endured. At this time, Alice Clark also heard a 'really brilliant' talk by Charlotte Perkins Gilman: 'I think she overstates her case but she does it with so sure and light a touch that it only stimulates your thoughts instead of establishing you in your old opinions.' In addition, she attended a reception for another visiting US suffragist then in London, Anna Shaw, 'a dear person'.[23] In these letters, too, she told of her plans to take part in the great demonstration being planned that summer by the NUWSS, the Women's Suffrage Pilgrimage. Groups of suffragists were to set off from all parts of Britain during July, holding suffrage meetings in towns and villages along their way, as they converged for a mass protest in London in August.

Laurence Housman also took part in the Pilgrimage, during which he recalled his only encounter with a violently hostile crowd. It occurred at a meeting in East Grinstead, when he became 'a cock-shy for rotten eggs and tomatoes'. His ill-treatment was said to have converted two former anti-suffragists to support for the cause, where his own speech had failed to do so, and he commented: 'It's nice to think that chickens gone wrong can sometimes be of more use in the world than ourselves. Thus we find our right place in the universe.'[24] Even anti-suffragists within the Liberal government appeared impressed by the Pilgrimage, and both they and the suffragist ministers each agreed subsequently to receive a NUWSS deputation. On both of these occasions the NUWSS emphasised the alliance which had been made between the movement for adult suffrage and that for women's suffrage. Margaret Robertson, chief organiser of the Election Fighting Fund campaigns, claimed that working men had taken note and were now 'inclined to regard opposition to women's suffrage as a Conservative and Liberal Plutocracy against Democracy'.[25]Afterwards, Alice Clark was able to tell her great-aunts about a recent NUWSS executive committee meeting where 'Everyone was able to report so many signs of progress since the Pilgrimage that we begin to be really hopeful of getting something done in the next Parliament.'[26]

Laurence Housman's continuing and open sympathy with the militants not surprisingly caused some tensions between himself and his constitutionalist colleagues throughout 1913. At one point he inquired of Sarah Bancroft Clark: 'Is my head on or off? I thought you would be writing to tell me whether I had been "constitution-ally" executed or no: but perhaps it is all too confidential.' His crime was to have subscribed to Clemence Housman's 'self denial card' for the WSPU. He had felt free to do so on the somewhat weak ground that the EFF committee had gone into suspension during the NUWSS's annual meeting, to be reconstituted the following week on even stronger anti-government lines. He also expressed the hope that the contribution he had made via Clemence Housman would 'go to militancy and not the Anti-Labour propaganda' on which the WSPU was by this time engaged.[27] On another occasion he reported the 'amusing suspicion' that his name was being deliber-ately excluded from reports in the *Common Cause* of NUWSS meet-ings and lists of speakers.[28]

His letters during 1913 provide further testimony of the unwel-come effects which his suffrage commitment was having on Laurence Housman's work as a writer. He reported that 'Suffrage events sadly disturb my mood for writing, and for the last fortnight I haven't got along at all well with the novel.' He wondered whether he should not for a while give up his house and his profession 'while the suffrage question is on, and simply go about the country as an itinerant preacher and firelighter just for my travelling expenses'. Several months later the problem continued: 'My book goes horribly slow, all because it does not and cannot rank first in my interest while suffrage things are on.' It would seem that suffrage speaking engagements became, in consequence, a sometimes welcome additional source of income for him: 'Cardiff has just asked me to lecture to it for gold in February . . . my impoverished pocket can't miss the chance.'[29]

By the autumn of 1913 he was back as part of a speaking tour among WSPU branches in the north of England. It is not clear, however, whether this participation had the endorsement of the WSPU leadership. The militant wing of the movement began to fragment after the expulsion of the Pethick Lawrences from its leadership at the end of 1912. They had sought to return the WSPU to its earlier populist methods and modes of protest, ones which had succeeded in gaining the movement much publicity, and substantial evidence of mass interest in the women's suffrage issue. Emmeline and Frederick Pethick Lawrence were persuaded that the present methods caused most harm to the WSPU's own members, while they alienated public opinion. Christabel Pankhurst, now living in exile in Paris, had not been convinced by their arguments, however. She was supported by Emmeline Pankhurst, who continued along her own path to martyrdom. But many WSPU branches away from the immediate control of the London leadership continued to welcome the Pethick Lawrences, alongside other WSPU dissidents. Hence, Laurence Housman found himself speaking alongside both Mrs Despard and Frederick Pethick Lawrence during his tour of northern WSPU branches in late 1913, suggesting that it may well have been an 'unofficial' programme, not one sanctioned by WSPU headquarters.[30]

Sylvia Pankhurst shared with other militants the growing unease with the suffering and loss of popularity which followed the escalation in violent methods endorsed by the leadership from 1912. So, she determined on re-building a popular base for the movement in the East End of London, where she sought to appeal especially to working-class supporters. The East London Federation of Suffragettes (ELFS), which she formed during 1913, was closely allied with the 'rebel' section of the Labour movement around the Daily Herald Leagues, led by George Lansbury. It sought to combine suffrage with socialist and Labour campaigning, an example being in its support of Irish trade union leaders during the Dublin lockout. Such associations brought about, in their turn, the expulsion of the East London Federation from the WSPU at the beginning of 1914.

It was at this time that other expelled or disaffected militants formed the United Suffragists, among the leading members of which were the Pethick Lawrences, Evelyn Sharp, Henry Nevinson, Barbara Ayrton Gould, Evelyn Sharp, a former colleague of Laurence Housman from *Yellow Book* days, and George Lansbury. Lansbury was himself a long-time sympathiser with the militants, and had resigned his seat and unsuccessfully fought a by-election in Bow and Bromley during 1912, in a failed attempt at that point to force the Labour Party towards a greater commitment to women's suffrage. That advance occurred the following year, as we have seen, though as a result of the policies of the NUWSS, while the WSPU leadership became increasingly antagonistic both to the Labour Party, and to the involvement of men in the suffrage campaign. By the beginning of 1914, then, George Lansbury too found himself out of favour with Emmeline and Christabel Pankhurst. Also at this time Laurence Housman first began to write for the *Daily Herald*, and met George

Lansbury, in his role as its editor. He offered this assessment of the Labour rebel:

> I sum him up as a rather sensual, strong-natured man with a very genuinely warm heart and an honest mind. A bit school-boyish and reckless and thoroughly enjoying life and his fellow men. He is one of the few men – not personal friends – whom I haven't resented throwing an arm around my shoulder. Generally I resent it as a great liberty: so I suppose I like him *au fond* more than a little.[31]

Other men previously close to the WSPU leadership attempted to maintain some dialogue, but faced the increasing hostility of Emmeline and Christabel Pankhurst at any attempt to moderate their reliance on extreme and clandestine acts of violence.

The complex cross-currents between both militant and consti-tutional wings of the suffrage movement, and between Labour and suffrage campaigning, were everywhere evident in the two years or so preceding the First World War. Alice Clark, as a member of the NUWSS leadership, could not help but become embroiled in the tensions which were generated among her colleagues by such cross-currents. East Bristol was among the constituencies which the NUWSS hoped to persuade the Labour Party to fight, for it was held by the anti-suffragist Cabinet Minister, Charles Hobhouse. This goal may even have been a factor in the recruitment of Alice Clark to London headquarters. The influential Bristol Society had been resisting NUWSS plans to make East Bristol an EFF constituency, that is one where it would help with the organisation of Labour Party support in any forthcoming election. No doubt to circumvent such opposition, the London leadership promoted the formation of a new branch in the constituency, the East Bristol Society. By this means it was able to introduce an EFF organiser responsible directly to the EFF committee, not to the hostile Bristol Society, which none the less continued to present problems throughout 1913. A planned campaign on behalf of the new Labour newspaper, the *Daily Citizen*, initially met with resistance, for example. But by the end of the year, Alice Clark was able to report to Catherine Marshall: 'We coaxed them round . . . I wanted to help Labour if we possibly could.'[32] Through such efforts many women Liberals in the area were brought into contact with the Labour movement for the first time, and were reportedly impressed with what they found. EFF work in East Bristol provided an example of the effectiveness of the new policy. It served to strengthen the forces of Labour in the constituency, so that the Labour Party seemed set to challenge Charles Hobhouse in the general election which was expected in 1915.

Initially, Alice Clark, like many of her colleagues on the EFF committee, was somewhat guarded in her attitude to the Labour Party, for there were continuing tensions between the leadership of the Labour Party and the NUWSS over the operation of the EFF. For one thing, there was a concern that the Labour Party sympathies of EFF organisers sometimes superseded their suffrage loyalties. It was equally the case that some prominent Labour MPs, including James Ramsay Macdonald, remained hostile to the women's suffrage as a middle-class demand, and wary of interference from an outside organisation.

A by-election in Keighley in 1913 brought some of these tensions out into the open. The EFF's chief organiser, Margaret Robertson, was incensed when the NUWSS headquarters could not bring itself to oppose the Liberal candidate, Sir Stanley Buckmaster, an old friend to the cause, after a Labour candidate somewhat belatedly entered the campaign. Her view was shared by other prominent NUWSS supporters of the EFF policy, like Margaret Ashton of the Manchester Society. She wrote to Catherine Marshall:

> I'm really relieved that you see the seriousness of the whole bother for I do not think Miss Clark does. We can't afford to be thrown by the Labour Party – we have only them to rely on (and a broken reed at that) for the next general elections.[33]

For her part, Alice Clark commented: 'We must retain our freedom to be influenced by the Suffragist actions of the Liberals.'[34] The NUWSS had been disappointed at the unwillingness of the Labour Party to embarrass the government over the issue. To substantiate her position she quoted Philip Snowden, whom she had consulted about the matter. It was his opinion that the EFF policy remained important as a way of 'causing the Liberals uneasiness in the country', but it was one which was unlikely to wring much more out of the Labour Party. Snowden believed that the miners were being friendly towards the suffragists only because they saw the value of NUWSS help during the elections, though Alice Clark herself commented: 'I think that even such friendliness is of great value to us.'[35]

Nor surprisingly, perhaps, Alice Clark reported to her great-aunts that these weeks had brought her 'much food for anxious thought.

So many difficulties arise.'[36] In consequence, she set about attempting to resolve the conflicts and tensions to which the work of the EFF was giving rise within the NUWSS leadership. She suggested that much misunderstanding might be avoided in the future if Margaret Robertson were brought on to the committee, or at least was required to attend its meetings so that she might 'bring us her ideas as she has them and hear the discussion on them and either convince us or be convinced'. She urged: 'They [the EFF organisers] do so much work that I think their point of view would be valuable and I don't think people get so far away if they can discuss things point by point.'[37] In fact, closer contact with EFF organisers appears to have served to move Alice Clark and others of like mind more towards the views of the organisers who had much more day-to-day contact with the rank-and-file of the Labour Party. Hence, in the North-West Durham by-election the EFF was used to oppose an old and tried friend within the Liberal Party in favour of the Labour candidate. Alice Clark reported to the Priestmans how 'great excitement' had been caused by the NUWSS's failure to back one of its own members in Aneurin Williams, the Liberal candidate: 'But after all Mr Stuart [the Labour candidate] is just as good and he was there before Mr Williams appeared.'[38]

A few weeks later Catherine Marshall announced to the annual conference of the Independent Labour Party that the NUWSS would honour any pre-existing commitments to Labour candidates, even should the Liberal Party make women's suffrage part of its programme for the next general election. This seemed to those who remained sceptical about the EFF policy to extend it in a way not sanctioned as yet by the membership of the NUWSS. Such opponents attempted to organise resistance to any further such extension of the NUWSS's commitment to the Labour Party at a general meeting in April, but without success. None the less, with the approach of a general election, and as leading Liberals became ever more uneasy about the cooperation between the Labour Party and the NUWSS, old Liberal loyalties among the NUWSS's rank-and-file began to re-assert themselves. Local secretaries wrote to tell of growing disaffection and resignations over the NUWSS's support for the Labour Party.

Opinion within the NUWSS became, then, increasingly polarised. On the one hand, there were those who continued to see the EFF policy as the best strategy for maintaining pressure on the Liberal Party, and holding Labour to its present pro-suffrage stand. On the other were those who refused to be part of such an aggressively anti-Liberal stance, and who argued that recent developments in the EFF campaign meant that the NUWSS could no longer claim to be non-party. Such opponents of the EFF within the NUWSS maintained that its branch societies would not acquiesce in a policy that required them to refuse to campaign on behalf of tried Liberal 'friends'. In one case, it was declared: 'It is hardly too much to say the future of our branch depends on the attitude we adopt [on election policy].' Other Liberal women, in contrast, thankfully continued to contribute to the EFF so as, in the words of one correspondent in the columns of the *Common Cause*:

> to purge my once beloved party – the party which still represents so much that is dear to me and is only going astray on *one* point – of those reactionaries and wobblers against whom I feel an indignation that no woman who is not a Liberal can fully share.[39]

The militants, as we have seen, were even more sadly divided. Nor was there any longer the light-heartedness and gaiety which had been so characteristic of the early years of militant campaigning. In his autobiography Laurence Housman recalled:

> The last two years before the war were a nightmare to which I look back with a memory of wearing anxiety almost as constant as what one experienced during the four years of war which followed. It had then become literally a fight to the death.[40]

This was especially so for Emmeline Pankhurst. These years for her were ones of repeated re-arrest and imprisonment, followed by hunger strikes, after each of which she was released more frail and broken in body, but still indomitable in spirit. Her supporters constantly expected news of her death, 'and a dreadful whisper went about in the Suffrage ranks that if Mrs Pankhurst died, a Cabinet Minister would die too. One, at least, among her followers had vowed to do it and hang for it.' It was concern for Mrs Pankhurst's ever-weakening condition which led Emily Wilding Davison to make the protest during the 1913 Derby that resulted a few days later in her own death from the injuries she had sustained.

For Laurence Housman such 'desperate heroism' came almost as a relief from the 'dark dread' of political assassination which hung over sympathisers of the WSPU. He was speaking in Hyde Park when news of the death of Emily Wilding Davison came, and recalled that the crowd gave 'a low murmur of sympathy'. It was his view that: 'In a strange way her act of self-immolation was popular; it caught the public imagination. . . . In the mind of many thousands hitherto careless or indifferent, it made the demand for Woman Suffrage a serious thing.' He remembered the two-mile-long procession which accompanied her body through London to her funeral as 'a procession of triumph, not of mourning'.[41]

From time to time, however, as the martyrdom of WSPU prisoners grew with harsh prison sentences, repeated hunger strikes, and continued forcible feeding, Laurence Housman would confess a sense of despair over the future of the campaign:

I am feeling not 'down' but very serious about suffrage things: for the more I study the situation the more it seems to me that men don't and won't care enough to get it through until terrible suffering has been presented to them as an object lesson by the women. That is to say 'militancy' of a kind, however much the women may direct the sharp point of it against themselves.

At the same time, he expressed the frustration he felt at not feeling free to join in such suffrage militancy. He believed that he could not morally give 'testimony in the same way', for he possessed all the qualifications for the vote, and found that 'seems to confuse the issue. And yet if Mrs Pankhurst dies I shall find it hard not to go to prison to relieve my conscience.' In the meantime he was engaged in trying to organise a men's suffrage deputation to the Prime Minister, though he believed it unlikely they would be received:

There, with our wretched 'constitutional' ways, we come to an end, while some of our finest women are wearing themselves to death. It is a humiliating position for men to be so tied by the general indifference of their fellows and yet not have the right to revolt.[42]

Clemence Housman, as we have seen, had already gone to gaol, however briefly, for her passive resistance through the non-payment of rates. And shortly, Lawrence Housman also felt driven to seek imprisonment by protesting the forcible feeding of suffragist hunger strikers. After a demonstration outside the House of Commons in which he found himself so 'hurled around' that he was grateful to be arrested, he was bound over to keep the peace for six months.

After refusing this condition for his release, he and the other demon-strators were remanded for a few hours. Then, once the court was empty of observers, they were brought back for a scolding, and released. As he himself noted, Laurence Housman was thus allowed to go scot-free for an offence for which women demonstrators were regularly sentenced to terms of imprisonment.[43]

Afterwards, he sent an account of the incident to Sarah Clark, one in which the tone of self-mockery failed to cloak altogether his sense of powerlessness to make any effective intervention. As he reported it, he was arrested by a 'big beefy ugly policeman', and afterwards:

> I wanted to kiss him because it would have shocked him so much more than having to arrest me. This is only to tell your Quakerish scrupulosity how very *Christian* it all was – so far as the combatants were concerned.

On his unconditional release, he commented:

> It is sickening to think that *I* was let go for doing what women have got three months for: and more horrible still to think that recently a man who seduced his own daughter of 13 and had a child by her only got that same sentence.

He believed a similar protest ought to be made by men every week, until the authorities were forced to imprison them: 'three known men going continuously to prison *might* have an effect so it seems to me'.[44] Yet, it was now clear that to secure such punishment, men would have to engage in a far greater degree of violence than he felt able to endorse. And such protests on the part of male militant sympathisers did not eventuate. Laurence Housman reported how the Men's League for Women's Suffrage declared such action on the part of one of its officials 'hurtful' to its reputation. He also detected an increase in the influence of those who wanted to cooperate more closely with the new Liberal suffrage organisations, beginning to be formed at this time. Laurence Housman himself opposed any such association, and was preparing to resign from the Men's League, and join the United Suffragists if this should eventuate.[45]

Questions of campaign methods and political strategy were not the only source of cross-currents of thought within the suffrage movement in these years. For many suffragists the demand had raised broader questions concerning citizenship and gender identity. We have seen how, over several generations now, suffragists had put forward alternative understandings of citizenship, ones which conformed more closely with their gendered identities as women. Laurence Housman's letters to Sarah and Roger Clark suggest, not surprisingly perhaps, that this project held implications, also, for thinking about manliness, and its relationship to citizenship. For Laurence Housman, and for others, it appeared impossible to examine the nature of manliness without examining also the nature and varieties of male sexuality. Discussion of both questions recurs in the letters between the Housmans and the Clarks. Frequently, this arose with reference to shared reading. At the end of 1912, for example, Laurence and Clemence Housman were reading August Strindberg's *Confessions of a Fool*, which he was to review for *Votes for Women*. He found the picture it provided of sexual relations between men and women was 'as plain and unvarnished a statement as we could wish for, dating back to the year 1870, or thereabouts, of that "sex-war" which is supposed to be the special product of the militant suffragist'.[46] The Housmans offered to lend the book to Sarah Clark, warning that she would find it disagreeable, 'yet suffragists should read what a typical Anti [anti-suffragist] man might swallow greedily'.[47]

Their friend evidently agreed to read it, too, for a few weeks later Laurence Housman was forwarding 'this nasty but interesting book', with the additional comment:

> You are one of the few people I can trust not to be misled by its ferocious one-sidedness. I have dear men-suffrage friends whom I could not trust with it for a moment. Roger I can under your guidance.

Consideration of sexual relationships between men and women evidently led Laurence Housman to question also the supposedly distinctive nature of the masculine and the feminine:

> It struck me while writing this that *Clem* is the right man for *me* in much the same way as Roger is for you: for I think she is as masculine as you and I as feminine as Roger. But Lord love us! . . . how we *are* getting on; for what an insult a decade or two ago it would have been to any man to tell him that he had anything feminine about him! And now – taken rightly – it is something of a compliment: nothing to be vain about, for he can't help it, being born so.[48]

The relationship between sexuality and gendered identities was also a subject of particular interest for him at this time, in part prompted again by shared reading with Clemence Housman. On this occasion, it was Ellen Key's *Love and Marriage*. Laurence Housman reported to Sarah Clark that they disagreed about the argument put forward there that 'woman love usually proceeds from the soul to the senses and sometimes does not reach so far', while the opposite was the case for men. Clemence Housman was doubtful about such a generalisation, but her brother pronounced it 'good and true'. Laurence Housman also found convincing Ellen Key's account of sexual difference with regard to chastity: 'I am reluctant to modify the ideal of absolute equality of conduct: but the springs of motive are different.' He argued that, in consequence, any reform of sexual relations between men and women would have to be based on 'reasonable lines of progression', for, in his view, the differing sexual needs of men and women would not be brought into greater harmony until men had 'evolved a good bit further'.[49] Elsewhere, he declared: 'In no modern community and under no code of laws has there ever yet been sex-peace worthy of the name.' In particular, he identified the physical demands which men made upon women, especially in terms of conjugal rights and their 'consuming desire for sexual possession', as the source of social deterioration. In contrast, he argued that 'the maternal interest is the sounder guide to the strengthening and preservation of the species'.[50]

Motherhood was something which had long fascinated Laurence Housman: 'it is the one architectural fact of life that a man is outside'. It was in this respect that he believed the 'male imagination really fails and lands one in the fundamental reason for "suffragitis" again'.[51] So he was particularly engaged by Ellen Key's discussion of motherhood in terms of its 'strongly sensuous element'.[52] He also confessed the unrealisable longings he had felt to become a mother when he wrote to commiserate with Janet Ashbee on a miscarriage:

> What a Mother Earth of grief you must feel! . . . These are the deep inwards of relationship with creation's plan which men can't share: and by so much we are inferior in consequence. You women are nearer to mother Earth, and the whole ordering of things – of that I have no doubt, and that is one of the whys for my wish to see women take hold of citizenship with both hands and mould things rather more their way than ours.

He believed that in a past life he might himself have been a mother:

'Anyway in this incarnation I have most motherly yearnings, never to be satisfied on the material plane.'[53]

An issue which became especially significant in suffrage polemic at this time was that of venereal disease. Christabel Pankhurst had published a shocking exposé, *The Great Scourge*, which argued that venereal disease was so widespread among men that celibacy was the only safe option for women. Though her figures were almost certainly somewhat exaggerated, a subsequent Royal Commission on Venereal Diseases did find considerable cause for concern. It reported evidence of the extent of ignorance of these diseases among women, an ignorance which the medical profession often fostered in order to protect erring husbands. It also gathered information which suggested the impact which such ignorance was making on both women's and children's health.

Laurence Housman himself encountered the growing interest in such questions during an international medical congress in London in 1913. He reported 'a sort of appalling staleness' after hearing discussion of a 'very difficult and rather unspeakable problem in sex matters', 'an intimate and painful sex-problem'. He also found, though, that the presence of women during the discussion had proved 'wonderful and fine . . . making it *better* by their presence in spite of the added painfulness'. At this sign 'I lifted up my heart and thanked God for the suffrage movement which has made such a thing possible. We move, we do move, and I'm glad to be alive here and now.' He had been pleased, too, that when he 'spoke for the woman's suffrage side of the solution there was a quite general agreement'. He received similar support when he insisted that women should form a part of any investigating committee to be established, though afterwards he commented: 'The difficulty is what women to ask . . . to be sure that we are getting those with absolutely open minds and yet not cranky or revolutionary extremists.'[54]

The focus of this discussion is not clear from his veiled references, but hinged in some way on varieties of sexual expression. A few months later he was telling friends about the formation of the British Society of Psychiatry which had arisen out of such discussion at the medical conference on 'the homogenic question'. He had been asked to attend this session by Edward Carpenter and 'put the suffrage point of view'. The immediate goal of the new organisation, almost certainly the body which was subsequently known as the British Society for the Study of Sex Psychology, was the 'translation of

German scientific investigations'. He consented to be on the committee of the new society

> on the condition that women – preferably women doctors – were included. . . . It is wonderful how open to a free discussion of everything I now find women – Suffragist women I mean. And of course it is the movement that has done it: even in the last two years the advance has been immense: and between now and six years ago it is as if a century had awakened . . . things are really getting on – and probably the fight for the apparently 'inessential' vote has been the essential cause of it.[55]

The British Society for the Study of Sex Psychology (BSSSP) was established as a group dedicated to exploring issues relating to sexuality. In its beginnings, the society included about eight women doctors, a few men doctors, two or three lawyers and four schoolmasters. Dr Hilda Clark was among those who lent it early support, and Laurence Housman hoped initially that she might be co-opted on to its committee.[56] Sarah and Roger Clark also took an interest in its proceedings. Laurence Housman reported after its inaugural meeting: 'All promises well for the future: the fear-barriers are broken down, and I think we have now got it quite fixed that our line is fearless *investigation* and the demand for *understanding:* but not propaganda on moralist lines.'[57] Lesley Hall has recently suggested the need to modify earlier views of the BSSSP as 'a crypto-homosexual rights organisation'. Her survey of its history suggests rather that it had 'a wider perspective', and that its prime goal was to foster 'a much broader re-conceptualisation of the meaning of sexuality within society'.[58] It did not engage in overtly political campaigning, but concentrated instead on promoting a greater understanding of 'expert' and 'scientific' opinion on such questions. Hence, Edward Carpenter gave an address on 'Inversion', one of the most common terms then applied to homosexuality, at its first meeting.

Same-sex, loving relationships were not uncommon among suffragists, male and female. Their existence was, and continues frequently to be noted in order to confirm pathological interpretations of the movement itself. So male suffragists were frequently derided at the time as effeminate, a charge intended to undermine their credibility, and prove the illegitimacy of the claim itself.[59] Similarly, George Dangerfield's early and influential account of these years portrays a lesbian current among suffrage militants as a symptom both of a social pathology, and the forces of unreason, in the re-emergence of 'primitive' patterns:

> To recover her womanhood woman must go out into the wilderness there to be alone with herself and her sisters . . . and it was from some secret yearning to recover the wisdom of women that the homosexual movement first manifested itself, in 1912, among the suffragettes.[60]

The matter had great actuality and immediacy for many in this period, and a significance not restricted to the militant wing of the movement. Hilda Clark's interest in the discussions within the BSSSP were almost certainly personal as well as professional. Her romantic friendship with Edith Pye had begun while she was completing her medical training in the women's hospital in Birmingham, and it continued for the rest of their lives. The friendship brought Edith Pye into a more active role in the suffrage movement, and had already proved a great support to Hilda Clark. These were testing years, as she established a career in medicine, and confronted the limits and possibilities of her profession when called on to supervise the medical care of close family and friends, including both Alice Clark and Edith Pye herself, when each succumbed to tuberculosis.

Same-sex love in this period was frequently conceived of in terms of 'comradeship', borrowing from a poem of Walt Whitman's, 'The dear love of comrades'. The phrase held a special resonance for the group of militant irregulars which included Emily Wilding Davison.[61] By 'comradeship' was implied a selfless kind of loving, spiritually and morally elevating to the giver, especially as it developed a more general capacity for loving humankind. It promised to make better citizens by fostering such fellow-feeling. The letters of Hilda Clark to Edith Pye make it clear that she understood their love as something different from both heterosexual love and maternal love – 'marvellous and beautiful and wholly good as both those are in their ideal forms'. Their relationship, she thankfully believed, to be quite 'independent of the outward circumstances on which the other two depend. There is nothing in life that I am more thankful for than that thou and I can have, and will one day perfect, the true spirit love.'[62]

While physical signs of affection were evidently a satisfying part of their relationship, Hilda Clark did not primarily understand it in sexual terms. Indeed, she rejoiced in how such 'spirit love' had released her from physical desires that she had earlier known:

> I used to feel the power to love was a bitter cruel thing like
> the power to bear children – dependent on outward circum-
> stances for its fulfilment – and I suppose it is so. Oh how hard
> it used to be to feel how one could love if one might – but
> one learned much from having it withheld.[63]

Their relationship was maintained through long periods of separation, and provided Hilda Clark with the strength she felt she needed
to maintain a single life: 'I do not feel nearly so dependent on
marriage to complete myself – though I know it would bring me a
world of new experiences and teach one to understand things that
perhaps one would not fully understand without.'[64] And she also
believed that such a life might develop in herself greater powers for
good:

> I think love is the only thing that carries beyond. . . . I learn
> to love by loving thee dear creature, dear friend that this
> outward world has brought me in contact with. I do try so
> hard to keep my love pure and unselfish – and not only
> outward. Dear Twin-soul.[65]

In such an idealised and idealistic relationship, Hilda Clark found
what proved for her the greatest liberation of all, a liberation from
some of the desires and demands attaching to a woman's body,
bringing with it also the promise of an enlarged conception of
citizenship.

10

WOMEN'S SUFFRAGE AND THE FIRST WORLD WAR

Walking on a beach in Dorset, one day in the early summer of 1914, Alice Clark fell into conversation with a laundry worker. Women's suffrage was their topic. Afterwards she wrote to Anna Maria and Mary Priestman of how this working-class woman had explained her involvement in the suffrage campaign: 'she felt very independent and quite worthy of having a vote. She had brought up a family on laundry work, apprenticed three sons and supported one who was an invalid, and never had either charity or poor relief'.[1] This working woman, then, thought of her claim to the franchise in terms of an independence established through her own labour, both productive and reproductive. It was a way of conceiving of citizenship which drew on the long-established radical notion of independence, a notion which, over the previous few decades, had undergone expansion in terms of the common property of women and men in their capacity to work. Women's suffragists expanded this conception of citizenship still further to incorporate the sexual labour particular to women: bearing children, loving men, and nurturing the young, weak and needy.

The more effective mobilisation of working-class suffragists, like Alice Clark's anonymous walking companion, became a key part of NUWSS strategy in the two years before war broke out, and various methods were adopted for reaching and registering that support. The two women had met at a Women's Suffrage Camp at Upwey, where Alice Clark's small home-town of Street had provided a fifth of all the participants. She was joined from time to time by other members of her family, including her mother, Helen Priestman Bright Clark, and her aunt Dr Annie Clark, both now in their seventies. Such events brought together suffragists from varying backgrounds and districts, in a relaxed environment where they could meet and exchange views, and build that cross-class solidarity among women so essential to the EFF strategy. During the camp, reading groups were organised, with a focus on aspects of social policy relating to women and children, and there was the opportunity of training for, and practising public-speaking on women's suffrage in the impromptu meetings held in the small villages and towns around the camp.

By 1914 the NUWSS could take satisfaction in the success of such efforts to maintain popular support for votes for women, and especially the support of organised labour, in the face of escalating violence on the part of militants, and the active harassment of Labour politicians. Shortly after announcing the EFF policy, the NUWSS had also established its Friends of Women's Suffrage scheme, aimed especially at organising and demonstrating support among those who could not afford its membership fees, or who did not feel free or ready, for whatever reason, to join formally a suffrage society. Such 'friends' were recruited either by house-to-house canvassing in working-class districts, or among the crowds of observers attracted by the local open-air meetings which were another function of the suffrage camps, summer schools and the cycle and caravan tours which the suffrage movement had also adopted in imitation of socialist modes of campaigning.

By such means the continuing commitment of organised labour to votes for women was sustained. But some sections of the Labour movement proved hard to win over, and the ambivalence of the miners' leaders was a particular cause for concern, as they controlled a large block of votes at Labour Party annual conferences. Part of the work of the EFF from 1913, in consequence, was directed at strengthening women's suffrage support in mining villages and among local union branches. Its success was evident at the Durham miners' gala in 1914. The incorporation of suffrage speakers in the plans for the gala was a notable departure, and women's suffrage was one of the themes taken up by miners' leaders in their addresses. One of these leaders was Robert Smillie, who had been the first to experience the WSPU's shift away from its socialist origins in the Cockermouth by-election of 1907, and on whose behalf Mary Gawthorpe had conducted her last major campaign as a Labour organiser. On this occasion, and despite the WSPU's now active hostility to the Labour Party, Robert Smillie declared his readiness to call a general strike in support of votes for women. Margaret Ashton of the Manchester Society expressed something of the new confidence such support brought to the leadership of the NUWSS. She was about to lead a Liberal deputation to the Prime Minister during the forthcoming National Liberal Federation conference, intending, as she declared, 'to *tell* him not to ask him anything'.[2]

The Liberal leadership was increasingly concerned both at the defections among its own women supporters, and the stalemate over franchise reform which had arisen from its failure to deal with the issue of women's suffrage. Not only were the Liberal Party's own interests seen to lie in the creation of a democratic franchise, but this was ground which the Labour Party was now seizing as its own. At the same time, the Liberal government's resort to political repression through censorship, forcible feeding, the Cat and Mouse Act, and threats to WSPU subscribers, had not secured an end to suffrage militancy. Indeed, the acts of individual militants were becoming ever more desperate, and a similar spirit was evident among some sections of male sympathisers. Militant demonstrators were also causing increasing inconvenience and threats to the dignity, if not the safety, of the establishment, from the mayor's parlour to Buckingham Palace. And so, led by David Lloyd George, the Liberal leadership set about taking a lead once again on the question of franchise reform, in the month or so preceding the outbreak of war.

In this, the government sought to profit from the fragmentation of the militant wing of the movement, by appealing especially to the democratic suffragist current of opinion evident among the dissident militants and their organisations. Hence, David Lloyd George conducted his negotiations through Sylvia Pankhurst and George Lansbury. He promised a new government Reform Bill, to include a women's suffrage clause on which the Liberal leadership would guarantee a free vote. As evidence of good faith, he interceded with Reginald McKenna, the Home Secretary, to prevent the re-arrest of Sylvia Pankhurst under the Cat and Mouse Act:

> She and her friends mean to throw in their lot with the constitutionalists against the Militants. This would be useful and unless she is guilty of some outburst – which is extremely improbable – would it not be desirable to leave her alone?

This request was sent with a covering note which suggested Herbert Asquith's complicity in these negotiations: 'Since writing enclosed letter, the Chancellor saw the Prime Minister who promised to see the Home Secretary and arrange matters with him.'[3]

In this period, the Prime Minister also received a deputation from the East London Federation of Suffragettes. The occasion enabled Herbert Asquith to use the representations of the working-class suffragists to concede that women's suffrage must come, but to indicate his determination that when it did, it would be as part of a thorough overhaul of the British electoral system: 'If the change has to come, we must face it boldly and make it thoroughgoing and democratic in its basis.' David Morgan has suggested that, with a general election looming, 'Asquith was firing the opening shot of the campaign.'[4] It presented a solution to the question which NUWSS leaders had been advocating in their dealings with the Cabinet for the previous year or so. Catherine Marshall had already put it to the Chancellor of the Exchequer that the promotion of 'a really effective demand for Adult Suffrage . . . at the same time as your land campaign . . . would be a grand programme on which to go to the country'.[5] Now, Sylvia Pankhurst pushed for even more definite evidence of the government's new commitment:

> What a splendid rally there would be if a Franchise Bill for Manhood and Womanhood suffrage were carried in this Parliament. If the Lords were to throw it out, it wouldn't matter at all – it would only be a temporary delay that would make the enthusiasm the greater and it would be the best rallying cry for the General Election.[6]

Not surprisingly, Christabel Pankhurst refused any part in these negotiations, or any acknowledgment of the significant concession which had been won from the Liberal leadership. But, by this shift the government gained the compliance of the ELFS and the United Suffragists, isolated the WSPU, and undermined whatever legitimacy might previously have attached to militant methods.

No doubt Laurence Housman had these developments in mind when he wrote optimistically to Sarah Clark late in June 1914, emphasising the importance of the more conciliatory attitude now evident among anti-suffragist ministers:

> Under the surface hopeful influences are at work: but I expect there must be more suffering and perhaps a tragedy before they come to a head. Nevertheless McKenna's speech was to me remarkably significant: and every politician I have talked to about it thinks so too.

In the meantime, he and Clemence Housman continued to subscribe openly to the WSPU, in the face of the declared intent of the authorities to seek damages from those who offered such support. He reported: 'We are disposing of all our worldly goods so as to challenge the threats of Government.'[7]

The leaderships of the NUWSS and Women's Liberal Federation were not initially included in the negotiations between suffragists and the Liberal leadership, no doubt because the primary concern was to secure the end of militancy. The leadership of both organisations was anyway dominated by democratic suffragists who might be relied upon to support a solution to the question in terms of a universal suffrage. None the less, some among the NUWSS's leadership were disturbed by the recognition which the government's dealings had given to a section of the militant wing. Like Sylvia Pankhurst, Catherine Marshall was convinced that revolutionary change must come to British society, and shortly. For her, the women's movement, the Labour movement and the movement for colonial freedom formed together a significant advance in human affairs. But she was also committed to securing radical social change by peaceful methods, and saw the citizenship of women as central to that goal: 'The great mission awaiting women is to help keep the great revolution which is coming on sane and humane lines. I believe women will have no small voice in determining the manner in which that revolution is brought about.' It was for this reason that she doubted the government's wisdom in lending legitimacy to the alliance between dissident militants and rebel socialists in the East London Federation of Suffragettes and United Suffragists: 'It is going to matter to the whole future of civilisation how the suffrage is won in England. It is vitally important . . . that it should not even appear as a concession to militancy.'[8]

Even so, Catherine Marshall and other democratic suffragists could not fail to be gratified by the advance which the government proposal represented, and the new unity it promised for their cause. It served only to confirm their commitment to the democratic suffragist perspective, and its pursuit through the work of the EFF. Some have argued that women's suffrage eventually came about as a result of women's participation in the mass mobilisation required by the 'total war' of the 1914–18 global conflict. The events described above would suggest that, if anything, the outbreak of war in August 1914 may have delayed the enfranchisement of women. This goal had attained a fresh actuality with the new Reform Bill being planned as part of the Liberal programme for the general election anticipated in 1915, and postponed because of the war until 1918.

Alice Clark was out of England at the time of these events, staying in Germany with an old family friend, the Professor of Sociology at Kiel University, Ferdinand Tönnies. They had corresponded regularly over the previous few years, and it seems likely that her presence there reflected their shared adherence to an internationalist perspective. Ferdinand Tönnies had become increasingly anxious about the possibility of war between their two countries, and had confided to Alice Clark his attempts to organise resistance to war among Germany's intelligentsia. A letter which Alice Clark received from another friend while staying in Germany urged the need 'to turn what one knows about brotherhood and unity of human beings into action, to live it actively'.[9] But such ideals were quickly submerged with the war fever which followed the declaration of hostilities on 4 August 1914.

Alice Clark now joined her closest colleagues among the leadership of the NUWSS in hoping to see the suffrage movement promote conciliation between warring nations. Democratic suffragists throughout the movement generally shared an internationalist outlook, and it was in this that the distinctiveness of their approach to citizenship now became apparent. They found themselves increasingly at odds with former colleagues whose ambitions for citizenship reflected, in contrast, a patriotic identity. The outbreak of war represented a most terrible defeat, then, for both internationalism and democratic suffragism. It put an end to the optimistic belief in human progress which had informed such an outlook, and yet again crushed hopes for a suffrage victory which had seemed so close. When Mary and Anna Maria Priestman died within days of each other in October 1914, their obituary recorded their ardent pacifism and how the South African war had 'distressed them so deeply that their health was permanently impaired'. The outbreak of a new and more awful conflict proved 'too much to bear and brought on illnesses from which they died within five days of one another'.[10]

The outbreak of war brought disillusion also to many militant supporters. Laurence Housman resigned from the Franchise Club, for example, when its members rejected his appeal for considerate treatment of German women stranded in Britain by the war. He felt that such attitudes were a betrayal of 'the international character' of the suffrage movement, which, like many democratic suffragists, he believed to have been one of the fundamental pillars of women's claim to citizenship.[11] The WSPU leadership further divided its supporters when it declared an end to all suffrage campaigning, and took an increasingly prominent role in recruitment drives for the armed forces and the munitions industry. Internationalism was a common value among militant 'irregulars', and, in consequence, many, like Rose Lamartine Yates, now broke away to form groups like the Independent Suffragettes of the WSPU as a voice for such opinion. For his part, Laurence Housman at last felt justified in joining with the dissident militants of the United Suffragists, among whom he found a consistent adherence to a democratic, inter-nationalist perspective on women's citizenship. Other dissident militant organisations, including the Women's Freedom League and the East London Federation of Suffragettes, also decided to continue their campaign for the vote, and to support a peaceful settlement of the war.

In the political context which attended the war, however, there was little opportunity of employment for suffrage or labour organisers out of sympathy with the war effort. Early in 1916, Mary Gawthorpe and her mother at last left England for a long-postponed visit to her married sister, who had emigrated to the United States some years before. She recorded herself as still 'somewhat like a shell-shocked soldier who wishes to get back to the work-standard quietly' at the time of her arrival there.[12] The change of scene evidently restored her to better health, however. She had old friends from suffrage days who were also then living in the United States, including Beatrice Forbes-Robertson Hale, who introduced her to leading members of the movement there. Mary Gawthorpe at last returned to suffrage campaigning some time in the autumn of 1916, when she joined the staff of the New York Woman Suffrage Party in Eyrie County. One of those who worked alongside her then later recalled that her press work in Buffalo was 'one of the most telling factors' in the November 1917 vote there for women's suffrage.[13]

For some time yet, Alice Clark, along with other internationalists, was able to continue her role within the leadership of the NUWSS. The commitment of such democratic suffragists to constitutionalism had reflected both a faith in the power of reason in human affairs, and a rejection of methods of violence and physical force. These were beliefs shared by Millicent Garrett Fawcett. But her consti-tutionalism was also informed by strong patriot values which now led her to resist the influence of the internationalists within the NUWSS. The British heritage of constitutional change was, according to her view, the greatest contribution which her country had to offer the world, and she interpreted the current conflict as one on behalf of democracy, reason and progress against Prussian absolutism and brutish militarism. So she sought a role for the NUWSS in support of Britain's war effort, as altogether of a piece with its commitment to the constitutional pursuit of women's citizenship, and the realisation of Britain's particular role in world history. While Millicent Garrett Fawcett resisted attempts on the part of her inter-nationalist colleagues to use the NUWSS to help stop the war, she did not abandon her commitment to gaining the vote for women. Pragmatism dictated that the campaign be suspended until franchise reform was once again on the political agenda, but her most immedi-ate aim meanwhile was to maintain the organisational strength of the NUWSS and, if possible, to avoid the further fragmentation and organisational decline which the war brought to the WSPU.

To these ends, internationalists and patriots within the NUWSS were united. Securing women's citizenship took on, if anything, an even greater urgency for those to whom the current situation exemplified, at least in part, the inadequacies of all-male polities, where women's needs, perspectives and values might be ignored at will. So patriots and internationalists within the NUWSS leadership managed, for some time, to maintain a semblance of unity by com-mitting the resources of their society to the relief of the distress occasioned by the social dislocation accompanying the outbreak of war. For the time being there was hunger, unemployment and need, especially among women and children, as men left for the front, many were thrown out of work, and prices began to rise. Such humanitarian endeavours were consistent with the goals of both groups, and NUWSS branches played a major role in many local relief committees. Alice Clark wrote home on the frustration of her work on one such committee, and 'how invincibly stupid' she found the officials in control of war relief provision.[14] But the strength and coherence of the NUWSS network of branches was preserved to a quite remarkable degree by such means, so that it was well able, when the time came, to take up the campaign for women's suffrage once more.

Nor did the NUWSS restrict its humanitarian efforts to the home front. One of its most successful operations was the Scottish Women's Hospitals Units, formed by Dr Elsie Inglis of the Edinburgh Society, which took suffragists into some of the worst of the war zones, and in the service of which a number lost their lives. Dr Hilda Clark was another member of the NUWSS who set out to provide medical relief, in this instance for civilian victims of the war in Europe. She proposed to the regular Quaker Meeting for Sufferings in September 1914 that the Society of Friends should 'support a movement to give medical and ambulance help to the non-combatants in France or Belgium'. Her proposal was taken up and she herself was among those sent to France by the Friends War Victims Relief Committee.[15] Under its auspices she helped establish maternity and children's hospitals for refugees, as well as sanatoria for tuberculosis sufferers. It was work which initially brought separation from Edith Pye, but within a few months she too joined the Quaker relief effort in France. Alice Clark also sought to prepare herself to help in this work, beginning training in London as a midwife at the beginning of 1915, while assuring her evidently worried mother that it was 'not nearly so hard as hospital work'.[16]

Two different approaches became evident among the NUWSS's internationalists in the first months of the war. First, there were the pacifists, among whom were Helena Swanwick and Isabella Ford, who wanted the NUWSS to lead an anti-war campaign. They were very soon also closely involved in the anti-war organisation, the Union for Democratic Control (UDC). This body attracted the support of leading Liberal and Labour politicians opposed to the war, including Charles Trevelyan and James Ramsay Macdonald. Its members believed that peace would have been preserved if there had been full democracies in Britain and Germany, and if foreign affairs were conducted openly, so that there had been a fully informed public opinion which might have been mobilised against such an outcome. It sought the immediate cessation of hostilities and arbitration between the two sides. The UDC attracted so much support from individuals and branches of the NUWSS, that some of the patriots feared their organisation was about to be entirely overtaken.

A second group of more moderate internationalists advocated using the NUWSS simply for an educational campaign on the causes and prevention of war in general, rather than any more contentious alliance with organisations which were aimed directly at ending the present war, or advocating pacifism. This compromise was promoted by Catherine Marshall, Alice Clark, and the NUWSS's secretary, Kathleen Courtney, in the hopes that it would prove acceptable to patriots, internationalists and pacifists alike. In the event, the internationalists secured the withdrawal of Millicent Garrett Fawcett's contentious resolution for a general meeting of the NUWSS, which had read: 'The British Empire is fighting the battle of representative government and progressive democracy all over the world and therefore the aim of the National Union as a part of the general democratic movement is involved in it.'[17] The moderate internationalists secured instead resolutions which argued for an educational campaign 'to keep public opinion sane'. They also endorsed a recent statement by Herbert Asquith of Britain's war aims as 'the enthronement of the idea of public rights as the governing idea of European politics', a 'repudiation of militarism', 'the independent existence and free development of the smaller nationalities', and finally 'the substitution for force . . . of a real European partnership based on the recognition of equal rights and established and enforced by a common will'. The NUWSS's rank-and-file supported this position, and also resolved on this occasion that the *Common Cause* should carry articles on the causes and prevention of war.[18]

This outcome left Alice Clark hopeful, for, as she wrote to Catherine Marshall, she felt the meeting 'had drawn people together instead of separating them'. None the less, she remained uncertain as to the best course to follow now:

> I wish I could see rather more clearly what the National Union ought to be at. . . . Obviously, our position as a Suffrage Society is very difficult. If the war is to last three years I doubt if we can keep our people together on Relief Work, unless we can take a stronger line.

Yet she evidently felt they did not have the strength to press their own position any more forcefully, while adding 'I rather wonder whether we are making the most of our connections with the Labour Party.' She hoped that her own appointment to the Women's Unemployment Sub-committee of the Southwark Relief Committee might help in this respect.[19]

As a middle way, she suggested the NUWSS might 'give more guidance to our members as to the objects we have in view in the prosecution of relief work . . . they want to be expressed with a voice that can reach the public generally'. In her own view, such efforts were not simply aimed at 'keeping women and children alive but at strengthening the position of women and developing their capacity and their sense of citizenship. But I don't believe we are saying so enough.' Beyond this, she also saw it as a proper role for the NUWSS to educate its members on the problem of 'Militarism' and 'the methods which are needed to protect humanity against a repetition of the horror of this war'.[20]

This letter also makes clear where her views differed from Helena Swanwick, Isabella Ford and Maude Royden, who wished to commit the NUWSS to an outright stop-the-war position like that of the UDC:

> I don't think it is our place to prescribe the means [for ending the war], but I do think it is our duty to encourage our members to think, just as I believed it was our duty to encourage our members to think about the means of preventing infant mortality and the abuses which the law permits to be inflicted on married women.

She summed up her view of matters thus: 'We have at one end Mrs Fawcett and doubtless many other people of less importance who are much more inclined to really militarist ideas than she is.' At the other end, she saw Maude Royden, Helena Swanwick and Isabella Ford 'who perhaps really think that England could have kept out of this and watched Germany beating France. At least the ardour of their non-resistance line gives colour to that.' She felt that the extremity of either view endangered the possibility of 'practical politics and the prevention of war in the future'.[21]

But she also believed that within the NUWSS there was 'a middle party who is bent only on the prevention of future wars'. Alice Clark hoped that, together with Catherine Marshall and Kathleen Courtney, it might prove possible to rally this body of opinion sufficiently to achieve 'a compromise which will be really of practical utility'. All three groups were equally loyal to the NUWSS, and 'I feel it will be worth Mrs Fawcett's rather unwilling acquiescence, the evident sacrifice which she felt she was making to preserve peace will induce the others to temper their ideals to practical aims.' The compromise position achieved at the November Council had yet to be ratified at the coming annual meeting, but Alice Clark was hopeful 'if we can get the resolutions well drafted'. To this end, she advocated extensive negotiations beforehand, so as to 'avoid red herrings' should the varying parties feel dissatisfied with the particular formulations of policy put forward on the agenda.

In the months that followed, however, Millicent Garrett Fawcett became increasingly sure of a large body of support for her own patriot perspective among the membership of the NUWSS. At the same time, many of her colleagues in the leadership were publicly identifying themselves more and more with pacifist and inter-nationalist perspectives on the war. In consequence, she became ever more intransigent in her opposition to *any* internationalist initiative on the part of the NUWSS, however non-confrontational. It was clear that the consensus reached at the November Council remained a fragile one, and that the divisions within the NUWSS leadership were only intensifying.

These were difficult months for Alice Clark, as she attempted to negotiate between the three distinct bodies of opinion among her closest colleagues. The resolutions drafted by herself, Catherine Marshall and Kathleen Courtney for the annual meeting were first altered by Millicent Garrett Fawcett, and then 'greatly improved in the Executive'. In the beginning, she was hopeful that she might serve as a consensus-broker and conciliator, like her great-aunt Priscilla Bright McLaren many decades before. She was pleased to be selected to play a key role in finding a formulation of the NUWSS's policy on the war behind which all parties might unite, reporting 'I was favoured in the Executive to redraft a very contentious resolution in a form which met with unanimous approval.' She maintained her hope, as a consequence, of securing the unity of the NUWSS:

> I think there are on the Executive people with as widely divergent views as any in the Union, so I hope the consent of the Executive will foretell the unity of the Council. The Resolutions are not drastic but make a foundation on which a sound public opinion may be built up.[22]

Such hopes foundered at the NUWSS's annual meeting in Febru-ary 1915 when it failed to ratify every element in the compromise which had been brokered in November. While NUWSS members declared their preference for arbitration over war, and support for 'a real international partnership based on the recognition of equal right and established and enforced by a common will,' they rejected the proposal to use their organisation for an educational campaign in support of such principles.[23] Helena Swanwick, Catherine Marshall and Kathleen Courtney all resigned at this point from the executive committee, while Maude Royden resigned as editor of the *Common Cause*.

For the time being other internationalists, including Alice Clark, remained in the hopes of upholding their perspective within the NUWSS's leadership. But matters came to a head over the question of whether or not the NUWSS should send delegates to an international congress of women in the Hague. This congress had grown out of an initiative from Dutch suffragists, seeking to use the united strength of women's movements around the world to bring an end to the war. Helen Priestman Bright Clark was among those who had given her active and vocal support for such an attempt. The internationalists believed that NUWSS participation would be fully consistent with the position adopted at its annual meeting, but Millicent Garrett Fawcett insisted that the congress was a peace conference, and that the executive had no mandate to take part in such a forum. She argued that any official association would damage 'the reputation of the National Union for common sense', and indicate a 'total aloofness from national sentiment'. Again, a compromise was agreed whereby individual NUWSS members might attend the congress, but not as representatives of the NUWSS.[24]

Many branches of the NUWSS, including the Clark family's local society in Street, rejected this compromise, however, and insisted on their right to send delegates to the Hague congress. Margaret Ashton reported that Manchester suffragists felt the executive 'were overstraining their powers and over-riding the Societies. It had seriously considered leaving the Union.'[25] Alice Clark was ill once more, and out of London at this time. She reported herself 'in bed in quiet in the sunshine of a revolving shelter', suggesting fears of a recurrence of the tuberculosis from which she had recovered three years before. She wrote to Catherine Marshall of these events: 'Your news appals me.' She agreed that a stand now had to be made against Millicent Garrett Fawcett, and that they should seek the endorsement of the societies for such rebellion. But she added, 'I doubt the fight being successful. All the backward and ignorant societies will follow Mrs Fawcett.' Though unable herself to attend the Hague congress, she supported NUWSS representation there, believing that 'this international women's movement is our greatest hope'. She offered secretarial and organising aid, and money, but added 'I am unable to do much in the fight if that is decided on. I am a poor fighter at any time, I hate it so much.'[26] The next day, having learned more of proceedings in London, she declared:

These new interpretations that separate societies mayn't act on their own seem to me to leave no choice but for such societies to leave the Union. . . . If complete liberty is not given to individual societies, the Union must break. Action as a whole is evidently impossible.[27]

Alice Clark wished that they might ' "evacuate" the sentimentality out of the Peace Movement. There is no need for it, our case is strong enough without.' Her experiences while training as a midwife in Battersea also led her now to question the adequacy of suffragism itself. She found the lives of the women she encountered there 'simply appalling and I do not think votes will help them much unless we can win for them some measure of personal freedom'. The position of these married, working-class women clearly represented for her the worst depths of women's subordination, for their personal freedom depended entirely on

> the good will and pleasure of their husbands. . . . Such dependence degrades them into slaves. After all what the vote means to us is Liberty, Freedom, and I think we must make it clearer to the world. To do this we must face this economic issue and be prepared to press for a solution.

These dual concerns, with the 'sentimentality' of the peace movement and the inadequacy of suffragism, together suggested to her the need for a new women's organisation, one which combined internationalism and an enlarged conception of women's citizenship which went beyond the vote for its own sake. Pragmatically, too, she believed 'we should arouse far more enthusiasm by the boldness of this demand which would catch hold of the imagination of the younger generation in a way votes for women does not'.[28]

She was now convinced that any new organisation 'if it is to be fruitful' must fully develop the 'feminist side' in its approach. She drafted a constitution for such a body which was to have as its dual objects the creation of a 'Permanent Peace among Nations', and the 'Parliamentary Franchise for Women'. It was a society which was to seek 'Liberty, Equality and Fraternity' for all 'irrespective of sex, class, or race'. Alice Clark evidently hoped that her proposed organisation would facilitate continuing cross-class campaigning among women, and that it might 'take in the Women's Co-op [Guild] en bloc, and at the same time enable them to continue their development without being over-shadowed by the middle-class'. She also anticipated that it would attract members from some of the NUWSS branches, the Fellowship of Reconciliation, the Christian pacifist group with which Maude Royden was associated, and the No Conscription Fellowship, the running of which Catherine Marshall took over when its male secretary was imprisoned.[29]

In the meantime, the executive committee had continued to bar formal NUWSS participation in the Hague congress. The resignation of more internationalists, including Alice Clark, followed, amid accusations of a 'tide which is converting the Union into a de facto autocracy, under the cover of a de jure democratic constitution'. A Special Council meeting, called in June 1915, resulted in a victory for the patriots, and a rejection of any role for the NUWSS in internationalist and pacifist undertakings.[30] A deep bitterness over these events remained evident in Millicent Garrett Fawcett's attitude to her former colleagues for years afterwards, despite the tenacious efforts which a number of the internationalists had made to find a compromise.

Though all the internationalists had resigned from the NUWSS's executive committee by this point, a number, including Catherine Marshall and Alice Clark, remained on the Election Fighting Fund for some time longer. By May, however, the new leadership of the NUWSS was interpreting the Council's resolution to suspend political activity as grounds also for bringing a halt to EFF organisation. Catherine Marshall, as secretary of the EFF, and Margaret Hills (formerly Robertson) as its chief organiser, immediately resigned as officers, although they remained as members of that committee. Catherine Marshall and Kathleen Courtney evidently hoped that the NUWSS's organisation and resources might now be divided between the democratic suffragists who remained committed to the EFF, and those who sought its winding up. According to this plan the EFF committee was to form the nucleus for a new women's organisation which would 'work for the general advancement of women's position, socially, industrially, economically and politically'.[31] No record remains of any discussions around such a proposal, and nothing resulted from it immediately. But it would seem to be linked in nature to Alice Clark's proposal for a new society, and was followed by the formation in Britain some months later of a section of the Women's International League for Peace and Freedom.

In the meantime, Alice Clark and Margaret Ashton remained on the EFF committee to argue that the NUWSS must honour earlier commitments made to the Labour Party. Catherine Marshall was allowed to make representations to a meeting of the committee in July 1915, and appears to have convinced the NUWSS leadership of the importance of keeping in close touch with the Labour leadership, and of the need to put the suspension of the EFF policy into as positive a light as possible. A struggle was maintained for some months more, however, concerning EFF activity in East Bristol and

Accrington, the only two constituencies where active support of the Labour candidate had been maintained. The first case was felt to be especially embarrassing by the patriots who now dominated the NUWSS leadership. The Labour candidate there, Walter Ayles, adopted a no-conscription platform after which they attempted to halt all registration work on his behalf. The East Bristol Society retaliated by threatening to withdraw altogether from the NUWSS. Catherine Marshall once more drew the executive's attention to pledges made earlier, and it decided on the wisdom of accepting her advice. Thus the NUWSS found itself providing election aid to a no-conscription Labour candidate. But Ray Strachey succeeded in otherwise securing the practical end of all other EFF activity at the NUWSS's general meeting in February 1916. At this point seven of the most committed democratic suffragists on the EFF committee resigned, including Alice Clark, Catherine Marshall, Margaret Ashton, and Isabella Ford. Somewhat dishonestly the new EFF committee wrote to Labour leaders claiming that this development involved no practical change in attitude of the NUWSS to the Labour Party. Arthur Henderson and W. A. C. Anderson sent cordial replies, though the latter's also contained a sting in the tail: 'You may be quite certain that whatever you decide to do in the future, there will be no change in our attitude on a question which is to us a matter of principle and not expediency.'[32] The EFF committee eventually wound itself up in November 1917, by which time women's suffrage was assured.

Few British suffragists were able to attend the Hague congress in the event. Even those who had succeeded in obtaining passports from the government found themselves trapped in Britain by government instructions which closed the North Sea to non-combatants. However, there were enough British suffragists already in Europe to give their movement some representation, and later in 1915 the British section of the Women's International League for Peace and Freedom (WILPF) was formed. There is no evidence of Alice Clark's involvement in its foundation. By the latter part of 1915 she had joined the Quaker relief effort in France. But it conformed to her original proposal for a new society, being committed to the dual aims of achieving citizenship for women, and a permanent arbitration mechanism for all international disputes. Not surprisingly, the WILPF attracted internationalist and democratic suffragists from all parts of the movement, including Helena Swanwick, Catherine Marshall, Kathleen Courtney, Maude Royden, Isabella Ford and

Margaret Ashton from the NUWSS, alongside Charlotte Despard from the Women's Freedom League and Emmeline Pethick Lawrence from the United Suffragists.

It was also an organisation which attracted the support of working-class women, especially socialist suffragists. Hannah Mitchell was one who took an active part in the WILPF in Manchester. Internationalism had always been central to her radicalism: 'All my life I had hated war.' In this, if not in her atheism, she was followed by her sixteen-year-old son who 'withstood all the recruiting appeals of the first months', instead taking a course in ambulance work. She later recalled 'I waited, in such agony of mind, that I look back on that time as a reprieved man might look back on the time spent in the condemned cell.' As the time for his call-up came near, 'I felt I couldn't bear to live if I knew he had killed another woman's son, but it was for him to decide, and I saw he was slowly making up his mind.' Her son applied for exemption from combatant service, and asked instead to be allowed to join the Royal Army Medical Corps. This was refused and he had to appear before the Conscientious Objectors' Tribunal.[33]

Fortunately, he appeared before a sympathetic magistrate, the same one whose sentence of a half-crown fine had led to Hannah Mitchell's own imprisonment in 1906. She had felt him sceptical of the honesty of the police witnesses then, and now he accepted her son's religious convictions as grounds to allow him to take up non-combatant duties. This was no easy option, for conscientious objectors frequently suffered emotional and psychological maltreatment, sent from home to communities where they were unknown and despised, and frequently set to work for which they were untrained. Hannah Mitchell's son suffered serious injury as a result of his employment in timber-felling in Ireland. When he returned home, Hannah Mitchell recalled, 'Although he said little of his experiences. . . . I knew he had suffered in spirit, and felt the tragedy of war very keenly.'[34]

Alice Clark's experience of the war also proved harrowing. It is not clear from existing evidence whether she completed her midwifery training after her health became a renewed matter for concern in the summer of 1915, but by the end of that year, Hilda Clark was writing home from France, telling of the strains they were under, their particular need for a driver, and her hope that Alice would 'consider the matter'.[35] For the time being, Alice Clark remained in London, furthering the work of the Quaker war relief in an administrative capacity there. It appears that her health continued to be a matter of concern among her family. By the end of 1916, however, she too was in France, and her letters home were studiedly reassuring: 'I am feeling a good deal better, but continue my idle existence, for at the moment they have no need of helpers.' A subsequent letter similarly emphasised the restricted nature of her duties in the maternity and children's hospital which Hilda Clark had established: 'My office at Bellevue is taking temperatures. It takes me about two hours every afternoon!'[36] As hostilities ceased, she saw yet another face of war and its consequences. As starvation spread among the peoples of the defeated powers, Alice Clark, Hilda Clark and Edith Pye joined the Quaker famine relief effort in Austria. This experience of war, together with her struggle for good health, left Alice Clark questioning the Quaker theology in which she had been raised.

Laurence Housman's war-time anguish arose most directly from the sufferings of those to whom he was close. Though an internationalist, it took the pain of war, as experienced among his friends, to make him a pacifist. One of these friends, with whom he had a long-standing relationship, refused to be 'forcibly enlisted', and was sentenced to six months imprisonment in Wormwood Scrubs. This friend was a former policeman, and not, according to Laurence Housman, a true conscientious objector, for he was not against the war. In fact, earlier he had sought release from the London police force in order to enlist, but this had been refused. The attempt to conscript him had followed his dismissal from the police force when he took a prominent role in attempts to form a policemen's union. It was conscription which he objected to, not military service as such. In prison, he was allowed no visitors and Laurence Housman told how his wife got no news, receiving from the prison only a package containing her husband's clothes, 'all in rags, as if they had been torn off his back'.[37]

He and the prisoner had been 'bosom friends' for over fifteen years, and he wrote to Roger Clark of how 'constantly now I have my mind's eye filled with the wonderful beauty and tenderness of him, and the thought of how he may be broken to pieces before we get him back again'. Laurence Housman's account of their friendship throws more light on the nature of his relationships with working-class men, and the meanings that he attached to same-sex love. The wife of the former policeman had known and consented to their relationship, and Laurence Housman represented it as a kind of proselytising for a more advanced form of masculinity. He recalled: 'He was just an ordinary working man to begin with, but so extraordinarily open to culture and ideas.' He felt it was his own influence which explained his friend's 'present rebellious attitude', and the conviction they had come to share 'that forcible government is an evil thing deriving mainly from the Devil'.[38] By this time Laurence Housman was already an active supporter of the No Conscription Fellowship, asking 'Quakers who have riches' to help, when Catherine Marshall reported that its funds were about to run out.[39]

Seeking to help his own particular friend among the conscientious objectors in prison, Laurence Housman turned to the new Chief Commissioner of Police, Sir Edward Henry, who proved more sympathetic. A compromise was suggested whereby the former policeman could volunteer for service in the military police force. This solution proved acceptable to all parties. Somewhat ironically, Laurence Housman's friend subsequently played a part in putting down a military mutiny in Aldershot. His story suggests the complex, if not contradictory, nature of masculine identities at this time, embodying a duty to defiant, manly self-assertion and self-rule against personal oppression, but an equally compelling duty to suppress the autonomy of other men once placed in a position of authority.

Laurence Housman later argued that it was such experiences during war-time which persuaded him eventually to pacifism. In particular, he emphasised his friendship with a German national as one which gave him a particularly intense insight into the anguish of war. This romantic attachment was formed in 1916, when he was in the United States promoting the proposal for a League of Nations that might arbitrate international disputes. 'Hans' was the husband of one of his hosts there, and like himself a committed internationalist. In his autobiography, Laurence Housman suggests that it was because of these shared ideals that they 'most improperly' became friends. In his published recollections such impropriety is suggested in terms of the transgression of patriotic, national identities, as German and Briton.[40] In his correspondence with Roger and Sarah Clark, however, he was able more openly to express the pleasure he found in the simultaneous transgression of other boundaries. This homosexual relationship with an alien member of a warring power represented for him an opportunity to defy conventional understandings of masculinity in a multitude of ways. He enjoyed referring to Hans as his 'Hun' friend, and celebrated his ability by means of this relationship to offer 'comfort to the King's enemies'. With some glee, he conjured up visions of the War Office censor reading his German friend's 'transports' in letters he sent to Laurence Housman after his return to Britain. Resorting as so often to a pun, Laurence Housman hoped his own instructions to moderate such transports would not similarly be misinterpreted by the censor as coded military information. He reflected, too: 'It is curious how much more intimate we seem to have become *since* we parted; but I suppose the circumstances of inter-racial hate being the fashion has given impetus to our "contradictoriness"!'[41]

As the war continued, though, he was less and less able to hide his pain at the separation, and the intensification of his anxiety when the United States entered the war in 1917, when no news came of 'that hostile alien' for some weeks. By this time, Sarah Clark was in the United States visiting her family, and Laurence Housman asked if she might gather any information as to his whereabouts and condition. It seems she was able to meet Hans, and to pass on reassuring news. He responded: 'it was such a restful joy to know you had seen my dear Hans and like him', and the news restored him to his more usual flippancy and light-heartedness.[42]

The Housmans and the Clarks maintained their interest in the activities of the British Society for the Study of Sex Psychology during the war. At one of the society's meetings Clemence Housman tried out her theory of sexual 'inversion', one which was essentially biological, and which posited as the norm the alternate birth in any biological family of male and female children. Drawing on the experience of her own siblings, among whom at least three had a same-sex preference, she suggested that this arose when a male or female child was born out of this normal order. The subject of homosexuality was discussed also on another occasion, and in such terms that Laurence Housman wrote to Sarah Clark how he 'wondered whether it would have shocked you. It did me a little.' But he added that the paper had been delivered in such a way that:

> the discussion it produced was very good, *very* open-spoken and unembarrassed. I am amazed what can be said, and disagreed with without horror and confusion, where good-will is the prevailing note. Some of our members are ultra liberationists.[43]

He contributed a pamphlet of his own at this time, entitled 'The Relation of Fellow-Feeling to Sex', which had begun as a lecture to the BSSSP. Once again, he said of this occasion 'the joy was that a mixed audience, men and women, took it without discomfort or embarassment. That is what the BSSSP is doing.' He once again articulated the link now in his mind between exploring differing sexualities and expanding conceptions of citizenship when he described this pamphlet to Janet Ashbee in these terms: 'it is my main contribution to the suffrage cause during war-time'.[44]

Laurence Housman also remained an active suffragist throughout the war. Franchise reform became a pressing issue once again from 1916, as the possibility of the call for an election grew, and with it the need to ensure that the armed forces were not disfranchised by their absence on the fields of war. Democratic suffrage opinion had so advanced by this time that influential branches and individuals within the NUWSS began to argue that a demand for universal suffrage should replace the more limited object of women's suffrage. Ethel Williams reported from Newcastle, for example, that 'the feeling of the society was entirely for Adult Suffrage'.[45] Within the Cabinet, likewise, the Labour leader, Arthur Henderson, used the situation to press once again for full adult suffrage. A conference of suffrage leaders and sympathetic MPs similarly demonstrated 'feeling for Adult Suffrage almost without exception'.[46]

Here again, the leadership of the suffrage movement found itself divided. That of the NUWSS, the Women's Freedom League and the United Suffragists initially resisted growing pressure for universal suffrage among their own rank-and-file. The WILPF and Sylvia Pankhurst's renamed Workers' Suffrage Federation, on the other hand, took up the demand for full adult suffrage. Subsequently, the United Suffragists put forward the suggestion of a Speaker's conference which might address the whole question of electoral reform, and itself rapidly moved towards reformulating its demands in terms of full adult suffrage. An all-party Speaker's conference was established in the autumn of 1916, with the goal of identifying the components of a franchise measure which would satisfy all those seeking such reform. The pressing need among women's suffragists was to maintain a united front with regard to their demand.

In the meantime the NUWSS commenced a new membership drive in 1917, and helped establish a joint committee of all the suffrage societies. Only the WSPU refused any part in the renewed campaign while the war continued. Though the suffrage organisations were not able to take part in the proceedings of the electoral reform conference itself, they were closely consulted by sympathisers among its members. It was on the advice of suffragist leaders that the conference adopted a formula which provided for a higher age restriction on women's right to vote, as the form of limitation least unacceptable within the movement generally. The conference recommendations included full adult suffrage for men on a residential qualification, and a measure of women's suffrage based on property and age qualifications.

Laurence Housman continued his participation in the campaign through the United Suffragists. As the time for the bill approached, he decided he must stay in London: 'If the bill goes through then I can be free.'[47] Discord among suffragists had inevitably followed on the recommendations of the Speaker's conference. Sections of the NUWSS immediately began a campaign against the restrictions proposed on women's voting rights. The NUWSS leadership itself campaigned to lower the age qualification for women, while emphasising the dangers of pushing for full equality. Sylvia Pankhurst refused any compromise at all on this principle, and other leading democratic suffragists, including Kathleen Courtney and Margaret Llewellyn Davies, similarly maintained their determination to campaign for full adult suffrage, at least until convinced that such a measure would not receive a majority in Parliament. Eventually, suffragists of all shades accepted the need for compromise if women's suffrage were to be secured, and only Sylvia Pankhurst continued to uphold the demand for full sexual equality in the franchise. When the Representation of the People Act became law in February 1918, all women over thirty who were on the local government register or who were graduates, at last gained the parliamentary franchise, alongside all adult men.

Plate 7   Alice Clark, *c.* 1922. By courtesy of the Clark Archive.

11

LAST WORDS
Women's suffragists and women's history after the vote

Elizabeth Wolstenholme Elmy lived just long enough to see women win the parliamentary franchise in 1918, though not long enough to cast a vote in the general election later that year. Her obituary in the *Workers' Dreadnought* reported that 'even in her extreme old age she rose during the small hours of the morning in order that all her housework and cooking for the day might be finished before nine a.m.'. After that she felt free to 'devote the rest of her time to toiling for the cause of women and progress'.[1] On the advice of those close to her, her funeral was 'held after the manner of the Society of Friends' as being 'most in accordance' with her own outlook, although she had never joined the Quakers. It was attended by representatives from the NUWSS, the Manchester Women's Trade and Labour Council, and the Women's International League for Peace and Freedom, suggesting that she had maintained her lifelong commitment to internationalism and pacifism alongside women's rights until the end, and that she may thereby have become alienated from erstwhile friends among the super-patriots in the WSPU leadership.[2]

Just three weeks before the general election at the end of the year, women also won the right to stand for Parliament. Eighteen women candidates came forward, including Christabel Pankhurst. Only Countess Marckiewicz, the Sinn Féin sister of Eva Gore Booth, was successful, but she was unable to take up her seat because she was then in prison for her efforts on behalf of Irish freedom. The first woman entered Parliament the following year when a Conservative, Nancy Astor, took over the former constituency of her husband in Plymouth.

The inter-war period is frequently read as one of disintegration or dormancy for the women's movement, though such interpretations are increasingly under challenge. A few of the leading figures in the pre-war suffrage movement remained at the forefront of organisations which continued to pursue the equal citizenship of women. The National Union of Women's Suffrage Societies took a new name, the National Union of Societies for Equal Citizenship, which indicated the wider brief which it now set itself. Its President, Eleanor Rathbone, articulated what she termed the 'New Feminism' as a concern to address the particular needs of women, especially married, working-class women, whose problems presented, in the view of New Feminists, the fullest measure of women's subordination. As such, the New Feminism is perhaps best understood as the legacy of the democratic suffragist current within the pre-war movement. The Women's Freedom League and the Six-Points Group, in contrast, held to a strictly equal-rights approach, placing a particular emphasis on achieving full civil and legal equality for women. Many suffragists, however, found quite new causes and concerns, especially in the movements for internationalism and colonial freedom, and against fascism. Yet others focused their political activities through parties.

All this might be interpreted as a fragmentation of the women's movement. But it might also be read as reflecting the diversity and breadth of women's political goals in this period, a division of labour among different groups pursuing particular aspects of women's new claims on citizenship, and women's attempts to re-formulate the nature of citizenship itself. The stories of Laurence Housman, Alice Clark, Hannah Mitchell and Mary Gawthorpe after 1918 would support such an interpretation. Their interests were diverse, and each in some way made a contribution to the emerging field of women's history.

LAURENCE HOUSMAN

During the war Laurence Housman had continued his passage leftwards, and by its end had become an occasional contributor to Sylvia Pankhurst's *Workers' Dreadnought*, as well as writing on behalf of anti-war groups and in support of independence for India. By 1918 he was resisting suggestions that he might stand as a Labour candidate. This resistance reflected his scepticism about many of the Labour leaders, especially James Ramsay Macdonald. Also, he confessed: 'I'd rather be out of active politics for a little: the suffrage business was an awful long parenthesis, and altered not only my views but my literary style. I shall never be the same man again!'[3] Even so, in 1919 he did finally join the ILP 'mainly because it was the one political party which had no use for war'.[4] In these years he also began to recover some of his earlier religious faith, and became increasingly sympathetic to the outlook of the Society of Friends. He contributed also, then, to the *Ploughshare*, a paper produced by the Quaker Socialist Society.[5] Under the influence of another of the Clark family, Alice's younger sister Margaret Clark Gillett, he also became involved in the campaign for prison reform, some of the roots of which reached back to Constance Lytton's *Prisons and Prisoners*.[6] And he maintained his commitment to the causes of colonial freedom, internationalism and pacifism.

In the early 1920s, he and Clemence Housman moved to Street. Sarah and Roger Clark now became two of their closest neighbours, as brother and sister built 'Longmeadow' in one of the Clarks' orchards. Thus they found themselves in an environment which provided 'the most sympathetic milieu for our declining years',[7] among Quaker friends of longstanding. In the 1920s Laurence Housman also played a part in the Glastonbury Festival, organised for a number of years by the composer, Rutland Boughton. At this point in his life he began to enjoy a certain literary success, rather than the notoriety which had marked his earlier career. Two of his cycles of plays, the first concerned with the life of St Francis of Assisi, and the second with the British monarchy in the nineteenth century, proved popular. The second also became a success in the United States, where Helen Hayes played the role of the queen in his *Victoria Regina* on Broadway.

His autobiography was written at this high point in his career as a writer. He had expected to die when he was sixty-seven – hence the title of his memoirs, and also the obituary of himself which he had already prepared for the *Manchester Guardian*, and for which he had insisted on immediate payment in order to be sure of enjoying the proceeds. In reviewing some of the reasons which might justify the writing of his autobiography, he chose to emphasise the unanticipated character of so much of it. This unexpectedness he credited especially to the suffrage movement, both for turning him from a somewhat languorous, self-absorbed litterateur into a political activist, as well as for breaking down the Victorianism which he felt had so marred his own early years. Mary Gawthorpe met her former 'co-worker of suffrage days' when he visited New York once again in 1936, at the time of his theatrical success there. She recalled how he told her about his plans for this autobiography, when he remarked: ' "Of course I shall not tell all." '[8]

His autobiography is reticent about his homosexuality, and about the freeing up of masculine and feminine identities which occurred over his lifetime – themes which are far more in evidence in his private correspondence. None the less, it does makes clear that he conceived of emancipation in terms of recognition of, and enjoyment in, the body. His campaigning on behalf of the citizenship of women and his involvement in the movement for homosexual law reform were each aspects of that understanding of emancipation. And this work led him in turn to join with those who sought a new world order through internationalism, the independence of subject peoples, and, in his last years, through nuclear disarmament – each reflecting a broadened understanding of the duties of citizenship as extending beyond the interests of the citizen's own nation state.

In 1952 Laurence Housman at last joined the Society of Friends, and a portrait of him still hangs in the meeting house in Street. He lived well into his nineties, and though his last years were marred by the loss of Clemence Housman in 1955, and by his own declining health, he evidently retained a zest for radical causes. *Peace News*, the journal of the Campaign for Nuclear Disarmament, carried pictures of his ninetieth birthday party on its front page in 1958.[9] In the obituary he had provided for the *Manchester Guardian*, he sought to answer those critics who charged him with having been 'too versatile', insisting that 'the author who works in a groove works in blinkers'. But his autobiography and his letters will almost certainly hold a more lasting interest for subsequent generations than his many novels, or his journalism. *The Times*'s obituary described him in these terms: 'a born radical under a conservative skin (a family inheritance), clothed in the formidable tradition of the Victorian era, he proceeded by degrees and at intervals, to shed that clothing', and he would surely have found much gratification in such an assessment.[10]

ALICE CLARK

The experience of war brought a second great rupture in the life of Alice Clark. Her association with humanitarian aid continued on into the early 1920s, and once again she worked alongside Hilda Clark and Edith Pye in Quaker famine relief.[11] Her main role remained the administration of the relief effort at its headquarters in

London, not in the field: fund-raising, selecting personnel, organising relief supplies, which included the purchasing of livestock from those countries where it was available, and arranging for the sale of the work of Austrian craftsmen. She herself visited Vienna several times during this period, where her industrial experience was considered especially valuable.

Once this work was finished, however, Alice Clark seems not to have kept up any formal role in humanitarian projects, in radical politics, or with the internationalism which remained a primary focus in the lives of her sisters and friends. Edith Pye played an active part in the WILPF in the inter-war period, for example, and in the mid-1930s she and Hilda Clark went out to provide medical aid for the victims of the civil war in Spain. Later still, Margaret Clark Gillett, the sister to whom Alice Clark appears to have been closest, became one of the founders of the Oxford Committee for Famine Relief which subsequently became Oxfam. In her last years Alice Clark resigned from the Society of Friends and pursued her study of Christian Science. She joined the mother-church in Boston, and helped found a Christian Science Society in Street. In this new religious direction: 'She felt herself liberated; she gained the experience of rising over what was threatening to conquer her.'[12]

After the war, Alice Clark was able to see the completion of another enterprise which had been interrupted by the war, when her pioneering study, *The Working Life of Women in the Seventeenth Century*, was at last published. It provided the first detailed investigation of women's involvement in economic life in this period. There, she brought forward evidence of women's greater participation in industry in the seventeenth century than in the nineteenth century. She also showed men playing a larger role in domestic life in the earlier period, and wives equally involved with their husbands in productive labour, effectively partners in family enterprises. Her seventeenth-century women, then, were characterised by their vigour, competence and enterprise, qualities which Alice Clark argued were developed by their fuller participation in economic life.

In Alice Clark's analysis, the oppression and demoralisation of labouring women had not followed from the establishment of capitalist modes of production, but from industrialisation. This process had produced on the one hand an idle and dependent group of women among the wealthy, and on the other, the grossly exploited women of the working classes. Her study exhibits a sense of regret at the passing of a system of production which had enabled women to combine their domestic responsibilities, especially the care of children, with economic activity. Subsequent writers have also been struck by her concern with the conditions of life, moral values and personal qualities of the women she studied, and the assertion of the spiritual poverty of modern life entailed in her account.

Her celebration of the lives of seventeenth-century women ignored the significance of the sexual division of labour to be found then, and the lesser power accorded women, while it also presented the family as the 'natural' unit of economic life. As such, *Working Life* appears limited by the standards of present-day feminist scholarship. None the less, it remains a work which continues to provide an important reference point for historians of this period, and one which has been reprinted twice in recent years.[13] At this time, Alice Clark intended to write a second volume. This was to look at women's experience of family life and education in the same period.[14] But after the war she did not pursue her possible career as a historian any further, again for reasons which remain obscure. Certainly, it was not easy for women, even with a more conventional educational history than Alice Clark's, to find a place in the history departments of universities at this time. The American historian of women, Anne Scott, recalls being shown Alice Clark's research notes when she visited the London School of Economics some decades after Alice Clark's death, but these papers have subsequently been lost, so this promised second work has now only a phantom existence.[15] There is nothing in Alice Clark's surviving correspondence to tell us either what it might have contained, or why she abandoned her historical endeavours.

Alice Clark made a further contribution to women's history, which was of particular significance for the history of the women's movement that had helped to shape her, and that she helped shape. Through the family archive she helped collect, she left a body of material that suggested the need for the re-interpretation of the suffrage movement which has been pursued in this book. This is especially so in terms of re-thinking the complex origins and nature of militancy in relation to long-established Quaker methods of passive resistance. The militant–constitutional distinction which has provided the main framework for the history of the suffrage campaigns in the twentieth century also comes into question, for it is unable to take account of the role of Alice Clark and her kinship and friendship circles. The democratic suffragist current within which she was able to find a way of melding her deepening disillusion with Liberalism, her progressive politics, and her Quaker values also takes on a fresh meaning as a form of constitutional militancy.

Once her book and her work for the Austrian famine relief effort were finished, Alice Clark returned full-time to her position as a director of the Clarks' family enterprise. She had never altogether abandoned her interest in, and concern for, business, retaining her place on the board of directors during her ten-year absence from the factory. So her return may have simply reflected a sense of freedom to return to her earlier career now the vote was won, the need for humanitarian aid was over, and her history was written and published. The wish to care for her ageing parents may have been another reason, for in these years, she returned also to the role of daughter-at-home.

Even so, this return to her old career bore evidence of the changes in her outlook wrought by the previous ten years. As a business manager in these years she proved forward-thinking and innovative. The practices of the Clark family as employers had long been 'patronal'. The company cared well for its work-force but the Clark family, as its directors, retained complete control over such care. When Alice Clark had first entered the firm in the last decade of the nineteenth century, the family's benevolence had been accompanied also by low wages and an anti-union stance on the part of her father . When she finally returned as a full-time business executive in 1922, her major interest became the establishment of a personnel department, something which became 'her own child'.[16] As the director most concerned with the personnel policies of the company, she gave continuing expression to her more radical view of economic relationships.

By this time C. and J. Clark employed some 1300–1400 workers and, under the direction of Alice Clark, the newly established personnel department concentrated on two major innovations: first, the establishment of a non-contributory pension scheme for all waged staff, as part of the commemoration of the jubilee of the foundation of the firm in its existing form; second, the development of more extensive staff educational and training programmes. This last innovation reflected especially Alice Clark's love of the craft of shoe-making, and her firm belief that English workers might be educated to a better appreciation of style and beauty in the products they were engaged in making. Young people beginning work in the factory at fourteen were provided with continuing half-time education until they were sixteen. In her last years, Alice Clark felt more and more strongly that a business should be run and profits apportioned for the benefit of all concerned in it. She saw that this would involve a limit being set to the rate of interest paid to shareholders on their capital, and she realised that there would be great difficulty in rendering such a limitation effective, but she believed that a solution of this difficulty is essential if we are to find our way to a juster social order.[17]

Alongside her responsibilities for personnel management, Alice Clark also supervised the closing room at the Street factory, which employed some 300 women. Here was secured the style and quality on which the firm built its name. In this capacity she was to play a further significant role, helping steer the company during the 1920s and 30s from a largely bespoke manufacturer to one making ready-made, fashionable goods, and developing distinctive and widely known brand names. In this position she also continued to evince her concern especially for the welfare of women in the factory and the local community, a concern which was evident in her will. When she died in 1934 she left funds for the building of a swimming-pool for women, where they might relax and find recreation. It can still be visited across the road from the company headquarters of C. and J. Clark in Street, and today it is open to all. There was nothing overtly political about Alice Clark's activities in the last years of her life, but they evidence none the less a continuing commitment to the pursuit of social justice, and to improving the lives of women, especially their working lives. While her nearest female kin enacted their citizenship through service in local government, voluntary associations and internationalist and humanitarian efforts, Alice Clark chose to realise hers through the opportunity provided her as that rare thing, a woman industrialist.

HANNAH MITCHELL

A similar dedication to improving the working and living conditions of women is evident in the career of Hannah Mitchell subsequent to 1918, one which was also part of her continuing commitment to radical politics. She disliked the decision of the Labour Party after the war to form a separate Women's Section: 'I believed in complete equality, and was not prepared to be a camp follower, or a member of what seemed to me a permanent Social Committee, or Official cake-maker to the Labour Party.'[18] So instead she remained a member of the Independent Labour Party, and as its candidate she successfully contested a local government election in 1923. There followed twelve years of service as a municipal councillor in Manchester, during which she used her position to work for improved housing and the provision of local public laundries to ease the burdens of domestic labour on working-class women, as well as libraries for recreation. She also served as a local Justice of the Peace in these years and on the Public Assistance Board, seeing both in terms of her ability to pursue her commitment to social justice. And she was also able to realise to some extent her earlier intellectual and literary ambitions, for she became a regular writer for the local press. Here she contributed significantly to knowledge of local folk-ways and to the preservation of the Lancashire dialect, for which, though not her own local tongue, she had developed a great appreciation. A collection of her writings from this period is held still in the Manchester Public Library Archives.

For reasons she does not explain, Hannah Mitchell gave up her local government activities in the mid-1930s, while continuing on as a JP. Possibly this change reflected her severance in this period from the ILP, though, according to her nephew 'her basic attitudes did not alter in these years'. This severance is something which she does not refer to at all in her autobiography.[19] The outbreak of a new global war provided the prompt and the opportunity for her to begin writing her autobiography, something which helped her through long, wakeful nights of bombing and fear. It is written with a directness and frankness which conveys something of her stern and unbending character. Her clear intention is to bear witness to the harshness of life for women in working-class communities in her life-time. The suffrage campaigns are recorded as the high point of her life as an activist, a formative experience in terms of confirming her own sense of self-worth through solidarity with others of her sex. It is an account which does not fit easily into the frameworks which dominated the history of the women's movement at the time she wrote – it gave a role and autonomy to working-class women in what was generally seen as a middle-class movement; it suggested the place of the suffrage movement in mainstream politics which did not sit well with the marginal standing accorded it in conventional histories; it offered an account of suffragism as reasoned, thoughtful and principled and challenged the pathological models favoured in so many existing histories.

Hannah Mitchell never became a national figure in the suffrage movement, or any of her other political activities, and her base remained provincial radicalism. Publishers were therefore uninterested in her memoirs during her own life-time. *The Hard Way Up* was not published until 1968, twelve years after her death, and many years after she herself had ceased trying to find a publisher. Subsequently, it was re-issued by Virago, and remains in print today. It has become a central text for a major revision in this field of history which got underway in the 1970s, and its insights provided a significant starting point (as well as a title) for the path-breaking study, *One Hand Tied Behind Us*, by Jill Liddington and Jill Norris.[20]

MARY GAWTHORPE

Material on Mary Gawthorpe's life after she moved to the United States is sketchy, and, for the present at least, fragmentary in nature. There is a short account of her subsequent career included in the summary biography she wrote in December 1931 for the Suffragette Fellowship's 'Book of Suffragette Prisoners'. This is accompanied by a set of testimonials as to her political activism during her first seven years in the United States. There are also occasional references to her subsequent life in *Up Hill to Holloway*, which otherwise finishes in November 1906. And there are some letters, mostly among the papers of American suffragists and radicals, which provide further glimpses into her later life.

Her work for the American suffrage movement came to an end in November 1917. Over the next six years or so, she was employed by a variety of radical and labour organisations, including the National Consumers League, in which again her work was remembered well by those associated with her. Her investigation into women's work in wartime, for the Delaware National Consumers' League, was said to have led to the campaign for a minimum-wage law in that state, for example.[21] Similarly, her campaigning on behalf of the forerunner to the Labor Party in Chicago suggested she had lost none of her old skills: 'As a speaker', one colleague from this time recalled, 'you were electric – arresting immediate attention and holding it by your direct intelligent appeal and sparkling humour.'[22] As a journalist, she apparently made unsigned contributions to the *New Majority*, and in the years immediately after the war was involved in trade union organising for the Amalgamated Clothing Workers of America in Rochester, New York. She took part, too, in the 1920 Chicago conference which attempted, without success, to form a third party, the Farmer-Labor Party. And she campaigned in the presidential campaign of Farley Parker Christensen in Indiana and Illinois. For almost two years she worked for a meagre salary as secretary of the League for Mutual Aid in New York, helping 'radicals, intellectuals and other troublesome people' needing loans, jobs or simply a gift: 'She worked for the love of the people and the advanced ideas and causes they served. We had to give her up finally to private life – at least a more private life and we all hated to part with her.'[23]

In Mary Gawthorpe's own words it was 'threatened overstrain' which again led her to give up work in 1922, after which, she stated, she lived 'more as a private citizen than as a public worker'.[24] The previous year she had married an American, John Sanders, thereby herself becoming a United States citizen. When she wrote her summary memoir for the Suffragette Fellowship in 1931, she described herself as an Associate Member of the New School for Social Research, a 'firm believer in the fullest civil liberties including medical, religious, political and all conceivable intellectual liberties which are effective agencies of the spirit within man', and 'opposed to taking life whether by war or by the avenue of capital punishment'.[25] *Up Hill to Holloway* makes mention of a short return she made to Britain in 1933 with her American husband, introducing him, among other things, to the cricket which she and her father had so enjoyed when she was a child. Some of her correspondence from the 1950s provides evidence of a further short visit then.

It seems likely that the interest of the Suffragette Fellowship in preserving some of the history of the movement provided the spur which led Mary Gawthorpe to write her longer account of her own recruitment to militancy. Heroic images of the suffrage militant were under challenge at this time, and members of the Suffragette Fellowship were intent on explaining her nature to subsequent generations. But Mary Gawthorpe also had a particular goal of her own in responding with the memoirs, records, and memorabilia being solicited by the Suffragette Fellowship in these years. She expressly collected the testimonials on which we rely for some account of her early career in the United States, as a corrective to the 'misleading footnote' about her in Sylvia Pankhurst's *The Suffragette Movement*.[26] This had only recently appeared and Mary Gawthorpe had helped to promote its circulation in the United States. Sylvia Pankhurst's history provided the first, and still the most detailed, account of the suffrage campaigns up until 1918, so it looked set to dominate historical understandings.

Dora Montefiore had complained with far greater directness about the way she had been written out of Sylvia Pankhurst's earlier chronicle of the WSPU, *The Suffragette*, published in 1911. The omission was corrected to a degree in Sylvia Pankhurst's new book.[27] For her part, Mary Gawthorpe must have been hurt at the way her role in the WSPU was diminished, and her subsequent career so dismissively written off. In particular, she insisted that *The Suffragette Movement* was inaccurate as to the details of her 1912 imprisonment, as well as ignoring her suffrage, labour and social reform activities in America.

Elizabeth Wolstenholme Elmy had been similarly disturbed by the first chronicles of the nineteenth-century campaigns as they began to appear from the 1890s. In those years, she made constant reference to the time she was spending organising the vast body of documentary material relating to the British women's movement which she had collected from its earliest days. Her aim was to write an alternative account of the movement to those then available, written by Millicent Garrett Fawcett, Caroline Ashurst Biggs, and Helen Blackburn, and hence written from the perspective of the national leadership. Their accounts systematically ignored the role of Elizabeth Wolstenholme Elmy and other Radical suffragists in the nineteenth-century movement; on occasion they even misrepresented events.[28] Apart from a brief essay in the *Westminster Review*, she never appears to have completed this task, and her large collection of papers, some of which she made available to Sylvia Pankhurst when she was writing her 1911 history, *The Suffragette*, were lost after her death.

The Suffragette Movement was clearly intended as some redress for the imbalance in earlier histories of the nineteenth-century movement, though in a way which tended to celebrate the role of Richard and Emmeline Pankhurst at the cost of neglecting the work of some of their closest colleagues. While *The Suffragette Movement* provides one of the most compelling and readable histories, and will remain a primary source of great importance in itself, it could not, in the nature of things, provide a complete or unbiased account of the suffrage movement. And the pre-eminence which it gives to members of the Pankhurst family does serve to hide from view the highly contested nature of suffrage militancy, and of the connections between women's citizenship and women's emancipation, as well as the enormous complexity of the relationship between militants and constitutionalists. The material which Mary Gawthorpe provided initially for the Suffragette Fellowship was evidently intended, then, as something of a corrective, as was her memoir of her early life.

Internal evidence suggests that *Up Hill to Holloway* was begun sometime in the latter part of the 1930s, possibly prompted by the efforts of the Suffragette Fellowship, and a re-acquaintance with the scenes and friends of earlier years that occurred with her first return visit to Britain. There Mary Gawthorpe provides her personal 'last word' on the subject, for though she does not directly criticise existing histories, she does offer a very different narrative of the suffrage movement from that to be found in Sylvia Pankhurst. Mary Gawthorpe's memoir suggests a far more complex identity for the designation 'suffragist', and more particularly 'militant suffragist', than any to be found in Sylvia Pankhurst's account. It shows Mary Gawthorpe-as-suffragist being formed by a complex combination of private suffering and public life. It also presents her as a figure already in her prime as a political campaigner by the time she encountered the WSPU. Her choice of 'militancy' over constitutionalism allowed her, whatever the central leadership intended, and those intentions do not always appear coherent or consistent, to continue to work among a milieu of independent-minded radicals. The personal bonds she formed in the process, the pre-existing political and social values she continued to espouse, involved a complex set of commitments which might encompass personal loyalty to members of the WSPU leadership, but which was not delimited by those loyalties. The rediscovery of such circles of 'free-lance' militants has, in its turn, prompted a re-evaluation of militancy itself, as in the account provided in *The Life and Death of Emily Wilding Davison*, by Liz Stanley and Anne Morley.

By 1911 it had become the case that her personal identity as a suffragist required that Mary Gawthorpe express solidarity with comrades other than the Pankhursts, and that she pursue an understanding of women's emancipation very different now to theirs. Part of her concern, then, in engaging in a re-making of the history of the movement was to show how being a suffragist was, for her, all of a piece with being a dutiful and caring daughter, an independent, autonomous woman, a dynamic and thoughtful member of a profession, and a member of the radical intelligentsia, intent on changing society in fundamental ways.

The WSPU, and the practice of militancy, especially in its later stages, made a particular appeal to authentics, and encouraged especially intense personal loyalties among those who engaged in its activities. Mary Gawthorpe was able to recognise the authenticity of many of the militant irregulars whom she encountered in her campaigning, and it was the moral community which she felt, even when not necessarily of one mind with them, which explains her own gradual distancing from the WSPU. Looking back on her own connection with *The Freewoman*, she wrote:

> This is not the place to interpret or explain my short association with Dora Marsden. . . . I have always been acutely concerned with the maintenance of free speech, free opinion and free thought and was 'for' Dora and anyone else on these terms.[29]

Her motives were ones of 'personal helpfulness and cooperation', the same motives which she claimed, not without irony, informed her efforts to help launch Sylvia Pankhurst's *The Suffragette Movement* in the United States. But she was clearly dissatisfied with the way the history of the movement was being formed. It failed to acknowledge adequately her own experience, or to convey the meaning which being a militant had held for her and some of her closest colleagues.

Mary Gawthorpe's letters to an old friend from suffrage days, Mary Dreier, provides some evidence as to the last decades of her life. The two had remained in touch, sharing not only a circle of friends among their generation of radicals, but also membership of a particular religious faith. The similarity of their political, moral and religious outlook is evident also in their mutual interest in the movement for nuclear disarmament, their antagonism to the McCarthy witch hunts of the 1950s, and the tentative hopes they placed in John F. Kennedy when he came to power. These letters indicate that Mary Gawthorpe remained in touch with some of her former 'comrades' in Britain, telling Mary Dreier that 'quite a number of my old friends took part in the Aldermaston March and one of them is in the leadership group over there' (almost certainly a reference to Mary Leigh, her old comrade among the irregulars of the WSPU).[30]

When Mary Gawthorpe's husband, John Sanders, became seriously ill in the early 1960s, Mary Dreier sent a contribution toward his medical expenses. The couple found they were able to manage without drawing on this, and so proposed using it instead to help with the publication costs of *Up Hill to Holloway*. It had been turned down by a series of publishers who felt it was not a commercial proposition, so Mary Gawthorpe arranged for its publication as 'a cooperative' undertaking with a small press in Penobscot, Maine.[31] It appeared the following year, just months before her husband's death. Its distribution was necessarily limited, and undertaken largely through her friendship networks, so it remains an inaccessible source for those interested in suffrage history.[32] In consequence, its impact on suffrage historiography has so far been limited, and Sylvia Pankhurst's narrative remains the dominant one among such primary sources. A last trace of her jaunty cheerfulness is to be found in a Thanksgiving message which she sent in 1971 to one of her former school pupils, whom she had known nearly seventy years before. Here she thanked him for his ' "resurrection" friendship' as 'one of the wonder experiences of my long life'.[33] She died the following year.

The concerns which prompted Mary Gawthorpe to engage in writing her memoirs proved justified. Mainstream historians have, until very recently, continued to accept the narratives which focus on the contribution and role of the Pankhurst family. They have also constructed stereotypes, often mocking and demeaning, which do no justice, either to the Pankhursts, or to dissident figures like Mary Gawthorpe, Hannah Mitchell, Laurence Housman and Alice Clark, all from time to time, and in their own distinct ways 'militant' suffragists. Equally, this focus has led, until recent years, to a neglect of the constitutional wing of the movement, and of the 'democratic suffragist' current which maintained a close relationship between the women's movement and the socialist and labour movements.

The thrust of Mary Gawthorpe's memoirs is to show that the significance of the campaigns often grew from the everyday tragedies of ordinary life, and that suffrage participation was often of a piece with a more general radicalism. The record of her career as a suffrage organiser suggests that daring and courage arose out of comradeship and solidarity among the lesser beings who made up a real force in the movement, and that what happened at a local level is often inexplicable in terms of the policies and directives from the London leadership. It also provides a much darker perspective on militancy, as a mode of campaigning with heavy physical and emotional consequences for those who chose this route, the ambiguous value of which the 'official' view cannot admit. Many, like Mary Gawthorpe, were burnt-out cases by the end of the WSPU campaigns, and almost certainly to no good purpose. Once militancy moved beyond civil disobedience and passive resistance, it provided an apparent legitimacy to the abuse of state powers by the Liberal government which followed. This was a fundamental failure of political strategy, as the Pethick Lawrences and Sylvia Pankhurst recognised in their separate attempts to return to the original course of militancy in 1913–14. Mary Gawthorpe and some of her closest suffrage associates also came to find inadequate the vision of emancipation which informed the demand for the vote. But again, only in recent years has the alternative, and self-styled 'feminist' vision which emerged after 1910 begun to receive the attention of historians.

The revival of interest in the history of the women's movement from the late 1960s was shaped by a sense of the discontinuities between 'first-wave' (or 'past') and 'second-wave' (or 'present-day') feminism. The stories told here suggest the complexity which is submerged in the category 'first wave'. While we increasingly recognise the pluralism of the contemporary women's movement as representing a range of 'feminisms', we have been less ready to explore the conflicting accounts of citizenship, and of emancipation, which divided the earlier women's movement. These stories also suggest some notable continuities between the women's movements of the past and of the present, most especially in the recognition to be found across time of the embodied nature of citizenship.

Historians who research suffrage history, especially in Britain, often encounter the question: 'Can there be anything left to say about the suffrage movement?' Yet new stories, like those told here, continue to re-emerge, and the past always proves too untidy for those histories we have already made. Such new stories often challenge existing frameworks, or render uncertain the categories and concepts we apply, or suggest new lines of enquiry. A brief account of how this history came to be put together illustrates how history-making is always partial and provisional in nature, and how happenstance and serendipity may also play a part in the work of the historian.

The choice of Laurence Housman as one of the suffragists discussed here, for example, simply reflected in the first instance my sense of a major gap presently in the literature on the suffrage movement, concerning the role of men within it. But reading his memoirs, his journalism and his letters suggested a relationship between the achievement of women's citizenship and the articulation of new masculine identities which has been raised here, but which remains in need of more extensive exploration. Such an act of interpretation was possible because of the correspondence which had been preserved by his friends, and which made it possible to fill some of the silences evident in his autobiography. A different self emerges in his letters, a warmer, more engaged figure than that presented in the autobiography. And the self he presents to his women friends is in subtle ways a different self to the one he presents when writing to men friends, though it has not been possible to explore those differences in this context. What is offered here, then, is an interpretation and blending of the selves I have found represented in two forms, autobiography and letters, expanded with a few insights gained from his pamphleteering, novel-writing, and journalism.

I set out, too, with the aim of looking at the suffrage activity of some lesser-known figures in the women's movement – their absences or marginality in some of the earliest histories raised questions which could only be answered by trying to piece together some new stories. Elizabeth Wolstenholme Elmy was an obvious candidate – someone who was evident at some point in the records of almost every major organisation, if neglected in subsequent chronicles. Though her own collection of papers has disappeared, her friend, Harriet McIlquham, had kept much of her correspondence between 1890 and 1910, and it was subsequently deposited in the British Library. It has been surprisingly little used by historians of the movement – reflecting, no doubt, the marginal standing of Elizabeth Wolstenholme Elmy in existing accounts, as well as the practical difficulties presented by her idiosyncratic handwriting. The account of her suffrage career presented here is told entirely from her own point of view, and that of others close to her. It cannot, in consequence, altogether explain why she so often fell foul of her colleagues in the movement. But it was my interest in democratic suffragism which took me to the papers of Alice Clark, and the chance find of a large body of correspondence from among her female kin, some of which threw a fresh light on the life of Elizabeth Wolstenholme Elmy. This body of material suggested, too, the existence of an alternative current of Radical suffragists, and more especially, the significance of the issue of coverture to Radical suffragism, and the deliberate appeal of Radical suffragists to working-class support.

A 'hunch' suggested that I might also find there correspondence with suffragists in the United States. When that was confirmed, the letters in turn directed me back to some largely unused published sources for the history of the British movement, in the autobiographies and histories written by suffragists in the United States. These cast the British movement in a somewhat different light from the contemporaneous chronicles produced by some of its own leadership, and served to confirm for me the actuality of the Radical current. A focus on the transatlantic links between Radical suffragists also suggested certain continuities between the nineteenth-century movement and twentieth-century suffrage militancy, and the complex origins and nature of militancy itself. Transnational history is a methodology which a number of historians have begun to pursue in the past few years, as far as I know, quite independently. It is suggesting noteworthy re-interpretions in national movements, as well as establishing more clearly the complex international links of the national women's movement.[34]

Jessie Craigen is the only suffragist discussed here who left very little first-hand testimony. The story I have told is formed almost entirely, then, by the representations which others made of her in their letters and press reports. It is formed, further, by the selection I made among those accounts, the way I have ordered them and contextualised them. Another historian would almost certainly read the same sources differently, and make a somewhat different pattern out of them. Once again, happenstance or serendipity led to the inclusion of her story here. I knew of her previously only as the author of a pamphlet which expressed especially forcefully a sense of sexual solidarity among women of different classes, and as a fleeting presence in Helen Blackburn's account of the nineteenth-century movement. Again, it was the frequent reference to her in letters in the Millfield papers which made me look for her in other records of the movement, and so piece together this sketch. It seems unlikely presently that any fuller account of Jessie Craigen is possible – working women rarely leave the kind of literary and documentary sources on which this kind of history-making relies. We have to be grateful for the different senses of self, as well as the material resources, which allowed Helen Taylor and the Priestman sisters to collect their own papers, and so preserve the only presently known primary sources regarding Jessie Craigen's part in the women's movement.

Hannah Mitchell is a rarity: a working woman who wrote an autobiography which eventually found a publisher and an extensive readership. Her account of her role in the suffrage movement has made an extraordinary impact on recent histories. Clearly, there were other working-class suffragists whose stories might prove equally challenging – if only they had left more traces for the historian to work with. It is also the case that the Hannah Mitchell you meet here reflects the face she chose to show the world. It is a tribute to her literary abilities that she manages to convey, within this spare account, something of the other selves she could see, looking back from the relative tranquillity and sense of self-worth she had achieved by late middle-age. But there is no significant body of correspondence in which to search for other faces of her. What I offer, then, is an interpretation of her particular story inflected by the other stories with which it has been woven together here.

Telling Mary Gawthorpe's story presented other difficulties. Her published memoirs finish in 1906, and the material she left with Rose Lamartine Yates seems to have been dispersed, or perhaps reclaimed on a return visit to Britain and then lost. Her husband pre-deceased her, and there were no children to keep her memory alive. On the other hand, her national reputation as a speaker meant that her suffrage activities were recorded regularly in the suffrage press at the time. And her engaging personality ensured that her memory stayed in the minds of other suffragists when they came to write their own autobiographies and memoirs. A growing recognition of suffrage history as contested ground was evident in the formation of the Suffragette Fellowship in the early 1930s. It was evident also in her own contribution to its archives, which makes it possible now to tell something of her life in the fifteen years or so after she left Britain. Thereafter, there is a gap in documentary sources until the 1950s, when some of her letters were preserved in the papers of an American friend. The same Mary Gawthorpe reveals herself in these letters as in her memoirs, a cheery, generous, lively-minded radical who seems never to have lost the high spirits of her youth. But these letters also reveal a committed and absorbing religious orientation, of which there are only hints in the memoirs. There, she points up the place of the established Church in her education and her sense of place in the local community of her childhood. She also suggests an interest at different times in theosophy and Christian Science. But it is impossible, with the sources presently available, to bring together her suffragism and her political radicalism with the religiosity revealed in the letters from her last years.

Alone among these inter-war survivors of the suffrage movement, Alice Clark left no memoirs or autobiographical writings. She had helped her mother in the collection and care of the substantial archive known as the Millfield papers, after the name of her family's home, and now housed in the archives of C. and J. Clark, Ltd. This collection contains the correspondence of several generations of women in the Priestman, Bright, and Clark families, as well as some of the correspondence from husbands, fathers and brothers. Both Helen and Alice Clark clearly had a sense of their value, and not simply in terms of the reverence for family history that is so notable an aspect of Quaker life. Both must have been well aware of how the activities of themselves and their female kin were effectively marginalised in histories of the women's movement produced prior to the First World War, and virtually written out in those that were published afterwards. Yet no effort was made by either at correction, no concern expressed with regard to such omission, at least in material which has so far come to light. It seems it was enough that they knew how they and their close kin had acted, and the motivations for those actions. Their own papers evidence little use for worldly recognition or celebrity.

Moreover, the personal papers of her own which Alice Clark left among this material are relatively meagre, so that the story told here remains sketchy in nature. And the reserve, noted in the short biography written by her younger sister, Margaret Clark Gillett, is evident both in photographs of her, and in those letters of hers which do survive. Only in those images taken in middle-age does she look directly at the camera, and even then the gaze seems self-contained, contemplative. The centrality of religious concerns, however, is evident from her biography, and from her letters. Perhaps because she was of more reflective a temperament, her letters do throw greater light on the links between her spirituality and her politics than can be determined for Mary Gawthorpe. They are thoughtful, too, about militancy and its morality. And her historical interests led her to express, in her letters, some sense of the continuities between earlier radical causes and women's suffrage. But, as we have already seen, her letters tell us little about the motivations which took her to the London School of Economics, or which led her to write what remains a major reference point in the history of women in the early modern period.

The lack of papers from the last decade or so of her life also means that her religious life in this period remains largely an enigma. And there is no evidence as to why she retreated from political activism. She seems not to have preserved any of her correspondence after her move to London in 1913. Was her life too busy? Did she, too, suspend a sense of personal life, as Mary Gawthorpe did, when she became a suffrage organiser? Or did this material simply go astray in the dislocations of war? Fortunately, some of her letters home in these years were preserved by members of her family. But when she herself returned permanently to Street to live, even this source runs out. It is difficult, therefore, to know what interests she had outside her work in her last years, how she viewed political developments at home and abroad, what interest she took in the continuing participation of her sisters in local government, in the international women's movement, in social reform and in humanitarian aid. For all these reasons, she remains perhaps the most enigmatic of those suffragists whose story is told here. It seems likely that she did not think her own life of likely interest to later generations, yet a revival of interest in the history of the suffrage movement, together with her own efforts in history-making, have meant that this proved not to be the case.

The materials of history are in many ways 'found'. I have worked from the documentary evidence which survives, tracking down that evidence by a process which reflects both an accretion of knowledge about possible sources, and chance. The questions I ask, similarly, are prompted by the gaps, silences and inconsistences in existing histories. The questions I am able to ask are structured by the discourses which surround me and in which I partake. My part has been to engage imaginatively with those found materials, to create new patterns and interpretations. I chose to present the outcome in the form of some stories which might fill some of those gaps and silences, address some of those inconsistencies. In some recent reflections on the writing and practice of history, Carolyn Steedman has concluded that it is an activity necessarily 'constructed around the understanding that things are not over, that the story isn't finished: that there is no end', though the historian must impose closures 'in order to finish arguments and books'.[35] Historical knowledge must always remain provisional, for new evidence, new ways of looking at evidence, may alter what we see, produce new interpretations, and make possible some fresh story-telling. So to answer the question which began this concluding section: there is unlikely ever to be a 'last word' on the history of the women's suffrage movement. There are ample seams of evidence yet to be mined, many questions yet to be answered, and any number of new stories to be told – the kaleidoscope keeps on turning.

NOTES

Where a source or collection has only been used on a few occasions, the name of the collection and its location are given in full in the relevant note. Where a source has been used more extensively the following abbreviations are adopted in the notes:

CA   Clark Archive, C. & J. Clark, Ltd., Street, Somerset
CMP   Catherine Marshall Papers, Cumbria Record Office
CRAJ   C. R. Ashbee Journals, King's College, Cambridge
ESCC   Elizabeth Cady Stanton Correspondence, Mabel and Frederick Douglass Library, the University of New Jersey at Rutgers
ESPA   E. Sylvia Pankhurst Archive, the Institute of Social History, Amsterdam
EWEP   Elizabeth Wolstenholme Elmy Papers, Add MSS 47447–52, British Library, London
FAC   Fawcett Autography Collection, the Fawcett Library, London Guildhall University
FHL   Friends House Library, Friends House, London
GP   Greenbank Papers, the Clark Archive, C. & J. Clark, Ltd., Street, Somerset
HCP   Hilda Clark Papers, Temp MSS 301, Friends House Library, Friends House, London
HP   Housman Papers, Street Public Library, Street, Somerset.
HTP   Helen Taylor Papers, in the J. S. Mill–H. Taylor Papers, the Archives of the British Library of Political and Economic Science, the London School of Economics
JBP   Jessie Baines Papers, photocopies held in the Fry Library, the University of Queensland
JEBP   Josephine E. Butler Papers, the Fawcett Library, London Guildhall University
MEDP   Mary E. Dreier Papers, Arthur and Elizabeth Schlesinger Library, Radcliffe College
MGFP   Millicent Garrett Fawcett Papers, the Fawcett Library, London Guildhall University
MP   Millfield Papers

MPLA   Manchester Public Library Archives

MWDP Mary Ware Dennett Papers, Arthur and Elizabeth Schlesinger Library, Radcliffe College

NUWSS National Union of Women's Suffrage Societies

SFCM   Suffragette Fellowship Collection

WFLMB Women's Franchise League Minute Book, microfilm from the Special Collections, Northwestern University, Illinois

I thank the following repositories and individuals for permission to quote from material used in this research: the British Library (Elizabeth Wolstenholme Elmy Papers); the British Library of Political and Economic Science (the Mill-Taylor collection); the Clark Archive, C. and J. Clark Ltd (the Millfield Papers); the Fawcett Library, the London Guildhall University (the J. E. Butler and H. McIlquham papers); the Friends' House Library (H. Clark Papers); the Huntington Library (the Harper collection); the Mabel and Frederick Douglass Library (Elizabeth Cady Stanton Correspondence), Rutgers University; Manchester Public Library Archives (Women's Suffrage collection); the Special Collections of Northwestern University, Illinois (Women's Franchise League Minutes); the Institute for Social History, Amsterdam (E. S. Pankhurst Archive); the Elizabeth and Arthur Schlesinger Library, Radcliffe College (the Mary Dreier Papers); Muriel Stevenson (J. Baines papers); Special Collections of the Vassar Libraries (Elizabeth Cady Stanton correspondence).

INTRODUCTION

1 L. Tickner, *A Spectacle of Women. Imagery of the Suffrage Campaign, 1907–14*, London, Chatto and Windus, 1987, p. 152.

2 K. A. K. Israel, 'Writing inside the Kaleidoscope: Re-presenting Victorian Public Figures', *Gender and History*, 1990, vol. 2, pp. 40–8, esp. p. 40.

1 FROM 'SURPLUS WOMAN' TO INDEPENDENT PERSON: Elizabeth Wolstenholme and the early women's movement

1 E. Ethelmer, 'A Woman Emancipator: A Biographical Sketch', *Westminster Review*, 1894, vol. CXLV, pp. 424–83, and see also *The Reformer's Year Book 1908*, which gives her date of birth as 1833, together with a sketch of her career; her obituary in the *Manchester Guardian*, 13 March 1918, which tells something of her family and career. Her obituary of Ben Elmy, 'Ignota' (her pseudonym), 'Pioneers! Oh, Pioneers!', *Westminster Review*, April 1906, pp. 415–17, together with a further obituary of Ben Elmy in an unidentified cutting from 10 March 1906, in the records of the *Congleton Chronicle*, and E. S. Pankhurst, *The Suffragette Movement. An Intimate Account of Persons and Ideals* (1931), London, Virago, 1977 repr. p. 31. All identify Ellis Ethelmer as Ben Elmy, but others have suggested it was a joint pseudonym of the couple, while S. Jeffreys, *The*

Spinster and Her Enemies, London, Pandora, 1985, chooses to assign it to Elizabeth Wolstenholme Elmy herself. I am especially grateful to A. John Condliffe, Editor and Managing Director of the *Congleton Chronicle*, for providing me with cuttings relating to Elizabeth Wolstenholme Elmy and Ben Elmy, and to Mary Lyndon Shanley, Vassar College, for suggesting this source to me.

2 M. Vicinus, *Independent Women. Work and Community for Single Women 1850–1920*, London, Virago, 1985, esp. ch. 1, 'The Revolt against Redundancy' provides an especially helpful and thought-provoking introduction to this topic.

3 H. Moyes, *A Woman in a Man's World*, Sydney, Alpha Books, 1971, p. 92 recalls that the term 'suffra*gette*'was coined by the *Daily Mail* journalist, Charles E. Hands, to identify the supporters of the recently formed Women's Social and Political Union (henceforth, WSPU), and their more aggressive forms of campaigning. It was subsequently taken up by the militants to distinguish themselves from the suffra*gists* of the National Union of Women's Suffrage Societies (henceforth the NUWSS), which chose to characterise itself as 'constitutional' (not as 'non-militant', as they were dubbed by the WSPU). The differences between the two wings of the movement, and the meaningfulness of these distinctions will be considered in later chapters.

4 D. Montefiore, *From a Victorian to a Modern*, London, E. Archer, 1927, p. 113.

5 Pankhurst, *Suffragette Movement*, p. 31.

6 Elizabeth Wolstenholme Elmy dated her involvement with the women's movement from 1861, in a letter to the journal of the WSPU, *Votes for Women*, 10 March 1910, p. 392.

7 B. Stephen, *Emily Davies and Girton College*, London, Constable, 1927, p. 106.

8 P. Levine, *Victorian Feminism 1850–1900*, London, Hutchinson, 1987, p. 15.

9 H. C. Robinson, quoted in S. R. Herstein, *A Mid-Victorian Feminist, Barbara Leigh Smith Bodichon*, New Haven, Yale University Press, 1985, p. 19.

10 Quoted in B. Taylor, *Eve and the New Jerusalem. Socialism and Feminism in the Nineteenth Century*, New York, Pantheon, 1983, p. 277.

11 Quoted in D. M. C. Worzala, 'The Langham Place Circle: The Beginnings of the Organized Women's Movement in England 1854–1970', Wisconsin Ph.D. thesis, 1982, University Microfilms International, p. 56.

12 Mrs Wolstenholme Elmy, 'A Woman's Plea to Women', Westminster, Women's Printing Society, 1886, p. 3, reprinted from the *Macclesfield Courier*, 8 November 1886.

13 E. J. Yeo, 'Social Motherhood and the Sexual Communion of Labour in British Social Science, 1850–1950', *Women's History Review*, 1992, vol. 1, pp. 63–88.

14 A. J. Hammerton, 'Victorian Marriage and the Law of Matrimonial Cruelty', *Victorian Studies*, 1989–90, vol. 33, pp. 269–92, esp. p. 291.

15 Herstein, *Mid-Victorian Feminist*, p. 78.

16 Both quoted in J. Rendall, 'Friendship and Politics: Barbara Leigh

Smith Bodichon (1827–91) and Bessie Rayner Parkes (1829–1925)' in J. Rendall and S. Mendus (eds) *Sexuality and Subordination*, London, Routledge, 1989, pp. 136–70, esp. pp. 143–4.

17 Quoted in Herstein, *Mid-Victorian Feminist*, pp. 127–8.

18 Ethelmer, 'Woman Emancipator', p. 425.

19 Ibid.

20 E. C. Wolstenholme, 'The Education of Girls, its Present and its Future', in J. Butler (ed.) *Woman's Work and Woman's Culture*, London, Macmillan, 1869, pp. 290–330, esp. p. 291.

21 Ibid., pp. 298, 318–19.

22 Quoted in Stephen, *Emily Davies*, pp. 108–9.

23 Quoted in A. Rosen, 'Emily Davies and the Women's Movement, 1862–1867', *Journal of British Studies*, 1979, vol. XIX, pp. 101–21, esp. p. 110.

24 'The Ladies Petition', *Westminster Review*, 1867, vol. XXI, pp. 63–79, esp. p. 63.

25 See for example H. Blackburn, *Women's Suffrage. A Record of the Women's Suffrage Movement in the British Isles with Biographical Sketches of Miss Becker*, London, Williams and Norgate, 1902, pp. 55–6, which omits mention of both Elizabeth Wolstenholme and the Manchester Society, and focuses instead on the attendance of Emily Davies and Elizabeth Garrett at the House of Commons to pass over the petition to Mill. The omission here is compounded subsequently on p. 59 which gives the date of the formation of the Manchester Society as 11 January 1867. This misleading account made it possible for Blackburn both to give all the glory of this first effort to the London Society, and to ignore Elizabeth Wolstenholme's role as secretary of the original committee in order to establish Lydia Becker as the original moving force in the Manchester Society. A corrective may be found in E. S. Pankhurst, *Suffragette Movement*, p. 30, not surprisingly, given that its author had consulted Elizabeth Wolstenholme Elmy when writing her earlier history, *The Suffragette*, London, Gay and Hancock, 1911, and had access to some of her papers. Further supporting documentary evidence for Elizabeth Wolstenholme Elmy's claim may be found in E. Wolstenholme to H. Taylor, 5 April 1867, HTP, vol. 14, f. 256 (a letter not in Wolstenholme's own hand but sent over her signature).

26 Quoted in Rosen, 'Emily Davies', p. 113.

27 Emily Davies, quoted in Stephen, *Emily Davies*, pp. 117–18.

28 F. M. Gladstone, *Aubrey House, Kensington 1698–1920*, London, Arthur Humphreys, 1920, esp. pp. 44–51; W. T. Malleson, 'Mrs Peter Taylor', *Englishwoman's Review*, no. CCLXXVIII, pp. 145–58.

29 C. Taylor to H. Taylor, July 1867, HTP.

30 'Enfranchisement of Women Committee', leaflet enclosed with C. Taylor to A. M. Priestman, 6 July 1867, 'Miscellaneous Papers. Political Papers' packet, Box 24, MP.

31 'Ignota' (Elizabeth Wolstenholme Elmy), 'Women's Suffrage', *Westminster Review*, 1897, vol. CXLVIII, p. 360.

2 'THE REVOLT OF THE WOMEN': Sexual subjection and sexual solidarity

1 I deliberately avoid the antinomies 'radical' and 'conservative' here, as all suffragists were offering such a challenge to the status quo that they must be seen as small-r 'radicals'. I prefer to make the distinction pursued here in terms of 'Radical suffragists', which indicates an adherence to a political current outside the women's movement, and 'moderate suffragists'. Radical suffragists were also distinguishable by their commitment to more inclusive forms of the suffrage demand.

2 This was acknowledged by L. Becker in a letter to E. Wolstenholme, 26 April 1868, copied in Lydia Becker's Letter Book 1868, M50/1/3, MPLA.

3 E. Wolstenholme to H. Taylor, 3 May 1868, HTP, vol. 14, f. 112.

4 H. Taylor to E. Wolstenholme [draft], n. d. [c. May 1869], HTP, vol. 14, f. 260.

5 From the *Newcastle Daily Chronicle* account of a paper she presented at the 1870 Social Science conference, reprinted in the *Englishwoman's Review*, October 1870, no. IV, p. 296.

6 According to one account, she resigned from the executive and the post of secretary of the Married Women's Property Committee in 1871, returning as secretary only in 1880. Certainly, in 1872, as we have seen she had left Congleton to fill her new post in London. But reports in the *Englishwoman's Review* continue to identify her as both secretary and committee member until the latter part of 1875.

7 P. Levine, ' "So Few Prizes and So Many Blanks": Marriage and Feminism in Later Nineteenth Century England', *Journal of British Studies*, 1989, vol. 28, p. 174.

8 W. T. Stead, quoted in J. Walkowitz, *Prostitution and Victorian Society: Women, Class and the State*, Cambridge, Cambridge University Press, 1980, p. 120.

9 E. M. Bell, *Josephine Butler. Flame of Fire*, London, Constable, 1962, p. 74. J. Butler, *Personal Reminiscences of a Great Crusade*, London, Horace Marshall, 1911.

10 Quoted in Walkowitz, *Prostitution and Victorian Society*, p. 93.

11 J. E. Butler, *Recollections of George Butler*, Bristol, Arrowsmith, 1892, p. 224.

12 Ibid.

13 Ibid.

14 A. M. Priestman to M. Priestman, 26 Sept 1870; E. W. Elmy to 'Dear Friend' [A. M. Priestman], 5 February 1903, Boxes 17 and 24, MP respectively.

15 Quoted in Walkowitz, *Prostitution and Victorian Society*, p. 108.

16 Quoted in Butler, *Personal Reminiscences*, p. 11.

17 P. B. McLaren to H. P. B. Clark, 8 October 1874, Box 35, MP.

18 Ibid.

19 A. M. Priestman to M. Tanner, 29 February 1872, and similar letters 7 March 1872, 24 October 1872, Box 17, MP.

20 See M. Shanley, *Feminism, Marriage and the Law in Victorian England*,

1850–95, London, I. B. Tauris, 1989, for an extended account of CALPIW.

21 *Englishwoman's Review*, January 1873, no. XIII, p. 60. For an especially helpful discussion of the attitude of nineteenth-century feminists to state intervention see M. J. D. Roberts, 'Feminism and the State in Later Victorian England', *Historical Journal*, 1995, vol. 38, pp. 85–110.

22 *Englishwoman's Review*, April 1874, no. XVIII, p. 271.

23 A. M. Priestman to M. Priestman, 20 October 1875, Box 17, MP.

24 Emma Paterson was a former book-binder who had gained considerable organisational experience in the London club movement for working-class men. Like Elizabeth Wolstenholme her hold on middle-class status, based on her father's occupation as a headmaster, had proved fragile. His income was low at £60 a year, and he died when Emma Paterson was sixteen. Consequently, she had to work to support herself and her family. Again like Elizabeth Wolstenholme, many of her views had been shaped by the free thought movement. And like Elizabeth Wolstenholme, she hoped for a new career as an employee of the women's movement. This opportunity proved short-lived, however, for her suffrage employers decided that her physical frailty and poor speech disqualified her from a continuing post. In 1873 she married, and it was during a wedding tour in the United States that she began to think about the possibilities for promoting greater trade union organisation among women in Britain.

25 Details of the objects, benefits and subscribers to the NUWW are to be found in two leaflets in the Manchester Public Library Archives, one undated but circa August 1874, M50/4/10/2, and another dated 1 July 1875, M50/4/10/1. First-hand testimony of its activities is to be found in the correspondence of A. M. Priestman, for example, A. Henry to A. M. Priestman, 2 May 1875 and 22 October 1875; M. Priestman to A. M. Priestman, 1 and 28 October, 5 December 1875, in Boxes 20 and 22, respectively, MP. This and subsequent paragraphs draw on these sources.

26 Alice Cliff Scatcherd is another Radical suffragist about whom little is presently known, but see the brief portrait in E. S. Pankhurst, *The Suffragette Movement. An Intimate Account of Persons and Ideals* (1931), London, Virago, 1977 repr., p. 19; J. Willoughby, 'Alice Cliff – a Local Woman Who Was Ahead of Her Time', *Morley News and Observer*, 6 March 1975, p. 7, with my thanks to Nesta Holden who found this source for me.

27 S. Boston, *Working Women and the Trade Union Movement*, London, Davis-Poynter, 1980, p. 30.

28 United Kingdom. Parliamentary Papers, vol. XXX, 1876. Report of the Factory and Workshops Acts Commission, vol. II, Minutes of Evidence, Cd 1443–1, with my thanks to Michael Roberts, Macquarie University for this reference. Ben Elmy's evidence makes curious reading today. He spoke as an employer, and argued that existing protective legislation limited his capacity to employ women workers, and that this in turn made him uncompetitive with regard to foreign silk-manufacturers, free from the safety measures required in British mills. That is to say, he

asserted the common interest of employer and worker in maintaining the viability of their industry, even at the expense of safety.

29 Boston, *Working Women*, p. 31.

30 S. Lewenhak, *Women and Trade Unions*, London, Ernest Benn, 1977, p. 71.

31 A. Scatcherd to L. Ashworth, 29 March 1875, Box 22, MP.

32 See E. W. Elmy to H. McIlquham, 23 August 1899, EWEP, vol. IV, 47452.

33 E. Ethelmer, 'A Woman Emancipator: a Biographical Sketch', *Westminster Review*, 1894, vol. CXLV, pp. 424–8, p. 426.

34 M. Priestman to A. M. Priestman, 15 Sept 1872, Box 14, MP.

35 E. W. Elmy to H. J. Wilson, 19 June 1887, JEBP. My thanks, once more, to Michael Roberts, for drawing this letter to my attention. Significantly, Elmy also recalled that in her early work for the Vigilance Association, 'I relied entirely upon the cooperation of country most especially north-country friends', and her reservations about London leaderships, and distrust of the corrupt and corrupting metropolis remained evident throughout her career in the women's movement.

36 J. S. Mill to G. C. Robertson, 15 November 1871, in John Stuart Mill, *The Collected Works. The Later Letters*, Volume 17, (F. E. Mineka and D. N. Lindley eds), Toronto, Toronto University Press, 1972, pp. 1853–5.

37 J. S. Mill to G. C. Robertson, 20 October and 31 October 1871, in *Collected Works*, volume 17, pp. 1842–3, 1848–9 respectively.

38 J. S. Mill to G. C. Robertson, 6 November 1871, *Collected Works*, volume 17, pp. 1849–52.

39 R. Strachey, *Millicent Garrett Fawcett*, London, John Murray, 1931, p. 52.

40 J. S. Mill to G. C. Robertson, 27 November 1871; J. S. Mill to J. E. Cairnes, 15 May 1872, both *Collected Works*, vol. 17, pp. 1855–7 and pp. 1894–5 respectively.

41 Quoted in M. Ramelson, *The Petticoat Rebellion. A Century of Struggle for Women's Rights*, London, Lawrence and Wishart, 1967, p. 92.

42 Ignota, 'Women's Suffrage', *Westminster Review*, 1897, vol. CXLVIII, pp. 357–72, esp. p. 360.

43 Quoted in E. S. Pankhurst, *Life of Emmeline Pankhurst. The Suffragette Struggle for Women's Citizenship*, London, T. Werner Lawrie, 1935, p. 25.

44 Quoted in H. Blackburn, *Women's Suffrage. A Record of the Women's Suffrage Movement in the British Isles with Biographical Sketches of Miss Becker*, London, Williams and Norgate, 1902, pp. 42–3.

45 Lydia Becker, 'Women's Suffrage', *Transactions of the National Association for the Promotion of Social Science*, 1877, pp. 701–4, esp. p. 702. She made a similar point in her paper on women's suffrage in the *Contemporary Review*, vol. 4, 1867, pp. 307–16.

46 L. Becker to 'Dearest' (annotation in her own hand shows the addressee to be E. Wolstenholme, though it is catalogued as to E. Pankhurst), 1 March 1874, ESPA.

47 P. B. McLaren to H. P. B. Clark, 29 March 1874, Box 35, MP. She also suggested that Ursula Bright's attempts at fund-raising were sometimes abrasive – possibly they were the cause of some of the umbrage taken by J. S. Mill and Harriet Taylor at applications for funds from the

Manchester Society – reporting that her sister-in-law had been 'very insulting' to her own aunt and uncle, the Penningtons, at a committee meeting of the NSWS 'calling out "Has Mr Pennington given nothing?" in her own peculiar way'.

48 Ethelmer, 'Woman Emancipator', p. 427.

49 B. Taylor, *Eve and the New Jerusalem. Socialism and Feminism in the Nineteenth Century*, New York, Pantheon, 1983, p. 282 suggests that the secularist movement was the main inheritor of the Owenite socialist legacy, a legacy which included a questioning of conventional family forms, and more particularly of women's position in marriage.

50 A. Besant, 'Legalisation of Female Slavery in England', a speech delivered to the first Annual Meeting of the British, Continental and General Federation for the Abolition of Government Regulation of Prostitution (another organisation started by Josephine Butler, and supported by Radical suffragists), reported in the *National Reformer*, 4 June 1876, p. 353. She went on to say that the secularist 'does not despise human passion, or pretend that he has no body', but sees in marriage 'a far higher and nobler humanity' than can be attained through celibacy. The Elmys' own views may also have been reflected in a series of translations from an Italian writer which Ben Elmy was shortly to publish. These looked forward to 'widening somewhat the present code for women, and restricting a good deal that for men', Ben Elmy (trans), 'The Cause of Woman', esp. Part III, *National Reformer*, 10 December 1876, pp. 371–2.

51 M. Estlin to M. Priestman, 12 March n. y. [in an envelope postmarked 1874], Box 20, MP.

52 E. Wolstenholme to Miss Priestman, 14 August 1874, Box 23, MP.

53 L. Ashworth to A. M. Priestman, 13 July 1874, Box 23, MP.

54 A. Henry to A. M. Priestman, 2 May 1875, Box 20, MP. This letter also refers to the Priestman sisters having been 'sent to Coventry', but it is not clear whether this has anything to do with the Elmys, or some quite separate problem.

55 S. Courtauld to A. M. Priestman, 5 September 1875, Box 20, MP.

56 Ajax, *National Reformer*, 20 June 1875, pp. 389–90; 'Congleton Christian Civilisation', ibid., 8 October 1876, pp. 225–6. A personal attack on Lydia Becker was also mounted in this paper, for declining to collect signatures for a petition against any further grant to the royal family: 'Yet Freethinkers and Radicals furnish Miss Becker with a large proportion of all the signatures in favour of Women's Rights, and will continue to do so, despite Miss Becker's refusal to give her help in favour of the over-taxed many', ibid., 30 January 1876, p. 74.

57 See her notice of a new Married Women's Property Bill in the *Englishwoman's Review*, August 1875, no. XXVIII, pp. 376–7. This is the earliest public use of her married name I have yet identified.

58 Enclosure in letter from I. M. S. Tod to Mrs Clarke (H. P. B. Clark), 16 November 1875, Box 22, MP (her emphases), which is also the source for the quotes in the next paragraph.

59 Ibid.

60 Ibid. This account of Josephine Butler's role in the controversy is not

altogether consistent with the one she herself gave to Millicent Garrett Fawcett (see note 62).

61 Ibid., 30 November 1875, Box 22, MP.

62 J. Butler to M. G. Fawcett, 8 December 1875, JEBP. Once again, I thank Michael Roberts for drawing this letter to my attention.

63 M. G. Fawcett to E. W. Elmy, 10 December 1875, FAC.

64 Pankhurst, *Suffragette Movement*, p. 32.

3 A 'STRANGE, ERRATIC GENIUS': Jessie Craigen, working suffragist

1 Quoted in H. Blackburn, *Women's Suffrage. A Record of the Women's Suffrage Movement in the British Isles with Biographical Sketches of Miss Becker*, London, Williams and Norgate, 1902, p. 42.

2 'Jessie Craigen', the *Englishwoman's Review*, 15 January 1900, no. CCXLIV, pp. 65–6, an obituary almost certainly by H. Blackburn, the then editor of that journal. See also H. Blackburn's reminiscences of Jessie Craigen in *Women's Suffrage*, p. 126. For the earliest report I have so far located on her suffrage lectures, see the *Englishwoman's Review*, January 1871, no. V, p. 5.

3 L. Becker to P. B. McLaren, 25 October 1879, quoted in Blackburn, *Women's Suffrage*, pp. 147–8. See the *Women's Suffrage Journal*, 1879, vol. X, pp. 119, 135, 169, for some further reports of Jessie Craigen's meetings that year.

4 This paragraph draws on the following accounts of the Free Trade Hall demonstration: C. A. Biggs, 'Great Britain', in E. C. Stanton, S. B. Anthony, M. J. Gage (eds), *History of Woman Suffrage* (6 vols, 1881–1922), vol. III (1886), New York, Source Books, 1970 repr., esp. pp. 867–8; B. Mason, *The History of the Women's Suffrage Movement*, London, Sherratt and Hughes, 1912, pp. 60–1.

5 Jessie Craigen's contribution is recalled in 'Jessie Craigen', p. 66 and *Women's Suffrage*, pp. 152–3, and reported in *Women's Suffrage Journal*, 1880, vol. XI, p. 45, and ibid., p. 35 for the reflections of 'JHC' (Jessie Craigen's middle name was Hannah, and this report repeats some of the images and phrases in her speech).

6 *Women's Suffrage Journal*, 1880, vol. XI, p. 35.

7 A. M. Priestman to M. Priestman, 22 October 1880, Box 17, MP; *Women's Suffrage Journal*, 1 October 1880, vol. XI, pp. 214–15.

8 M. Priestman to A. M. Priestman, 13 July 1880; M. Priestman to A. M. Priestman, 5 February 1881, Box 14, MP.

9 Quoted in M. Shanley, *Feminism, Marriage and the Law in Victorian England 1850–95*, London, I. B. Tauris, 1989, p. 63.

10 E. C. W. Elmy, 'The Law of England with Regard to the Property and Status of Married Women', *Journal of the Vigilance Association*, 15 June 1881, pp. 52–4, esp. pp. 54, 52.

11 *Journal of the Vigilance Association*, 15 July 1881, p. 61.

12 See, for example, her articles and letters in the *Journal of the Vigilance*

Association, 15 May 1881, pp. 42–3; 15 October 1881, pp. 86–7; 15 September 1883, pp. 94–5; 15 September 1881, p. 79.

13 A. M. Priestman to P. B. McLaren, 12 March 1905, Box 17, MP.

14 L. Becker to L. A. Hallett, 2 April 1880 (Lilias Ashworth had married George Hallett, a Conservative Anglican, in 1877 further confirming fears that she was steadily retreating from her early radical proclivities); L. Becker to J. Stansfeld, 26 May 1880, both quoted in Blackburn, *Women's Suffrage*, pp. 149, 150.

15 A. M. Priestman to M. Priestman, 6 July 1881, Box 17, MP.

16 S. J. Tanner, *How the Women's Suffrage Movement Began in Bristol Fifty Years Ago*, Bristol, Carlyle Press, 1918, p. 14, with my thanks to June Hannam for this source.

17 A. M. Priestman to Margaret Tanner, 12 March 1881, Box 17, MP.

18 A. Scatcherd to A. M. Priestman, 16 January 1885, Box 22, MP.

19 'Jessie Craigen', p. 66.

20 See fragment (in the hand of Jessie Craigen and with other correspondence from her) to Mary Priestman, n. d., unnumbered box, MP; the view of Lydia Becker, reported in P. B. McLaren to H. Taylor, 15 March 1881, f. 165, vol. XIII, HTP.

21 A. M. Priestman to M. Priestman, 9 July 1881, Box 17, MP.

22 J. Craigen to H. Taylor, 19 August 1882, HTP, vol XVIII, f. 162.

23 P. B. McLaren to H. Taylor, 21 September 1882, HTP, vol. XIII, f. 171.

24 A. M. Priestman to P. B. McLaren, 25 August 1882, Box 17, MP.

25 Typescript copy of E. C. Stanton to H. S. Blatch, [November],1882, Library of Congress.

26 P. B. McLaren to E. C. Stanton, 14 November 1882, Elizabeth Cady Stanton Papers, Special Collections, Vassar College Libraries, with my thanks for permission to draw on this material.

27 U. Bright, 'Letter of Mrs Jacob Bright . . .', 22 November 1882, n. p., n. d., MPLA M50/2/20/2.

28 U. M. Bright to E. C. Stanton, 2 July 1883, ECSC. Somewhat oddly, Ursula Bright also confessed that her husband would not like her to speak at the demonstration even if she were able to attend, as 'He is afraid of me losing my domestic character and being dragged into a round of public work.'

29 M. Ramelson, *The Petticoat Rebellion. A Century of Struggle for Women's Rights*, London, Lawrence and Wishart, 1967, p. 92.

30 Quoted in I. H. Harper, *The Life and Work of Susan B. Anthony* (1898, 3 vols), New York, Arno, 1969 repr., vol. 2, pp. 546, 565.

31 Quoted in T. Stanton and H. S. Blatch, *Elizabeth Cady Stanton, as Revealed in her Letters, Diary and Reminiscences* (2 vols), New York, Harper Brothers, 1922, vol. 2, pp. 208–9.

32 P. B. McLaren to E. C. Stanton, 17 July 1883, ECSC; P. B. McLaren to H. P. B. Clark, 19 January 1884, Box 36, MP.

33 A. Scatcherd to A. M. Priestman, 22 February 1884, Box 22, MP.

34 P. B. McLaren to H. P. B. Clark, 9 October 1883; H. P. B. Clark to P. B. McLaren, 10 October, 12 October 1883, Boxes 36 and 50, respectively, MP.

35 A. Scatcherd to A. M. Priestman, 27 October 1883, Box 22, MP.

36 Biggs, 'Great Britain', pp. 874–5.

37 P. B. McLaren to H. P. B. Clark, 5 November 1883, Box 36, MP.

38 H. Blackburn to A. M. Priestman, 15 November 1883; P. B. McLaren to H. P. B. Clark, 2 February 1884, Boxes 19 and 36 respectively, MP.

39 For example, T. Stanton (ed.) *The Woman Question in Europe*, London and New York, G. P. Putnam, 1884, Introduction, pp. v–vi suggests some sense of Anglo-Saxon superiority among United States and British suffragists, both in the way the book is organised, and in the stance taken towards women's movements in other parts of the world.

40 M. B. Lucas to A. M. Priestman, 10 January 1884; P. B. McLaren to H. P. B. Clark, 19 January 1884, Boxes 23 and 36, MP respectively.

41 P. B. McLaren to H. P. B. Clark, 2, 9, 17, 20 February, Box 36, MP.

42 H. P. B. Clark, M. G. Fawcett, P. B. McLaren and I. M. S. Tod to W. E. Gladstone, March 1884, MPLA, M50/2/1/37; A. M. Priestman to P. M. McLaren, 28 February, 9 March 1884, Box 17, MP.

43 P. B. McLaren to H. P. B. Clark, 9 February, 13 March 1884, Box 36, MP.

44 H. P. B. Clark to P. B. McLaren, 24 May 1884, Box 50, MP.

45 P. B. McLaren to H. P. B. Clark, n.d., Box 36, MP.

46 E. W. Elmy, letter to *The Times*, 24 May 1884, which refused it publication, reprinted in J. Lewis (ed.) *Before the Vote was Won. Arguments for and against Women's Suffrage*, London, Routledge and Kegan Paul, 1987, pp. 404–8.

47 A. Scatcherd to A. M. Priestman, 20 November 1884, 16 January 1885, Box 22, MP.

48 Ibid., 24 March 1886, Box 22, MP.

49 Ibid., 14 March 1886; and see also a further letter on this question on 29 March 1886, Box 22, MP.

50 W. T. Stead to Anna Maria Priestman, 12 March 1886, Box 23, MP.

51 F. Newman to A. M. Priestman, 30 March, 26 June, 30 September 1887; 4, 10 and 14 October 1887; and A. M. Priestman's Account Book for the 'Jessie Craigen Lecture Fund', Boxes 21 and 11, MP respectively.

52 A. M. Priestman to P. B. McLaren, 19 May 1898, Box 17, MP. The only other obituary I know for Jessie Craigen, beside that in the *Englishwoman's Review*, is that in the *Zoophilist*, 1 November 1899, vol. 19, p. 152. This gives her age at death as 57, but her death certificate gives it as 64. It also declared that 'As a woman of the people she exercised a great influence over the working classes. . . . We shall miss her courageous and outspoken advocacy . . . her racy and eloquent speeches.' My thanks to Irene Cassidy for locating these documents for me.

4 'THE GRANDEST VICTORY': Married women and the franchise

1 T. Stanton and H. S. Blatch, *Elizabeth Cady Stanton as Revealed in her Letters, Diary and Reminiscences*, 2 vols, New York, Harper Brothers,

1922, vol. 2, pp. 235, 270; E. C. Stanton, *Eighty Years and More: Reminiscences, 1815–1897*, New York (1898), New York, Schocken, 1970 repr., pp. 399, 422–3; P. B. McLaren to E. C. Stanton, 17 November 1887, ECSC.

2 Compare 'Women's Suffrage', 'The Enfranchisement of Women' with E. C. W. Elmy, 'Married Women and the Electoral Franchises', *Journal of the Vigilance Association*, 15 August 1883, pp. 81–3; 15 February, 1885, pp. 9–10 and 15 March 1886, pp. 21–2, respectively.

3 'The Annual Meeting', *Journal of the Vigilance Association*, 1 October 1886, pp. 80–4.

4 E. Stanton, *Eighty Years*, p. 408; E. C. Stanton to the Priestman sisters, 21 February and 26 February 1888, Box 23, MP.

5 P. B. McLaren to H. Taylor, 21 January 1888, 6 March 1888, HTP, vol. 13, f. 173, and f. 175 respectively; H. Taylor to S. B. Anthony, 7 March 1888, C. Smitt Collection, Huntington Library, Los Angeles; E. Stanton, *Eighty Years*, p. 410, which provides also a sympathetic portrait of May Dilke.

6 L. Becker's editorial in the *Women's Suffrage Journal*, 1889, vol. 20, p. 48, when describing the NSWS split, argued that the married women's claim for the vote was an 'uncalled for and gratuitous obstruction' to the demand for women's suffrage. 'The Women's Suffrage Crisis', *Personal Rights Journal*, April 1889, pp. 26–7, records the dissidents' intervention at the first annual meeting of the CNSWS, an episode again generally ignored in the standard histories of the suffrage movement for this period.

7 A. Scatcherd to A. M. and M. Priestman, 26 February 1886, Box 22, MP.

8 For Richard Pankhurst's account of the formation of the Women's Franchise League, which acknowledges Elizabeth Wolstenholme Elmy, Alice Scatcherd, and Harriet McIlquham as its founders, see Women's Franchise League, 'Report of Proceedings at the Inaugural Meeting, London July 25th 1889', London, Hansard Publishing Union, 1889. E. S. Pankhurst, *The Suffragette Movement. An Intimate Account of Persons and Ideals* (1931), London, Virago, 1977 repr, p. 95 serves to emphasise the role of her parents at the expense of those who actually undertook this task. H. S. Blatch and A. Lutz, *Challenging Years. The Memoirs of Harriet Stanton Blatch*, New York, G. P. Putnam, 1940, p. 73, instead emphasises the role of Ursula Bright, and the Women's Franchise League's *First Annual Report 1889–90*, ESPA 341, records that the Brights organised the preliminary meeting which led to its formation. Thereafter, Ursula and Jacob Bright held aloof from the new society for a while, for reasons which remain unclear, see E. W. Elmy to H. McIlquham, 9 May 1889, 5 June 1890; and her reminiscences of this period in ibid., 19 September 1904, 27 September 1904, in EWEP, vols I and VI, respectively.

9 Stanton and Blatch, *Elizabeth Cady Stanton*, vol. 2, p. 288 n. 4. Elizabeth Cady Stanton's endorsement of the League and involvement in its business in 1890 is evident also in the 'Programme for the the the Women's Franchise League International Conference, 16–17 July 1890', proof copy in Harriet McIlquham papers, Fawcett Library, London. This

conference was apparently prompted by a gathering of international jurists in London for the International Conference on Peace and Arbitration, Women's Franchise League, *First Annual Report 1889–90.*

10 Women's Franchise League, 'Report of Inaugural Meeting', records that among the League's early leadership were also Clementia and P. A. Taylor, Josephine Butler, Emmeline Pankhurst and Florence Fenwick Miller from among a second generation of Radical suffragists.

11 Women's Franchise League, 'Report of Meeting in Support of "The Women's Disabilities Bill" ', London: Hansard Publishing Union, 1889, MPLA M50/1/32/3, and *First Annual Report 1889–90.*

12 Women's Franchise League, 'Inaugural Proceedings', p. 22. For a further account of the League's programme see F. F. Miller, 'On the Programme of the Women's Franchise League', London, Hansard Publishing Union, 1890 and Mrs J. Bright, 'The Origins and Objects of the Women's Franchise League of Great Britain and Ireland', in M. W. Sewall (ed.) *The World Congress of Representative Women*, Chicago, Rand McNally, 1894, pp. 415–20. Other sources for the activities of the League are in occasional, irregular reports and correspondence in the *Personal Rights Journal*, the *Women's Gazette and Weekly News*, the *Women's Herald*, the *Women's Penny Paper*, and the *Women's Signal*, which last provides the only documentary source I have so far been able to identify for its final years.

13 Stanton and Blatch, *Elizabeth Cady Stanton*, vol. 2, p. 262.

14 Mrs W. Elmy, 'Foreign Investments and British Industry', n. p., Wyman and Sons, 1888, comprising four letters reprinted from the *Manchester Courier*, December 1887, and see also her 'A Woman's Plea to Women', London, Women's Printing Society, 1886, reprinted from the report of a paper read before the Congleton Fair Trade League in the *Macclesfield Courier*, 8 November 1886. Moreover, Harriet McIlquham, her friend and associate in forming the League, was a Liberal Unionist.

15 E. W. Elmy to H. McIlquham, 26 May 1890, 5 June 1890, 27 October 1906, EWEP, vol. I and vol. VII respectively.

16 J. Walkowitz, *City of Dreadful Delight. Narratives of Sexual Danger in Late-Victorian London*, London, Virago, 1992, p. 67. Florence Fenwick Miller is another figure who has been surprisingly neglected in studies of the nineteenth-century women's movement, but see R. T. Van Arsdel, 'Florence Fenwick Miller 1854–1935. A Life of Many Choices', unpub. manuscript held at the Fawcett Library, London Guildhall University.

17 E. W. Elmy to H. McIlquham, 9 October 1890, 29 October 1890, EWEP, vol. I.

18 Ibid., 27 October 1890. Pankhurst, *Suffragette Movement*, p. 96, presents a different interpretation of Elmy's departure from the League which is misleading both in terms of the timing of these events, and in falsely suggesting a change of position on the inclusion of married women in the suffrage demand by Elmy. Women's Franchise League, *First Annual Report*, suggests Elmy's resignation followed the cooption of Ursula Bright and others on to the Executive.

19 E. W. Elmy to H. McIlquham, 9 October 1890, EWEP, vol. I; WFLMB, 25 July 1890.

20 WFLMB, 23 April and 29 May 1891; also 24 November 1890; 2

January 1891; 2 February 1891; 18 March 1891; 4 December 1891; 25 April 1893; 18 May 1893; 16 March 1894; 9 June 1894.

21 For example, WFLMB, 15 September 1890; 2 February 1891; 3 February 1892; 18 May 1892; 9 June 1894. Lilias Ashworth Hallett also reported some attempt to re-unite with the Parliament Street Society in the spring of 1891, and passed on Eva McLaren's account of proceedings at a joint conference when 'Dr Pankhurst showed signs of his intention to boss the whole business', leading the larger society to decline, L. A. Hallett to M. G. Fawcett, May 1891, MPLA, M50/2/1/141.

22 WFLMB, 2 February 1891; 18 March 1891 (which suggests that its income for the previous year was a little over £350); 4 May 1891; 11 November 1891; 12 April 1894, and see also E. W. Elmy to H. McIlquham, 27 October 1889, EWEP, vol. 1.

23 WFLMB, 15 September 1890; 2 February 1891; 18 March 1891; 23 April 1893.

24 Bright, 'Origins and Objects', pp. 416, 418. Ursula Bright did not herself attend the Congress, and her paper was read for her by Jane Cobden Unwin, as a representative of the League.

25 Ibid., pp. 416, 417, 420.

26 Women's Franchise League, 'Report of Inaugural Proceedings', p. 22.

27 M. Dilke, *The Nineteenth Century*, 1889, vol. 26, pp. 97–103.

28 This perspective is evident also in R. Haldane, 'Some Economic Aspects of Women's Suffrage', *Contemporary Review*, 1890, vol. 58, pp. 830–8. Haldane was at this time a rising young Liberal politician and in 1889 and 1890 introduced into Parliament the Women's Franchise League's Women's Disabilities Removal Bill.

29 Recalled in Blatch and Lutz, *Challenging Years*, p. 79. See also S. B. Anthony and I. H. Harper, *History of Woman Suffrage* (6 vols, 1881–1922), vol. 4 (1886), New York, Source Books, 1970 repr., pp. 310–11 which gives the text of part of her paper 'Woman and the Economic Factor' to the National-American Convention in Washington in 1898, and compare also D. Kirkby, *Alice Henry. The Power of Pen and Voice. The Life of an Australian-American Labour Reformer*, Cambridge, Cambridge University Press, 1991, which identifies these new ideas as 'industrial feminism'.

30 E. W. Elmy to H. McIlquham, 23 April 1891, EWEP, vol. 1.

31 Ibid., 21 March 1891.

32 Mrs. W. Elmy, 'The Decision in the Clitheroe Case and its Consequences', Manchester, Manchester Guardian Printworks, 1891; 'Women's Emancipation Union. An Association of Workers to Secure the Political, Social, and Economic Independence of Women', Congleton, November 1891, with my thanks to David Doughan, the Fawcett Library, London Guildhall University for locating this last for me.

33 See for example, the use of 'worker' in 'Women's Emancipation Union', and see also E. W. Elmy to H. McIlquham, 23 July 1891, 30 October 1901, EWEP, vol. I.

34 E. W. Elmy to H. McIlquham, 29 December 1895, 14 December 1895, EWEP, vol. II. The five named for the 'inner Cabinet' were Harriet

McIlquham, Caroline Smith and her daughter Julia (Caroline Smith was a sister of George Holyoake, once again suggesting the links between some secularists and the women's movement), Mrs J. G. Grenfell from Bristol (and another old friend of the Priestman sisters), and the temperance campaigner, Lady Florence Dixie, one of the WEU's financial mainstays.

35 E. W. Elmy to H. McIlquham, 14 January and 25 March 1892, EWEP, vol. I, and see her similar arguments on behalf of a subsequent compromise formula, E. W. Elmy, 'Women's Suffrage', *Shafts*, April 1897. The controversy over this bill led to accusations that the Women's Franchise League 'had become a mere annexe to the Fabian Society': J. H. Levy to Mrs Bright, 2 April 1892, ESPA 341.

36 Ibid., 16 April, 18 May and 23 June 1892, in the last of which she also quoted from a report in the *Daily News*, 25 April 1892.

37 Ibid.

38 WFLMB, 2 May, 23 May, 5 August, 28 September, 19 October 1892; U. Bright to E. Pankhurst, 20 November 1893, ESPA, 325.

39 E. W. Elmy to H. McIlquham, 3 July 1992, EWEP, vol. I; Ignota, 'Pioneers! Oh, Pioneers!', obituary of Ben Elmy, *Westminster Review*, pril 1906, pp. 415–7.

40 U. Bright to E. Pankhurst, 5 November 1893, ESPA, 325.

41 E. W. Elmy to H. McIlquham, 17 and 21 November 1893, EWEP, vol. I. She also dismissed Ursula Bright's claims that the League had distributed half a million leaflets: 'People need not pretend to the impossible.'

42 W. McLaren to M. G. Fawcett, 21, 26 November 1893, 29 December 1893, 8, 11, 13 January 1894, MPLA, M50/2/1/207–211.

43 U. Bright to E. Pankhurst, 27 November 1893, ESPA, 325.

44 Ibid., 5 April 1894. It is noteworthy that H. Blackburn, 'Great Britain' in S. B. Anthoy and I. H. Harper, *History of Woman Suffrage*, vol. IV (1902), New York, Source Book Press, 1970 repr., pp. 1012–23, relegates any notice of the Local Government Act to an addendum on p. 1022.

45 E. W. Elmy to H. McIlquham, 5, 7, and 8 June 1894, EWEP, vol. II.

46 G. Lewis, *Eva Gore Booth and Esther Roper. A Biography*, London, Pandora, 1988, p. 84.

47 U. Bright to E. Pankhurst, 10 July 1894, ESPA, 325.

48 E. W. Elmy to H. McIlquham, 23 November 1895: H. McIlquham to A. M. Priestman, 17 December 1895, EWEP, vol. II.

49 D. Rubinstein, *Before the Suffragettes. Women's Emancipation in the 1890s*, Brighton, Harvester Press, 1986, pp. 233, p. x.

5 AMONG THE 'INSURGENT WOMEN': Hannah Mitchell, socialist and suffragist

1 H. Mitchell, *The Hard Way Up. The Autobiography of Hannah Mitchell, Suffragette and Rebel*, (ed. G. Mitchell 1968), London, Virago, 1977 repr., p. 90.

2 Ibid., pp. 90–1.

3 Ibid., p. 88.

4 Ibid., p. 82.

5 Ibid., pp. 67–8.

6 Ibid., p. 79.

7 Ibid., p. 80.

8 Ibid., p. 88.

9 Ibid., p. 114.

10 Ibid., p. 88.

11 Jill Liddington and Jill Norris, *One Hand Tied Behind Us. The Rise of the Women's Suffrage Movement*, London, Virago, 1978, pp. 15–16.

12 Mitchell, *The Hard Way Up*, pp. 99–100.

13 Ibid., p. 89.

14 Ibid., p. 102.

15 Ibid., pp. 112–13.

16 Ibid., p. 86.

17 Ibid., p. 98.

18 *Women's Signal*, 7 January 1897.

19 *Women's Franchise*, 15 April 1897.

20 Ibid., 29 April 1897.

21 Ibid., 1 July 1897.

22 U. Bright to E. Pankhurst, 30 May, 1 June, 26 June, 10 July 1894, ESPA, 325.

23 Ibid., 16 June 1894.

24 E. S. Pankhurst, *The Suffragette Movement. An Intimate Account of Persons and Ideals* (1931), London, Virago, 1977 repr., p. 120.

25 A. Clark to H. P. B. Clark, 20 May 1898, Box 75, MP.

26 E.W. Elmy to H. McIlquham, 25 February, 2 March 1894.

27 Quoted in R. Strachey, *Millicent Garrett Fawcett*, London, John Murray, 1931, p. 158. M. Cozens had also organised an ill-fated Hyde Park demonstration prior to the St James Hall meeting in support of Rollit's Bill: see M. Cozens to Mrs Bright, 2 April 1892, ESPA 341.

28 WEU leaflet, n. d., EWEP, vol. II, f. 198. WEU branches were here recorded in Birmingham, Glasgow, Coventry, Islington, Leeds, Oxford, Edinburgh, Dumbarton, Greentown, and Newton Stewart.

29 Ibid., and E. W. Elmy to H. McIlquham, 10 and 15 June, 2 October 1895, EWEP, vol.II.

30 Ibid., 6 July 1896.

31 Ibid., 26 February 1896.

32 Ibid., 9 and 13 September, 30 October, 4 November 1896, the last item of which is in EWEP, vol. III.

33 Ibid., 6 July 1896.

34 See the *Women's Signal*, 27 May 1897 for a report of the first annual meeting of the Union, and Union of Practical Suffragists, 'Leaflet No XII', the Fawcett Library, London Guildhall University, with my thanks to David Doughan for locating this, and other leaflets for me.

35 E. W. Elmy to H. McIlquham, 2 February, 26 February 1896, EWEP, vol. II.

36 H. S. Blatch and A. Lutz, *Challenging Years. The Memoirs of Harriot Stanton Blatch*, New York, G. P. Putnam, 1940, p. 73.

37 The classic example of this approach remains G. Dangerfield's influential account, *The Strange Death of Liberal England* (1935), London, Paladin, 1970 repr., and see also A. Rosen, *Rise Up Women. The Militant Campaigns of the Women's Social and Political Union, 1903–14*, London, Routledge and Kegan Paul, 1974.

38 See D. Montefiore, *From a Victorian to a Modern*, London, E. Archer, 1927, pp. 72–83 and Dora Montefiore's letter on tax-resistance in *The Women's Signal* 17 June 1897. Like Elmy her unconventional private life was to prove a source of discord in radical movements; see C. Collette, 'Socialism and Scandal: the Sexual Politics of the Early Labour Movement', *History Workshop Journal*, no. 23, 1987, pp. 102–11.

39 E. G. Booth, 'The Women's Suffrage Movement among Trade Unionists' in B. Villiers (ed.) *The Case for Women's Suffrage*, London, Fisher and Unwin, 1907, p. 50.

40 E. W. Elmy to H. McIlquham, 12 February 1905, 2 July 1905, vol. VI.

41 Ibid., 28 October 1904.

42 Ibid., 8 May 1905.

43 In the early years of the WSPU, Elizabeth Wolstenholme Elmy conceived of its supporters as 'insurgent women', rather than as 'militants', see for example her 'Song of the Insurgent Women', 14 November 1905, EWEP, vol. VII.

44 Quoted in G. Parker, 'Introduction' to E. Stanton, *Eighty Years. The Reminiscences of Elizabeth Cady Stanton* (1898), New York, Schocken Books, 1971 repr., p. xix and E. DuBois, 'Woman Suffrage and the Left: An International Socialist-Feminist Perspective', *New Left Review*, 1991, no. 186, pp. 20–45, esp. p. 28.

45 Ibid.

46 T. Stanton and H. S. Blatch, (eds), *Elizabeth Cady Stanton in her Letters, Diary and Reminiscences*, 2 vols, New York, Harper Brothers, 1922, vol. 1, p. xviii.

47 E. W. Elmy to H. McIlquham, 25 January 1905, vol. VI, EWEP.

48 Mitchell, *The Hard Way Up*, p. 126.

49 Ibid., p. 127.

50 E. Pankhurst, *My Own Story* (1914), London, Virago, 1979 repr. pp. 42–3.

51 Mitchell, *The Hard Way Up*, pp. 130–1.

52 Ibid., pp. 136–7.

53 Ibid., p. 139.

54 Ibid., pp. 148–9.

55 Ibid., pp. 149–50.

56 Montefiore, *From a Victorian*, pp. 72–4.

57 Pankhurst, *Suffragette Movement*, p. 187.

58 Ibid., pp. 187–8, 208.

59 Ibid.

6 'A MERRY, MILITANT SAINT': Mary Gawthorpe and the argument of the stone

1 M. Gawthorpe, *Up Hill to Holloway*, Penobscot, Maine, Traversity Press, 1962, pp. 1–15, 36; and M. Gawthorpe, 'Book of the Suffragette Prisoners', typescript questionnaire, 1931, p. 1, SFCM.

2 Gawthorpe, *Up Hill*, pp. 26–7, 32.

3 Ibid., pp. 104–5, 59–60.

4 Ibid., p. 65.

5 Ibid., pp. 156–7.

6 Tom Steele, personal communication with the author.

7 Ibid., p. 197.

8 Ibid., p. 206.

9 J. Clayton, *The Rise and Decline of Socialism in Great Britain 1884–1924*, London, Faber and Cryer, 1926, pp. 155–6.

10 Gawthorpe, *Up Hill*, p. 207.

11 C. Pankhurst to M. Gawthorpe, 1 March 1906, quoted in ibid., pp. 209–10.

12 Ibid., p. 214.

13 Ibid., p. 219.

14 See F. W. Pethick-Lawrence and J. Edwards (eds) *The Reformers' Year Book*, London, Clarion Company, 1908, p. 232, for a short account of Mary Gawthorpe's career in the previous few years.

15 Gawthorpe, *Up Hill*, pp. 222–4.

16 L. Moore, 'The Woman's Suffrage Campaign in the 1907 Aberdeen by-election', *Northern Scotland*, 1983, vol. 5, pp. 155–178, esp. pp. 158, 160, which rightly emphasises the importance of local studies.

17 Gawthorpe, *Up Hill*, pp. 227–8; *Women's Franchise*, 1 August 1907.

18 E. W. Elmy to H. McIlquham, 28 August and 3 September 1906, EWEP, vol. VI.

19 H. Mitchell, *The Hard Way Up. The Autobiography of Hannah Mitchell, Suffragette and Rebel* (ed. G. Mitchell 1968), London, Virago, 1977 repr., pp. 158, 159.

20 E. W. Elmy to Harriet McIlquham, 3 November 1906, EWEP, vol. VII.

21 Ibid.

22 Mitchell, *Hard Way Up*, pp. 160–1.

23 Gawthorpe, *Up Hill*, p. 160.

24 M. Gawthorpe, 'The Book of Suffragette Prisoners', p. 125, SFCM.

25 Ibid.

26 Mitchell, *Hard Way Up*, p. 163; Gawthorpe, *Up Hill*, p. 249.

27 Quoted in a cutting from the *British Journal of Nursing*, 20 January 1906, and see the cutting from the *Manchester Guardian*, 15 January 1906, MPLA, M50/2/1/219.

28 'Complimentary Banquet to the Suffragists', a programme held at the Fawcett Library, London Guildhall University.

29 E. S. Pankhurst, *The Suffragette Movement. An Intimate Account of Persons and Ideals* (1931), London, Virago, 1977 repr., p. 98.

30 H. Swanwick, *I Have Been Young*, London, Gollancz, 1935, p. 192.

31 R. West, 'The Freewoman', *Time and Tide*, 16 July 1926, reprinted from *Equal Rights*, and again in D. Spender (comp.), *Time and Tide Wait for No Man*, London, Pandora Press, 1984, p. 64.

32 E. P. Lawrence to J. Baines, 14 November 1907, JBP. My thanks to Judith Smart, Royal Melbourne Institute of Technology for sharing her research on Jennie Baines with me.

33 Mitchell, *Hard Way Up*, pp. 168–9.

34 Gawthorpe, 'Book of Suffragette Prisoners', SFCM.

35 C. Pankhurst to J. Baines, 28 August, 1907, JBP, and see also E. Pankhurst to S. Robinson, 22 June 1907, reproduced in Mitchell, *The Hard Way Up*, pp. 247–8. By this point Dora Montefiore had already been expelled from the WSPU, uneasy about the new direction in militancy. Her 'heterodox' sexual history, and a taste for cocaine lozenges, also counted against her, see F. E. Rowe to H. McIlquham, 26 September 1905, 9 January 1907, H. McIlquham Papers, Fawcett Library.

36 E. W. Elmy to H. McIlquham, 10 October 1907, EWEP, vol. VII. Emmeline Pankhurst's wish to displace Edith How-Martynd and C. Despard as joint secretaries of the WSPU also seems to have been an issue, see F. E. Rowe to H. McIlquham, 24 September 1907.

37 M. E. Gawthorpe, 'Votes for Men' (1907), London, Women's Press.

38 E. Pankhurst, *My Own Story* (1914), London, Virago, 1979 repr., p. 96.

39 I. O. Ford to M. G. Fawcett, 14 February 1908, MGFP.

40 *Votes for Women*, 7 May, 4 and 18 June, 1908.

41 Ibid., 2, 23 July 1908.

42 Ibid., 14, 21 and 28 January 1909.

43 *Common Cause*, 24 June 1909.

44 Ibid., 21 January 1909; H. Swanwick, *I Have Been Young*, London, Victor Gollancz, 1935, p. 192.

7 WOMEN'S SUFFRAGE AMONG THE BOHEMIANS: Laurence Housman joins the movement

1 The comment is that of C. R. Ashbee reporting how Laurence Housman had walked from Hereford to London as a protest against railway travel (although his baggage was put on a train), early December 1903, CRAJ.

2 L. Housman to Mrs [J.] Ashbee, 10 September 1905, CRAJ. Laurence Housman and Janet Ashbee kept up a life-long correspondence, some of which survived in the journal kept by her husband, C. R. Ashbee.

3 L. Housman, *The Unexpected Years*, London, Jonathan Cape, 1937, pp. 140–1.

4 Quoted in J. Hunt, 'Laurence Housman, the Younger Brother', *Journal of the Housman Society*, 1990, vol. 16, pp. 6–19, esp. p. 17, with my thanks to Pam Burroughs, formerly Librarian of Street Public Library for her help in locating material regarding Clemence and Laurence Housman.

5 Ibid., p. 8.

6 Ibid., p. 9.

7 A. Crawford, *C. R. Ashbee. Architect, Designer and Romantic Socialist*, New Haven, Yale University Press, 1985, p. 92, which provides also an account of the cultural and social circles in which Laurence Housman moved.

8 Hunt, 'Laurence Housman', p. 14.

9 L. Housman to J. Ashbee, 9 February 1908, CRAJ.

10 L. Housman to J. Ashbee, n. d. (June 1908), CRAJ.

11 Housman, *Unexpected Years*, p. 259.

12 Ibid., pp. 263–4.

13 Ibid., p. 49.

14 L. Housman to J. Ashbee, 24 June 1908, CRAJ.

15 L. Tickner, *A Spectacle of Women*, London, Chatto and Windus, 1987, p. 14. This study provides a superb analysis of the role of artists, writers and actors in the suffrage campaign, see esp. pp. 23, 69, 71, 94, 117, where the role of the Housmans is recorded.

16 Housman, *Unexpected Years*, pp. 247, 262–4.

17 Ibid., pp. 274–5.

18 Ibid., p. 267.

19 Ibid., p. 270.

20 Ibid., p. 267.

21 C. Pankhurst to Mrs Baines, 23 September 1909, JBP.

22 Ibid.

23 Reported in *Votes for Women*, 18 February 1909.

24 M. Gawthorpe to M. W. Dunlop, 10 October 1909, SFCM.

25 *Votes for Women*, 15, 22, 29 October 1909.

26 E. P. Lawrence to Miss Marsden, 1 December 1909, JBP.

27 Quoted in S. S. Holton, *Feminism and Democracy. Women's Suffrage and Reform Politics*, Cambridge, Cambridge University Press, 1986, p. 65, where I discuss the 'democratic suffragist' perspective on women's suffrage in more detail.

28 R. West, 'A Reed of Steel', in *The Young Rebecca*, J. Marcus, ed., London, Macmillan, 1992, pp. 243–62, esp. p. 254.

29 R. West, letter to the *Daily Herald*, 11 September 1912, reprinted in *The Young Rebecca*, pp. 369–71. The NUWSS's journal, the *Common Cause*, 16 December 1909, offered a similar assessment.

30 *Votes for Women*, 18 March 1910. See also the *Common Cause*, 10 February 1910, which reports an 'exceedingly witty' speech which she made at the Free Trade Hall, Manchester.

31 M. Gawthorpe, 'Book of Suffragette Prisoners', SFCM; West, 'Reed of Steel', p. 64.

32 This account is based on C. Lytton, *Prisons and Prisoners*, London, William Heinemann, 1914, esp. pp. 203, 227, 235.

33 *Votes for Women*, 7 October 1910.

34 Dora Marsden, quoted in L. Garner, *A Bright and Beautiful Spirit*, Aldershot, Avebury, 1990, p. 31.

35 Ibid., p. 36.

36 Housman, *Unexpected Years*, pp. 276, 269.

37 Ibid., pp. 45, 48–9; *Common Cause*, 3 March 1910.
38 Housman, *Unexpected Years*, p. 284.
39 Quoted in Garner, *Bright and Beautiful Spirit*, p. 55.
40 Quoted in ibid., p. 56.
41 Quoted in ibid., p. 58.
42 Quoted in ibid., pp. 50, 120, n. 10.
43 N. Cott, *The Grounding of Modern Feminism*, New Haven, Yale University Press, 1987, pp. 3–16, discusses the adoption of the term 'feminism' in this period, and pp. 38–9 provides an account of comparable developments among members of the Heterodoxy group in the United States.
44 A. N. Chew, 'Let the women be alive', from a letter to the *Freewoman*, 18 April 1912, reproduced in *The Life and Writings of Ada Neild Chew*, (comp. D. N. Chew), London, Virago Press, 1982, pp. 235–8.
45 Unsigned copy, Editor, Literature Department (Mrs Bjorkman), to M. Gawthorpe and D. Marsden, 24 February 1912, MWDP, M138.
46 Quoted in Garner, *Bright and Beautiful Spirit*, p. 51.
47 Mary Humphry Ward, quoted in ibid., p. 6.

8 'ON THE HORNS OF A DILEMMA': Alice Clark, liberal Quaker and democratic suffragist

1 A. Clark to the Priestman sisters, 24 June 1910, Box 75, MP.
2 Manuscript memoir of Alice Clark, CA.; M. C. G. (Margaret Clark Gillett), *Alice Clark of C. & J. Clark, Ltd., Street, Somerset*, privately published (c. 1934), p. 8.
3 A. Clark to M. Priestman, 5 May 1910, Box 75, MP.
4 Almost certainly as discussed in K. Pearson, *The Ethic of Freethought and Other Addresses and Essays*, London, Adam and Charles Black, 1890.
5 A. Clark to P. B. McLaren, 23 June 1898, Box 75, MP.
6 Ibid., 8 May, 15 May, 30 May 1905, Box 75, MP.
7 This apt phrase is borrowed from B. Lehane, *C. &. J. Clark, 1825–1975*, Street, C. &. J. Clark, 1975, p. 4.
8 A. Clark to P. B. McLaren, 26 February 1906, Box 75, MP.
9 A. Clark to the Priestman sisters, 12 December 1906, Box 75, MP.
10 J. Roe, *Beyond Belief. Theosophy in Australia, 1879–1939*, Sydney, University of New South Wales Press, 1986, p. 168, and see also pp. 178–80 which look more closely at how Charlotte Despard's feminism was inflected by her theosophy.
11 *Daily News*, 1 March 1907, cutting, together with numerous letters of support and other cuttings regarding Alice Clark's tax-resistance, Box 76, MP. It appears she halted this process after legal advice that the authorities might move against her father's property to secure payment.
12 A. Clark to the Priestman sisters, 25 July 1907, Box 75, MP.
13 A. Clark to M. Priestman, 14 November 1907, Box 75, MP.
14 A. Clark to the Priestman sisters, 26 June 1908, Box 75, MP.
15 Ibid., 18 November 1908.
16 Ibid., 10 October 1909. G. M. Trevelyan, *Garibaldi and the One Thousand*, London, Longman, Green, 1909 had recently been published and

was possibly the prompt to this reflection. A few years later Alice Clark was to help Trevelyan with his life of John Bright, undertaking some research for him among her family papers.

17 M. C. Gillett to Alice Clark, 4 September 1909, Box 77, MP.
18 S. B. Clark to A. Clark, 16 January 1910, GP.
19 Ibid., 27 January 1910, GP.
20 A. Clark to the Priestman sisters, 21 June, 24 June 1910, Box 75, MP.
21 M. C. Gillett to A. Clark, 28 November 1910, Box 77, MP.
22 C. Despard to A. Clark, 18 October 1910; A. Clark to the Priestman sisters, 27 November 1910, Boxes 77 and 75, MP, respectively.
23 L. Housman, *The Unexpected Years*, London, Jonathan Cape, 1937, pp. 268, 271.
24 Ibid. pp. 271–2.
25 Ibid., pp. 272–3.
26 Ibid., pp. 271–2.
27 L. Housman to Sarah Clark, 11 April (postmark, 1912), HP; R. Clark to A. Clark, 12 November 1912, Box 77, MP.
28 L. Housman to J. Ashbee, 4 December 1910, CRAJ.
29 Housman, *Unexpected Years*, pp. 286–9.
30 Quoted in A. Born, 'Clemence Housman, 1861–1955', typescript, 1978, HC.
31 L. Housman to J. Ashbee, 16 October 1911, CRAJ.
32 C. P. Scott, Memoranda, 15 June 1911, Add Mss 50901, British Library.
33 H. N. Brailsford telegrams to C. P. Scott, 25, 26, 27 November 1911, Kathleen Courtney papers, Fawcett Library.
34 M. G. Fawcett to J. R. Macdonald, 28 January 1912, James Ramsay Macdonald papers, Public Record Office, 30/69/1156/62–4.
35 E. S. Pankhurst, *The Suffragette Movement. An Intimate Account of Persons and Ideals* (1931), London, Virago, 1977 repr., p. 360.
36 H. A. Franklin to Herbert Samuel, 12 February 1912, Hugh Franklin Papers, Fawcett Library.
37 Case of William Ball. Report by Sir George Savage, MD, F. R. C. P. United Kingdom. Parliamentary Papers, 1912, Cd 6175, in the Fawcett Library.
38 Pankhurst, *Suffragette Movement*, p. 228n.
39 M. Gawthorpe to Mrs Bjorkman, 27 March 1912, MWDP, M138.
40 Ibid.
41 M. Gawthorpe, 'The Book of Suffragette Prisoners', SFCM.
42 Quoted in L. Garner, *A Brave and Beautiful Spirit. Dora Marsden, 1882–1960*, Aldershot, Avebury, 1990, p. 82.
43 *Freewoman*, 26 September, 1912, pp. 375–9 (the use of the masculine pronoun in such a context was not questioned at this time).
44 M. Gawthorpe to Mrs Bjorkman, 11 June 1912, 19 July 1912, MWDP, M138.
45 L. Housman to S. B. Clark, 7 December 1913, HP.
46 S. B. Clark to A. Clark, 11 and 13 June 1912, GP.
47 A. Clark to H. P. B. Clark, 24 November 1911; A. Clark to the Priestman sisters, 29 November 1911, both Box 75, MP.
48 M. Chaytor and J. Lewis, 'Introduction', to Alice Clark, *The Working*

Life of Women in the Seventeeth Century (1919), London, Routledge & Kegan Paul, 1986, p. x.

49 A. Clark, *The Working Life of Women in the Seventeenth Century*, London, George Routledge, 1919, p. lviii.

50 *The Standard*, 28 December 1912, Friends' House, Cuttings P.P. 178. Two years before, Anna Maria Priestman had organised a petition to the Yearly Meeting of the Society of Friends, seeking an expression of sympathy with the women's suffrage cause, Friends' House Library Ms Box X2/16.

9 MEN, WOMEN'S SUFFRAGE AND SEXUAL RADICALISM, 1912–14

1 L. and C. Housman to S. Clark, in Clemence's hand, n.d. (postmarked 6 December 1912), HP.

2 H. Swanwick, *I Have Been Young*, London, Victor Gallancz, 1935, p. 225.

3 B. Harrison, 'The Act of Militancy: Violence and the Suffragettes, 1904–1914', in his *Peaceable Kingdom. Stability and Change in Modern Britain*, Oxford, Clarendon Press, 1982, p. 30.

4 L. Housman, *The Unexpected Years*, London, Jonathan Cape, 1937, pp. 275–6.

5 Ibid., p. 279.

6 L. Housman to S. Clark, 24 May (postmarked 1912), HP.

7 Housman, *Unexpected Years*, pp. 281–2.

8 Ibid., p. 282.

9 L. Housman to S. Clark, 5 March 1913, HP.

10 Ibid., n. d. (postmarked 8 April 1913).

11 Ibid., 6 December (1912).

12 *Common Cause*, 11 April 1912, 4 July 1912, respectively.

13 S. Oldfield, *Spinsters of this Parish. The Life and Times of F. M. Mayor and Mary Sheepshanks*, London, Virago, 1984, p. 147.

14 H. Clark to E. Clothier, 28 January 1913, GP.

15 *Manchester Guardian*, 23 January 1913.

16 A. Clark to the Priestman sisters, 27 January 1913, Box 75, MP.

17 C. Marshall, draft circular to members of the National Union of Women's Suffrage Societies, February 1913, Catherine Marshall papers, CMP.

18 NUWSS Minutes, 28 January 1913.

19 *Common Cause*, 7 February 1913.

20 H. Clark to E. Clothier, 28 January 1913, GP.

21 NUWSS Minutes, 7 March 1913; see also 'Circular on Policy', following the February council meeting of the National Union, MGFP.

22 A. Clark to H. P. B. Clark, 26 November 1913, Box 75, MP; J. Vellacott, *From Liberal to Labour with Women's Suffrage. The Story of Catherine Marshall*, Montreal and Kingston, McGill–Queen's University Press, 1993, p. 255.

23 A. Clark to the Priestman sisters, 12 and 19 May 1913, Box 75, MP.

24 L. Housman to S. Clark, 20 August (postmarked 1913), HP.
25 Quoted in D. Morgan, *Suffragists and Liberals. The Politics of Woman Suffrage in England*, Oxford, Basil Blackwell, 1975, p. 125.
26 A. Clark to the Priestman sisters, 2 August 1913, Box 75, MP.
27 L. Housman to S. Clark, 5 March 1913 (though bound as at 1912), HP.
28 Ibid., 20 August (postmark 1913).
29 Ibid., n. d. (postmark 22 March 1913), 9 August 1913, 21 December 1912.
30 Ibid., 9 August 1913, 6 December 1912.
31 Ibid.
32 A. Clark to C. Marshall, 17 November 1913, CMP.
33 M. Ashton to C. Marshall, 26 November 1913, CMP.
34 A. Clark to C. Marshall, 28 November 1913, CMP.
35 Ibid., n. d. (circa late November–December 1913).
36 A. Clark to the Priestman sisters, 4 December 1913, Box 75, MP.
37 A. Clark to C. Marshall, 28 November 1913, CMP.
38 A. Clark to the Priestman sisters, 14 January 1914, Box 75, MP.
39 M. Garnett, A. Harrington, and E. Bowman to C. Marshall, n. d. (circa July 1914), CMP; *Common Cause*, 4 July 1912.
40 Housman, *Unexpected Years*, pp. 295–6.
41 Ibid.
42 L. Housman to S. Clark, 28 June 1913, HP.
43 L. Housman, *Unexpected Years*, p. 283.
44 L. Housman to S. Clark, n. d. (postmarked 2 March 1914), HP.
45 Ibid., 2 March 1914, 3 April 1914, 7 May 1914.
46 Ibid., 21 December 1912, together with a cutting from *Votes for Women*, n. d. (circa December 1912).
47 Ibid., n. d. (postmarked 6 December 1912, and in C. Housman's hand).
48 Ibid., 21 December 1912.
49 Ibid., n. d. (postmarked 8 April 1913).
50 L. Housman, 'Sex-War and Woman's Suffrage', a lecture for the Women's Freedom League, at the Essex Hall, 7 May 1912, December 1913. Some of the images in the speech, which focus on stallions and mares, throw some doubt on his reputation for an ability to raise such questions in public with particular taste and delicacy, c.f. n. 55 below.
51 L. Housman to J. Ashbee, 8 November 1910, CRAJ.
52 L. Housman to S. Clark, n. d. (postmarked 8 April 1913). Earlier he had written to Janet Ashbee saying 'I want some "mother facts" explained to me', L. Housman to J. Ashbee, 12 August 1912, CRAJ.
53 L. Housman to J. Ashbee, n. d. (bound as August 1914), CRAJ.
54 Ibid., 20 August 1913; 7 December 1913.
55 Ibid., 7 December 1913. Earlier C. R. Ashbee, who openly discussed his attachments to other men with his wife, had a few months earlier told how Laurence Housman had recently spoken on homosexuality: 'He spoke ever so delicately on that question, but only one of *our* type could have used words of such chivalry and refinement to women', C. R. Ashbee to J. Ashbee, May 1913, CRAJ.
56 Ibid., 13 July 1914.

57 She does not, however, appear to have become formally a member of the society until 1917, personal communication from Lesley Hall.

58 L. Hall, 'The British Society for the Study of Sex Psychology, 1913–1947: "A Note of Interrogation" ', *Journal of Contemporary History*, October 1995.

59 See, for example, Malcolm Muggeridge's account of his father's attitude to women's suffrage in his introduction to A. Raeburn, *The Suffragette View*, Newton Abbot, David and Charles, 1976.

60 G. Dangerfield, *The Strange Death of Liberal England* (1930), London, Paladin, 1970 repr., esp. pp. 136–41.

61 L. Stanley and A. Morley, *The Life and Death of Emily Wilding Davison*, London, Women's Press, 1988, pp. xiv, 133–4

62 Typescript fragment, H. Clark to E. Pye, annotated 29 July 1908, Folder 1908, 1909, 1910, Box 1, HCP.

63 Ibid., 29 July 1908.

64 Ibid., 8 April 1910.

65 Ibid., 30 January 1910.

10 WOMEN'S SUFFRAGE AND THE FIRST WORLD WAR

1 A. Clark to the Priestman sisters, 3 June 1914, Box 75, MP.

2 M. Ashton to C. Marshall, 31 July 1914, CMP.

3 D. Lloyd George to R. McKenna, 6 July 1914, C/5/12/9, LGP, House of Lords Record Office.

4 Quoted in D. Morgan, *Suffragists and Liberals. The Politics of Woman Suffrage*, Oxford, Basil Blackwell, 1975, pp. 131, 132–3.

5 C. Marshall to D. Lloyd George, 29 August 1913, C/9/5/20, LGP.

6 S. Pankhurst to D. Lloyd George, 21 July 1914, C/11/1/74, LGP.

7 L. Housman to S. Clark, 21 June 1914, HP.

8 C. Marshall to F. Acland (a friend and junior minister in the Liberal government), 23 June 1914, CMP.

9 E. New to Alice Clark, 30 July 1914, Box 76, MP.

10 Quoted in the entry for Anna Maria Priestman in the *Dictionary of Quaker Biography*, Friends House Library, London. Ursula Bright died the following year.

11 L. Housman, *The Unexpected Years*, London, Jonathan Cape, 1937, pp. 297–8.

12 M. Gawthorpe, 'The Book of Suffragette Prisoners', SFCM. Her hopes to visit the United States 'for the voyage sake' and as part of her process of convalescence were evident from 1912, M. Gawthorpe to Mrs Bjorkman, 27 March, 11 June 1912, MWDP, M 138.

13 M. Gawthorpe to V. Whitehouse, 5 November 1917, Vira Whitehouse papers, Schlesinger Library, Radcliffe College, suggests she had been in this post for the previous 14 months.

14 A. Clark to H. P. B. Clark, 12 October 1914, Box 75, MP.

15 Hand List, 'Central Organisations A-E', Friends House Library, Friends House.

16 A. Clark to H. P. B. Clark, 14 February 1915, Box 75, MP.
17 NUWSS executive committee minutes, 4 November 1914, CMP.
18 Annotated agenda for the Provincial Council meeting of the NUWSS, 12 November 1914, and report of the debate, CMP.
19 A. Clark to Catherine Marshall, 15 November 1914, CMP.
20 Ibid.
21 Ibid.
22 A. Clark to H. P. B. Clark, 5 January 1915, Box 75, MP.
23 NUWSS, Annual Report, 1915; NUWSS Minutes, 18 February and 4 March 1915.
24 NUWSS, 18 March 1915.
25 Ibid, 23 April 1915.
26 A. Clark to C. Marshall, 29 March 1915, CMP.
27 Ibid., 30 March 1915.
28 Ibid., 29 and 30 March 1915.
29 Ibid., 3 July 1915.
30 NUWSS Minutes, 15 April, 30 April, 6 May, 20 May, 14 June 1915, and see also Mrs Fawcett's letter to the membership, 23 April 1915, MGFP. Other resignations at this time included those of Isabella Ford and Maude Royden.
31 'Draft Resolution Proposed by Miss Marshall as a Basis for Discussion', n. d. (May 1915), CMP.
32 W. A. C. Anderson to the NUWSS executive, 14 April 1916, MGFP.
33 H. Mitchell, *The Hard Way Up. The Autobiography of Hannah Mitchell, Suffragette and Rebel* (1968), London, Virago, 1977 repr.
34 Ibid., p. 142.
35 'The Kid' (Hilda Clark) to E. Clothier, 17 November 1915, 1914–16 folder, Box 1, HCP.
36 A. Clark to H. P. B. Clark, 14 October 1916, 14 December 1916, Box 75, MP.
37 L. Housman to R. Clark, n. d., postmarked 31 July 1917, HP.
38 Ibid.
39 Ibid., 4 July 1917, HP.
40 Housman, *Unexpected Years*, p. 314.
41 L. Housman to R. Clark, 9 March, 30 April, postmarked 1917, HP.
42 L. Housman to S. Clark, 27 July 1918, HP.
43 Ibid., 27 October 1917, HP.
44 L. Housman to J. Ashbee, 22 February 1917, CRAJ.
45 NUWSS Minutes, 20 July 1916.
46 H. W. Nevinson, Diaries, 19 and 21 August 1916, Henry Wood Nevinson Papers, Bodleian Library.
47 L. Housman to S. Clark, 27 October 1917, HP.

11 LAST WORDS: Women's suffragists and women's history after the vote

1 Obituary of Elizabeth Wolstenholme Elmy, *Workers' Dreadnought*, 23 March 1918.

2 Obituary of Elizabeth Wolstenholme Elmy, *Common Cause*, 22 March 1918, with my thanks to David Dougham, Fawcett Library, for this reference.

3 L. Housman to S. Clark, 31 January 1918, HC.

4 L. Housman, *The Unexpected Years*, London, Jonathan Cape, 1937, p. 331.

5 L. Housman to S. Clark, 26 May n. y., HC.

6 Ibid., 24 January 1919, HC.

7 L. Housman, *Unexpected Years*, p. 331.

8 M. Gawthorpe, *Up Hill to Holloway*, Penobscot, Maine, Traversity Press, 1962, p. 21.

9 Cutting from *Peace News*, HC.

10 Quoted in J. Hunt, 'The Younger Brother', *Journal of the Housman Society*, 1990, vol. 16, p. 6.

11 As well as its effort in Austria, the Society of Friends also became part of the Fight the Famine Council, formed to help the starving population of Germany.

12 Christian Science Society, Street, 'How the Seed was Sown in Street', 1936, with my thanks to Yvonne Fettweis, Manager of the Church History Department, the Church of Christ Scientist, Boston, for identifying this material for me.

13 Compare the analysis in M. Chaytor and J. Lewis, 'Introduction' to A. Clark, *The Working Life of Women in the Seventeenth Century* (1919), London, Routledge & Kegan Paul, 1982, and A. L. Erickson, 'Introduction' to A. Clark, *The Working Life of Women in the Seventeenth Century* (1919), London, Routledge, 1992.

14 Clark, *Working Life*, p. viii.

15 A. Scott, personal communication 1993.

16 Manuscript memoir of Alice Clark, CA.

17 M. C. G. (Margaret Clark Gillett), *Alice Clark of C. and J. Clark Ltd., Street*, n. d. (c.1934), p. 17.

18 H. Mitchell, *The Hard Way Up. The Autobiography of Hannah Mitchell, Suffragette and Rebel* (ed. G. Mitchell 1968), London, Virago, 1977 repr., p. 189.

19 Ibid., G. Mitchell, 'Introduction', p. 28.

20 J. Liddington and J. Norris, *One Hand Tied Behind Us. The Rise of the Women's Suffrage Movement*, London, Virago, 1978.

21 M. Gawthorpe, 'The Book of Suffragette Prisoners', pp. 129–35, SFCM.

22 Arthur Garfield Hays to M. Gawthorpe, 4 August 1931, ibid., p. 135.

23 Roger N. Baldwin to M. Gawthorpe, 14 August 1931, ibid., p. 135.

24 M. Gawthorpe, 'The Book of Suffragette Prisoners', SFCM.

25 Ibid.

26 Ibid.

27 D. Montefiore, *From a Victorian to a Modern*, London, E. Archer, 1927, p. 51.

28 M. G. Fawcett, 'England' in T. Stanton (ed.) *The Woman Question in Europe*, New York and London, G. P. Putnam, 1884, presents perhaps an especially clear case of the way the history of the movement was being contested. This account was misleading in as much as it quite

deliberately obscures the controversy over the exclusion of married women from the suffrage demand. Stanton's footnotes also suggest that a second reader whom he had consulted, most likely Ursula Bright, had alerted him to certain omissions in this account, notably with regard to the work of the Married Women's Property Committee which she and Elizabeth Wolstenholme Elmy had brought to a successful conclusion in 1882.

29 Gawthorpe, 'Suffragette Prisoners', p. 136.

30 M. Gawthorpe to M. Dreier, 26 April 1958, MEDP, Box 7, Folder 110.

31 Ibid., 7 December 1961.

32 The copy I consulted is held by the library of Murdoch University, Western Australia, and is, to my knowledge, the only publicly available copy in Australia.

33 M. Gawthorpe to L. Dockray, Thanksgiving, 1971, the Blue Moon Collection of Pankhurst Memorabilia, Murdoch University Library, Perth, Western Australia.

34 For example, I. Tyrrell, 'American Exceptionalism in an Age of International History', *American Historical Review*, 1992, vol. 97, pp. 1031–55 and his *Woman's World, Woman's Empire. The Women's Christian Temperance Union in International Perspective 1880–1930*, Chapel Hill, University of North Carolina Press, 1991.

35 C. Steedman, 'History and Autobiography. Different Pasts', in her *Past Tenses. Essays on Writing, Autobiography and History*, London, Rivers Oram Press, 1992, pp. 41–50, esp. p. 48.

NOTES ON FURTHER
READING

This book has drawn on a wide selection of documentary sources, and I have concentrated on recording these in my notes, as a guide for other researchers. It would be impossible to acknowledge all my debts to other writers in this and relevant fields without very lengthy notes. The bibliography which follows is intended as a guide to some possible further reading; it seeks to acknowledge some, but by no means all, of my debts to other scholars, and for that reason largely comprises works not cited in the end notes. The reader may most easily locate a full bibliographic reference by checking the index under the name of the author.

A helpful, concise overview of the position of women in this period is P. Thane, 'Late Victorian Women' in T. R. Gourvish and A. O'Day, *Later Victorian Britain, 1867–1900*, London, Macmillan Education, 1988, pp. 175–208; J. Purves (ed.), *Women's History, 1850–1945*, London, UCL Press, 1995, looks at a range of topics for this period. L. Davidoff and C. Hall, *Family Fortunes. Men and Women of the English Middle Class, 1780–1850*, London, Routledge, 1992, and L. Davidoff, *Worlds Between. Historical Perspectives on Gender and Class*, Cambridge, Polity Press, 1995, look at the formation of the gender relationships which shaped the lives of the first generation of middle-class suffragists discussed here. M. J. Peterson, *Family, Love and Work in the Lives of Victorian Gentlewomen*, Bloomington, Indiana University Press, 1989, explores the lives of women in families of professional men, for a subsequent generation. P. Jalland, *Women, Marriage and Politics, 1860–1914*, Oxford, Clarendon Press, 1986, draws on the papers of fifty women from the political elite in this period, and focuses especially on their experience of marriage, childbirth, spinsterhood and in the role of political wives. B. Caine, *Destined to Be Wives. The Sisters of Beatrice Webb*, Oxford, Clarendon,

1986, compares the varying experience of women from one well-to-do, middle-class family who lived from the later nineteenth to early twentieth centuries.

On the value of the study of friendship to women's history and biography, see L. Stanley and A. Morley, *The Life and Death of Emily Wilding Davison*, London, Women's Press, 1988. P. Levine, *Feminist Lives in Victorian England*, Oxford, Blackwell, 1990, also emphasises the importance of pre-existing friendship networks for the formation of the women's movement, not least in the creation of a distinct feminist culture. C. S. Rosenberg, 'The Female World of Love and Ritual: Relations Between Women in Nineteenth Century America' and 'The New Woman as Androgyne: Social Disorder and Gender Crisis, 1870–1936', both reproduced in her *Disorderly Women. Visions of Gender in Victorian America*, Oxford, Oxford University Press, 1985, pp. 53–76, pp. 245–96, have been among the most influential articles on women's friendships in this period. The notion of 'romantic friendship' is reviewed in L. Stanley, 'Romantic Friendship? Some Issues in Researching Lesbian History and Biography', *Women's History Review*, 1992, vol. 1, pp. 193–216 and M. Vicinus, 'Lesbian History: All Theory and No Facts or All Facts and No Theory', *Radical History Review*, 1994, vol. 60, pp. 57–75.

R. Strachey, *The Cause. A Short History of the Women's Movement in Great Britain* (1928), London, Virago, 1978 repr., provides a useful overview, though with occasional inaccuracies, and written from the perspective of one of the more conservative of constitutional suffragists. H. Burton, *Barbara Bodichon 1827–1891*, London, John Murray, 1949, provides an additional account of the Langham Place circle. B. Caine, *Victorian Feminists*, Oxford, Oxford University Press, 1992, analyses and compares the feminism of Frances Power Cobbe, Emily Davies, Josephine Butler and Millicent Garrett Fawcett. O. Banks, *Becoming a Feminist: The Social Origins of First-Wave Feminism*, Brighton, Wheatsheaf Books, 1981, undertakes a broader analysis of three generations of women's rights activists. Each of the following provides a helpful comparative perspective on the British movement: J. Rendall, *The Origins of Modern Feminism. Women in Britain, France and the United States, 1780–1860*, London, Macmillan, 1985; R. Evans, *The Feminists*, London, Croom Helm, 1977; O. Banks, *Faces of Feminism*, Oxford, Martin Robertson, 1979; C. Bolt, *The Women's Movement in the United States and Britain from the 1790s to the 1920s*, Amherst, University of Massachusetts Press, 1993.

Some other of the activities undertaken by members of the

Langham Place circle are explored in A. J. Hammerton, *Emigrant Gentlewomen. Genteel Poverty and Female Emigration, 1830–1914*, Canberra, Australian National University Press, 1979; S. Fletcher, *Feminists and Bureaucrats. A Study of the Development of Girls' Education in the Nineteenth Century*, Cambridge, Cambridge University Press, 1980.

J. Rendall, ' "A Moral Engine?" Feminism, Liberalism and *The English Woman's Journal*' in J. Rendall (ed.) *Equal or Different*, Oxford, Blackwell, 1987, pp. 112–40, analyses further the ideas put forward in that journal. P. Levine, ' "The Humanising Influences of Five O'Clock Tea", Victorian Feminist Periodicals', *Victorian Studies*, 1989–90, vol. 33, pp. 293–306, emphasises the importance of such activities for creating a collective identity and a language of their own. D. Doughan and D. Sanchez, *Feminist Periodicals 1855–1984. An Annotated, Critical Bibliography of British, Irish, Commonwealth and International Titles*, Brighton, Harvester Books, 1987, is an essential resource for identifying the periodical literature of the women's movement.

J. Manton, *Elizabeth Garrett Anderson*, London, Black, 1958, provides a good introduction to the kinship and friendship circles of the Garrett sisters, while R. Strachey, *Millicent Garrett Fawcett*, London, Murray, 1934, and D. Rubinstein, *A Different World for Women. The Life of Millicent Garrett Fawcett*, Brighton, Harvester Wheatsheaf, 1991, each provide much fuller accounts of her life and career than that to be found in M. G. Fawcett, *What I Remember*, London, Fisher and Unwin, 1924. Lydia Becker has been a neglected figure in recent histories of the women's movement, but see J. Parker, 'Lydia Becker: Pioneer Orator of the Women's Movement', *Manchester Region History Review*, 1991, vol. 5, pp. 13–20; A. Kelly, 'Lydia Becker and the Cause', Lancaster, Lancaster University Centre for North Western Studies, 1992. B. Caine, 'John Stuart Mill and the English Women's Movement', *Historical Studies*, 1982, vol. 18, pp. 52–67, and 'Feminism, Suffrage and the Nineteenth Century Women's Movement', *Women's Studies International Forum*, 1982, vol. 5, pp. 537–50, look at some of the issues which divided the early suffrage committees. A. P. W. Robson, 'The Founding of the National Society for Women's Suffrage', *Canadian Journal of History*, 1973, vol. 8, pp. 1–22, presents a somewhat different account.

The extent and nature of the Bright circle is traced in S. S. Holton, 'From Anti-Slavery to Suffrage Militancy. The Bright Circle, Elizabeth Cady Stanton and the British Women's Movement', in

C. Daley and M. Nolan, *Suffrage and Beyond. International Feminist Perspectives*, Auckland, Auckland University Press, 1994, pp. 213–33. C. Midgley, *Women Against Slavery. The British Campaigns, 1780–1870*, London, Routledge, 1992, discusses the links between abolition and women's rights in Britain, while K. K. Sklar, ' "Women Who Speak for an Entire Nation": American and British Women Compared at the World Anti-Slavery Convention, London, 1840', *Pacific Historical Review*, 1990, vol. 59, pp. 453–99, provides a valuable comparative study. G. Malmgreen, 'Anne Knight and the Radical Subculture', *Quaker History*, 1982, vol. 71, pp. 100–13, provides further insights into the links between Chartism and the women's movement. Alongside such links, however, there is increasing recognition in recent work of the ways in which British feminism incorporated 'cultural racism' and became incorporated into the imperial mission. See, for example, C. Hall, *White, Male and Middle Class. Explorations in Feminism and History*, Oxford, Polity Press, 1992; V. Ware, *Beyond the Pale. White Women, Racism and History*, London, Verso 1992; A. Burton, *The Burdens of History. British Feminists, Indian Women and Imperial Culture, 1863–1915*, Chapel Hill, University of North Carolina Press, 1994; *Women's History Review*, 1994, vol. 3, special issue called 'Feminism, Imperialism and Race: A Dialogue between India and Britain'. For a subtle discussion from the Australian perspective, see M. Lake, 'Between Old Worlds and New: Feminist Citizenship, Nation and Race, the Destabilisation of Identity' in C. Daley and M. Nolan, *Suffrage and Beyond. International Feminist Perspectives*, Auckland, Auckland University Press, 1994, pp. 277–94.

I discuss the ethos of the suffrage movement more generally in S. S. Holton, *Feminism and Democracy. Women's Suffrage and Reform Politics in Britain, 1897–1918*, Cambridge, Cambridge University Press, 1986, pp. 9–26. My article ' "To Educate Women into Rebellion". Elizabeth Cady Stanton and the Creation of a Transatlantic Network of Radical Suffragists', *American Historical Review*, 1994, vol. 99, pp. 1113–36, explores the shared ideas of Radical suffragists in Britain and the United States. B. Harrison, *Separate Spheres. The Opposition to Women's Suffrage in Britain*, London, Croom Helm, 1978, examines the arguments of the anti-suffragists. Local government as a significant, though previously neglected, aspect of women's political emancipation is examined in detail in P. Hollis, *Ladies Elect. Women in English Local government 1865–1914*, Oxford, Clarendon Press, 1987.

The contours of Radical Liberalism have recently received extensive, fresh analyses in E. F. Biagini, *Liberty, Retrenchment and Reform. Popular Liberalism in the Age of Gladstone 1860–80*, Cambridge, Cambridge University Press, 1992, and M. Finn, *After Chartism. Class and Nation in English Radical Politics, 1848–1874*, Cambridge, Cambridge University Press, 1993. This last work identifies Jacob Bright and Richard Pankhurst as among those who sought to move beyond older traditions of middle-class radicalism, as represented by figures like John Bright. Neither, however, addresses the links between Radical Liberals and the women's movement in any detail. C. Rover, *Women's Suffrage and Party Politics in Britain, 1866–1914*, London, Routledge and Kegan Paul, 1967, discusses the relation of women's suffrage to party politics in broader terms.

The question of the relationship between the subjection of women and marriage in modern western society is explored at the theoretical level in C. Pateman, *The Sexual Contract*, Stanford, California University Press, 1988, esp. chs 5 and 6, and that account informs the analysis pursued here. A. J. Hammerton, *Cruelty and Companionship*, London, Routledge, 1992, looks at the ideals and the actuality of marriage in nineteenth-century Britain. L. Holcombe, *Women and Property: Reform of the Married Women's Property Law in Nineteenth Century England*, Toronto, Toronto University Press, 1983 is a further study of this question which emphasises the inter-relatedness of the demand for the vote and for married women's property rights. R. J. Morris, 'Men, Women and Property; the Reform of the Married Women's Property Act', in F. M. L. Thompson (ed.) *Landowners, Capitalists and Entrepreneurs. Essays for Sir John Habakkuk*, Oxford, Clarendon Press, 1994, pp. 171–91, examines the legislation in detail, and argues that women's growing role in the control and direction of a family's consumption was a more significant factor in reform than concerns about sexual equality. C. Shammas, 'Re-assessing the Married Women's Property Acts', *Journal of Women's History*, 1994, vol. 6, pp. 9–30, reviews the history of these reforms in the United States, places them in terms of commercial expansion and the corporatisation of business, and concludes that they did promote wealth-holding among women. S. K. Kent, *Sex and Suffrage in Britain, 1860–1914*, Princeton, Princeton University Press, 1987, argues that some sense of a sex-war was fundamental to the feminist enterprise in this period. C. Dyhouse, *Feminism and the Family in England 1880–1939*, Oxford, Basil Blackwell, 1989, examines feminist critiques of the family.

Further accounts of the campaigns to repeal the Contagious Diseases Acts may be found in P. McHugh, *Prostitution and Victorian Social Reform*, London, Croom Helm, 1980, while M. Trustram, *Women of the Regiment: Marriage and the Victorian Army*, Cambridge, Cambridge University Press, 1984, provides a different context for viewing the issue. S. S. Holton, 'State Pandering, Medical Policing and Prostitution. The Controversy within the Medical Profession over the Contagious Diseases Legislation 1864–86', *Research in Law, Deviance, and Social Control*, 1989, vol. 9, pp. 149–70, explores the debate among medical men on this issue.

S. O. Rose, *Limited Livelihoods, Gender and Class in Nineteenth-Century England*, London, Routledge, 1992, analyses the position of women industrial workers.

H. Goldman, *Emma Paterson*, London, Lawrence and Wishart, 1974; N. C. Soldon, *Women in British Trade Unions 1874–1976*, Gill and Macmillan, 1978, provide further background on the Women's Protective and Provident League. Understandings of the role of working-class women in the suffrage movement have undergone considerable change in recent years. Compare, for example, R. S. Neale, 'Working-class Women and Women's Suffrage' in his *Class and Ideology in the Nineteenth Century*, London, Routledge and Kegan Paul, 1972, pp. 143–95, and B. Hill, 'The Emancipation of Women and the Women's Movement', *Marxist Quarterly*, January 1956, pp. 40–57, with more recent accounts. S. S. Holton, 'Silk Dresses and Lavender Kid Gloves: the Wayward Career of Jessie Craigen, Working Suffragist', *Women's History Review* vol. 6, 1996, pp. 125–146 discusses material on Jessie Craigen which came to light after this book had been completed.

For a more wide-ranging account of ideas on free love, see C. Rover, *Love, Morals and the Feminists*, London, Routledge and Kegan Paul, 1970. The circumstances of the Elmys' marriage are discussed more extensively in S. S. Holton, 'Free Love and Victorian Feminism. The Divers Matrimonials of Elizabeth Wolstenholme and Ben Elmy' *Victorian Studies*, 1994, vol. 37. 199–202.

On the creation of the Women's Liberal Federation in 1887, out of the local Women's Liberal Associations, see L. Walker, 'Party Political Women: A Comparative Study of the Liberal Women and the Primrose League, 1890–1914', in J. Rendall (ed.) *Equal or Different. Women's Politics 1800–1914*, Oxford, Basil Blackwell, 1987, pp. 165–91. On the tensions within the WLF over policies on women's suffrage, see C. Hirshfield, 'Fractured Faith: Liberal Party

Women and the Suffrage Issue in Britain, 1892–1914', *Gender and History*, 1990, vol. 2, pp. 173–97.

On the emergence of the social purity perspective on sexual reform, see D. Gorham, ' "The Maiden Tribute of Modern Babylon" Re-examined: Child Prostitution and the Idea of Childhood in Late-Victorian England', *Victorian Studies*, 1978, vol. 21, pp. 357–79. See also F. Mort, *Dangerous Sexualities. Medical–Moral Politics in England since 1830*, London, Routledge and Kegan Paul, 1987. L. Bland, *Banishing the Beast. Sexuality and the Early Feminists*, New York, New Press, 1995.

S. S. Holton, 'Women and the Vote', in J. Purvis (ed.) *Women's History, 1850–1945*, London UCL Press, 1995, pp. 277–306, provides a brief survey of this field of suffrage history.

A. Kenney, *Memories of a Militant*, London, Edward Arnold, 1924, provides the perspective of one working-class, socialist suffragist who remained loyal to Christabel and Emmeline Pankhurst throughout the suffrage campaigns. T. Thompson, *Dear Girl. The Diaries and Letters of Two Working Women, 1897–1917*, London, Women's Press, 1987, includes the impressions of working-class suffragists who took an active interest in the suffrage campaigns, among their many other varied interests. On Jessie Baines, see J. Smart's entry in *The Australian Dictionary of Biography*, Melbourne, Melbourne University Press, 1966–1991, vol. 7, pp. 145–6.

J. Lewis (ed.) *Labour and Love. Women's Experience of Home and Family, 1850–1940*, Oxford, Basil Blackwell, 1986, and E. Ross, *Love and Toil: Motherhood in Outcast London*, Oxford, Oxford University Press, 1993, throw light on many aspects of the sexual politics of working-class life in this period. S. S. Holton, 'The Suffragist and "the Average Woman" ', *Women's History Review*, 1992, vol. 1, pp. 9–24, examines how suffragists brought together issues of personal politics and participation in public life in three autobiographies.

Some valuable localised studies of the women's suffrage movement include: L. Leneman, *A Guid Cause. The Women's Suffrage Movement in Scotland*, Aberdeen, Aberdeen University Press, 1991; C. Murphy, *The Women's Suffrage Movement and Irish Society in the Twentieth Century*, London, Harvester Wheatsheaf, 1984; L. Ryan, 'Traditions and Double Moral Standards: the Irish Suffragists' Critique of Nationalism', *Women's History Review*, vol. 4, 1995, pp. 487–504; C. Lloyd-Morgan, 'From Temperance to Suffrage' and K. Cook and N. Evans, ' "The Petty Antics of the Bell-Ringing Boisterous Band"? The Women's Suffrage Movement in Wales, 1914–1939', both in A.

V. John (ed.) *Our Mother's Land. Chapters in Welsh Women's History, 1830–1939*, Cardiff, University of Wales Press, 1991, pp. 135–58, and pp. 158–188, respectively.

T. Steele, *Alfred Orage and the Leeds Arts Club, 1893–1923*, Aldershot, Scolar Press, 1990, explores the intellectual and political life of Leeds at the turn of the century. J. Hannam, *Isabella Ford*, Oxford, Basil Blackwell, 1989, is essential reading on socialist–suffragist politics in Leeds. S. S. Holton, *Feminism and Democracy. Women's Suffrage and Reform Politics, 1900–1918*, Cambridge, Cambridge University Press, 1986, discusses the question of adult suffrage v. women's suffrage, and explores the relationship between militant and constitutionalist suffragists in this period.

There is no published history of the Women's Freedom League, but there are two biographies of Charlotte Despard which provide helpful accounts of its history: A. Linklater, *An Husbanded Life. Charlotte Despard: Suffragette, Socialist and Sinn Feiner*, London, Hutchinson, 1980; M. Mulvihill, *Charlotte Despard. A Biography*, London, Pandora, 1989. A brief biography of Teresa Billington Greig, together with reprints of some of her writings, is to be found in C. McPhee and A. Fitzgerald, *The Non-Violent Militant. Selected Writings of Teresa Billington Greig*, London, Routledge and Kegan Paul, 1987. Her career is also assessed in a collective biography of some suffrage leaders, B. Harrison, *Prudent Revolutionaries. Portraits of British Feminists Between the Wars*, Oxford, Clarendon Press, 1987.

J. Weeks, *Coming Out: Homosexual Politics in Britain from the Nineteenth Century to the Present*, London, Quartet Books, 1977, and M. Roper and J. Tosh, *Manful Assertions. Masculinities in Britain since 1900*, London, Routledge, 1991, provide valuable introductions to these fields of study. On sexual radicalism in this period, see S. Rowbotham, *A New World for Women: Stella Browne, Socialist-Feminist*, London, Pluto Press, 1977; S. Rowbotham and J. Weeks, *Socialism and the New Life: The Personal and Sexual Politics of Edward Carpenter and Havelock Ellis*, London, Pluto Press, 1977; R. Brandon, *The New Women and the Old Men. Love, Sex and the Woman Question*, London, Martin Secker and Warburg, 1990. S. S. Holton, 'Manliness and Militancy: Men's Protest and the Gendering of the Suffragette Identity' in A. V. John and C. Eustance, *The Men's Share*, London, Routledge, forthcoming 1996, looks at the experience of male militant suffragists, especially in terms of gender identities.

For more detailed accounts of the participation of writers and actors in the suffrage movement, see J. Holledge, *Innocent Flowers.*

Women in the Edwardian Theatre, London, Virago, 1981; S. Oldfield, *Spinsters of the Parish. The Life and Times of F. M. Mayor and Mary Sheepshanks*, London, Virago, 1984; N. Auerbach, *Ellen Terry. Player in Her Time*, London, J. M. Dent and Sons, 1987; S. Stowell, *A Stage of Their Own: Feminist Playwrights of the Suffrage Era*, Manchester, Manchester University Press, 1992; A. V. John, *Elizabeth Robins. Staging a Life, 1862–1952*, London, Routledge, 1995.

Discussion continues over the meaning and significance of militancy. For some recent contributions to this debate, see B. Harrison, 'The Act of Militancy' in his *Peaceable Kingdom. Stability and Change in Modern Britain*, London, Clarendon Press, 1982; M. Vicinus, *Independent Women. Work and Community for Single Women, 1850–1920*, Chicago, Chicago University Press, 1985; L. Stanley and A. Morley, *The Life and Death of Emily Wilding Davison* , London, Women's Press, 1989; S. S. Holton, ' "In Sorrowful Wrath". Suffrage Militancy and the Romantic Feminism of Emmeline Pankhurst' in H. L. Smith (ed.) *British Feminism in the Twentieth Century*, Aldershot, Edward Elgar, 1990, pp. 7–24 and compare A. Oakley, 'Millicent Fawcett and her 73 Reasons' in her *Telling the Truth about Jerusalem. A Collection of Essays and Poems*, Oxford, Basil Blackwell, 1986, pp. 18–35, which offers a thoughtful account of the constitutionalist position. J. Purvis, 'The Prison Experiences of the Suffragettes in Edwardian Britain', *Women's History Review*, 1995, vol. 4, pp. 103–34, questions some of the stereotypes about militant prisoners. H. Kean, *Deeds not Words: the Lives of Suffragette Teachers*, London, Pluto Press, 1990, provides a broader context for the story of Mary Gawthorpe.

J. Lidderdale and M. Nicholson, *Dear Miss Weaver. Harriet Shaw Weaver, 1876–1961*, London, Faber, 1970, tells the story of *The Freewoman* from the vantage point of one of its subsequent backers. L. Garner, *Stepping Stones. Feminist Ideas in the Women's Suffrage Movement, 1900–18*, Heinemann Educational Books, 1984, includes a concise account of its history.

E. Isichei, *Victorian Quakers*, London, Oxford University Press, 1970, provides a helpful overview of the humanitarian, political and philanthropic endeavours of Quakers in this period. P. Lovell, *Quaker Inheritance, 1871–1961. A Portrait of Roger Clark of Street Based on His Own Writing and Correspondence*, London, Bannisdale Press, 1970, provides many insights into the family life and political, cultural and industrial interests of the Clarks during Alice Clark's life time.

L. P. Hume, *The National Union of Women's Suffrage Societies, 1897–1914*, New York, Garland Publishing, 1982 provides an institutional history of the constitutionalist society and campaigns. H. Swanwick, *I Have Been Young*, London, Victor Gollancz, 1935, gives an autobiographical perspective from a constitutional suffragist prominent in these years. S. Fletcher, *Maude Royden. A Life*, Oxford, Basil Blackwell, 1989, provides an account of another prominent constitutional suffragist alongside whom Alice Clark was to work in the NUWSS. J. Liddington, *The Life and Times of a Respectable Rebel. Selina Cooper, 1864–1946*, London, Virago, 1984, traces the life of a working-class, socialist suffragist who in the years prior to the First World War became an organiser for the National Union of Women's Suffrage Societies.

C. Dyhouse, *Feminism and the Family in England 1880–1939*, Oxford, Basil Blackwell, 1989, looks at the influence of the Fabian Society on some of the early women historians. J. Lewis, *Women and Social Action in Victorian and Edwardian England*, Aldershot, Edward Elgar, 1991, compares the ideas and work of five women social activists, Beatrice Webb, Helena Bosanquet, Octavia Hill, Mary Humphry Ward and Violet Markham, to reveal the variety of ways in which women might conceive of citizenship in this period.

E. S. Pankhurst, *The Home Front. A Mirror to Life in England during the World War*, London, Hutchinson, 1932, is an autobiographical account of politics and social conditions during the war. On women's role in the peace movement, and the links between the suffrage movement and internationalism see J. Vellacott, 'A Place for Pacifism and Transnationalism in Feminist Theory: The Early Work of the Women's International League for Peace and Freedom', *Women's History Review*, 1993, vol. 2, pp. 23–56; A. Wiltsher, *Most Dangerous Women*, London, Pandora, 1985; J. Liddington, 'The Women's Peace Crusade. The History of a Forgotten Campaign' in D. Thompson (ed.) *Over Our Dead Bodies. Women against the Bomb*, London, Virago, 1983, pp. 180–98; L. J. Rupp, 'Constructing Internationalism: The Case of Transnational Women's Organisations', *American Historical Review*, 1994, vol. 99, pp. 1571–1600. B. M. Solomon, 'Dilemmas of Pacifist Women: Quakers and Others in World War I and II' in E. P. Brown and S. M. Stuard, *Witness for Change. Quaker Women over Three Centuries*, New Brunswick, Rutgers University Press, 1989, pp. 123–48, discusses the role of Quaker methods of consensus-generation in the deliberations of women's international organisations in this period. H. Clark, *War and Its Aftermath. Letters from Hilda Clark, M.B., BSc., From France, Austria and the Near East 1914–24*, privately printed c. 1954, is Edith Pye's edited collection of her companion's letters from various war zones. E. Sharp, *Unfinished Adventure. Selected Reminiscences from an Englishwoman's Life*, London, John Lane, 1934, provides a further eye-witness account of the famine in Europe by another former suffragist who became involved in the relief effort. See also G. Braybon and P. Summerfield, *Out of the Cage. Women's Experience of Two World Wars*, London, Pandora, 1987, and A. Woollacott, *On Her Their Lives Depend. Munition Workers in the Great War*, Berkeley, California Press, 1994, for the experience of women war workers.

Various aspects of the way in which the history of the twentieth-century suffrage movement was constructed are beginning to receive attention, see for example J. Marcus (ed.) *The Pankhursts and Women's Suffrage*, London, Routledge and Kegan Paul, 1987. For continuing controversy and debate surrounding the life of Sylvia Pankhurst, and treatments of militancy, see R. Pankhurst, 'Sylvia Pankhurst in Perspective. Some Comments on Patricia Romero's *E. Sylvia Pankhurst: Portrait of a Rebel*', *Women's Studies International Forum*, vol. 11, 1988, pp. 245–62; I. Bullock and R. Pankhurst, *Sylvia Pankhurst. From Artist to Anti-Fascist*, London, Macmillan, 1994. 'Introduction'; K. Dodd, 'The Politics of Form in Sylvia Pankhurst's Writing' in her edited collection, *A Sylvia Pankhurst Reader*, Manchester, Manchester University Press, 1993, pp. 1–31 and her 'Cultural Politics and Women's Historical Writing. The Case of Ray Strachey's *The Cause*', *Women's Studies International Forum*, 1990, vol. 13, pp. 127–37; H. Kean, 'Searching for the Past in Present Defeat: The Construction of Historical and Political Identity in British Feminism in the 1920s and 1930s', *Women's History Review*, 1994, vol. 3, pp. 57–80. S. S. Holton, 'Now You See It, Now You Don't: the Place of the Women's Franchise League in Contending Narratives of the Suffrage Movement', in M. Joannou and J. Purvis (eds), *New Perspectives in Women's History*, Manchester, Manchester University Press, 1966 forthcoming. For a thoughtful review of recent developments in women's history and suffrage history, see P. Grimshaw, 'Women's Suffrage in New Zealand Revisited: Writing from the Margins', in C. Daley and M. Nolan (eds) *Suffrage and Beyond. International Feminist Perspectives*, Auckland, Auckland University Press, 1994, pp. 25–41.

For contrasting accounts of developments in the women's movement from 1914 see J. Alberti, *Beyond Suffrage. Feminists in War and Peace, 1914–29*, London, Macmillan, 1989; M. Pugh, *Women and the Women's Movement in Britain, 1914–1959*, London, Macmillan, 1992;

S. K. Kent, *Making Peace. The Reconstruction of Gender in Interwar Britain*, Princeton, Princeton University Press, 1993.

There is little beyond the following path-breaking article on the role of women as historians in Britain in this period, M. Berg, 'The First Women Economic Historians', *Economic History Review*, 1992, vol. XLV, pp. 308–29, but for an earlier period, see B. Hill, *The Republican Virago: The Life and Time of Catherine Macauley*, Oxford, Clarendon Press, 1992. For a comparative perspective from the United States, see G. Lerner, 'A View from the Women's Side', *Journal of American History*, 1989, vol. 76, pp. 446–56; J. W. Scott, 'American Women Historians, 1884–1984', in her *Gender and the Politics of History*, New York, Columbia University Press, 1988, pp. 178–98; N. Cott, *A Woman Making History: Mary Beard through her Letters*, New Haven, Yale University Press, 1991, which also recounts Mary Beard's role in the British suffrage movement while living for a time in Manchester, where she came to know Emmeline Pankhurst. C. Dyhouse, *No Distinction of Sex? Women in British Universities 1870–1939*, London, UCL Press, 1995, examines the position of women more generally in the academic profession.

INDEX

DATE DUE

MAR 0 2001			

HIGHSMITH #45115